1968

MILTON ON HIMSELF

MILTON ON HIMSELF

Milton's utterances upon himself and his works

Edited with an Introduction and Notes

BY

JOHN S. DIEKHOFF

With a New Preface for this edition
by the editor

HUMANITIES PRESS
New York
1965

First published 1939

Reprinted 1965, with a new preface, by
Humanities Press Inc.
by special arrangement with the author

Library of Congress Catalog Card Number: 65-25276

Printed in U.S.A. by
NOBLE OFFSET PRINTERS, INC.
NEW YORK 3, N. Y.

AD PATREM

PREFACE TO THE SECOND EDITION

Milton on Himself was first published in 1939, perhaps not the most auspicious time in the light of the state of the nation, the state of the world, and the state of Milton's reputation and vogue. I do not remember in what year it went out of print, but it was a long time ago. During the past few years it has sometimes sold in the used book market at a considerable premium over new book prices. I have paid a premium for it myself. I need hardly say that it is gratifying to learn from a knowledgeable publisher that a continuing demand for it warrants re-issue a quarter of a century after its original publication. It is also gratifying to realize that I would not change it much if I could. After all, Milton wrote it, not I. Any use it served twenty-five years ago, it can serve now.

In the original preface, I observed that the book might be regarded as part of the process of "de-Massonizing" Milton. It is that certainly, but it is also part of a process of freeing Milton from other critics and biographers as well. In the earlier preface I also said that the book is an attempt to see Milton directly. That is an oversimplification. The volume is a means by which we can see Milton as he wished to be seen in a number of different contexts.

In the first and sixth Prolusions the young man seeks (and responds to) the goodwill of his fellow collegians. In the "Letter to a Friend," in its alternative versions, Milton works quite deliberately to present himself favorably to a chiding mentor. *Ad Patrem* shows him as he wished his father to see him. The sonnets to Lawrence and to Cyriack Skinner, perhaps sent as dinner invitations, reveal another private person. This is the genial Milton described by John Aubrey: "he would be chearfull even in his Gowtefitts; & sing."[1] When we read these sonnets, as when we read the private correspondence, we are reading someone else's mail. But for the most part in this volume we find the public Milton, Milton as he wished to appear to the public in the heat of controversy, as part of the rhetoric of controversy.

1 Helen Darbishire, *The Early Lives of Milton*, p. 5, London, 1932.

That Milton placed high value on the good opinion of his school-mates, his friends, his teachers, his father, the public whom he addressed, and the world at large emerges very clearly. But he wrote also for himself, whose good opinion he valued above any other's—and whose good opinion he enjoyed. This also emerges.

To see Milton as he wished to be seen or as he saw himself is not quite to see him directly, however. What Milton says about himself is important to our understanding of him, but he wrote no auto-biography and what he said about himself is no substitute for a biography.

The chief purpose of literary biography, I think, is greater under-standing of the writer's work. Milton was a complex and fascinating man—primarily a poet, but many things besides. If he had not been poet as well as politician, theologian, and political and religious pamphleteer, his biography would still be worth writing and worth reading, but its interest would be different and it would be read by a different audience. Those who study the life of Milton study it for the most part because he was a poet and they seek better under-standing of his poems. Literary biography is one form of literary criticism.

Every critic writes his own poem. The *Paradise Lost* of Denis Saurat is different from that of E. M. W. Tillyard; the *Paradise Lost* of William Empson is different from that of C. S. Lewis, and very different from that of John Milton.

Nevertheless, most readers (while hardly consciously building their own poem) prefer at least to start with the poet's poem—with Milton's *Paradise Lost*. The books about it have as part of their purpose the reconstruction of Milton's poem for readers of a different generation. Arnold Stein states the purpose:

> . . . we must remember that we, like Milton, also have our roots in time . . . The critical task is perhaps more like the poet's, to make the past present. I have not tried to be a seventeenth-century reader of *Paradise Lost*. I have tried to accept my role as a twentieth-century reader who is a student of seventeenth-century literature . . . I have honestly tried to enter Milton's mind and to submit myself to his work, but I have thought I could do so best

if I did not surrender (or attempt to deceive myself that I had) the discipline and sensibility I have gained from other poets. . . .[2]

Elsewhere Stein describes his basic orientation toward Milton as that of Hanford, Hughes, Woodhouse, Parker, and Allen, but with differences.

". . . being younger than they, I have also been exposed to some different interests. Some of my reading has gone in different directions, and we have read the same books at different times and with different eyes. The Milton they have given us cannot be quite the same Milton who is emerging to my contemporaries. He will not be the same Milton to my juniors. How could it be otherwise? And who would want to deny each age its immediate and individual claim on a great poet?"[3]

Thus every critic, and to some extent every reader, striving to grasp the poet's poem constructs his own.

Every biographer constructs his own hero or mock-hero. Helen Darbishire quotes the complete biography of Milton from Winstanley's *Lives of the most famous English Poets*:

John Milton was one, whose natural parts might deservedly give him a place amongst the principal of our English Poets, having written two Heroick Poems and a Tragedy; namely Paradise Lost, Paradise Regain'd and Sampson Agonistes; But his Fame is gone out like a Candle in a snuff, and his Memory will always Stink, which might have lived in honourable repute, had he not been a notorious Trayter, and most impiously and villanously bely'd that blessed Martyr, King Charles the First.[4]

Anthony à Wood, who finds him "a man of parts, . . . therefore more capable than another of doing mischief, especially by his pen . . . ," observes that Milton "did great matters to obtain a name and

2 Arnold Stein, *Answerable Style: Essays on Paradise Lost*, Preface, p. viii. Minneapolis, Minnesota, 1953.
3 Arnold Stein, *Heroic Knowledge*, Preface, pp. ix-x. Minneapolis, Minnesota, 1957.
4 Darbishire, *Early Lives*, Introduction, p. x.

wealth."[5] And Miss Darbishire comments that "no falser word has been said of Milton,"[6] although he did win great name, and for a time wealth, and disdained neither.

The anonymous biographer, on the other hand, who certainly knew Milton better than Anthony à Wood did, says that

> He had naturally a Sharp Witt, and steddy Judgment; which helps toward attaining Learning hee improv'd by an indefatigable attention to his Study; . . . Yet did hee not reckon this Talent but as intrusted with him; and therefore dedicated all his labours to the glory of God, & some public Good; Neither binding himselfe to any of the gainfull Professions, nor having any worldly Interest for aim in what he taught.[7]

Modern biographers differ as much in the reading of Milton's life as these early biographers and as much as modern critics differ in the reading of his poems. Liljegren and Saurat, from the continent, saw a different Milton from that of Sir Walter Raleigh or Mark Pattison. Belloc and Hanford know different Miltons. The list could be as long as the list of biographers, just as the list of different poems could be as long as the list of critics.

The student of Milton will read critics and biographers, will be helped and hindered in his task of knowing Milton, will choose those from whom he can best learn. With their help, as part of the process of reconstructing a *Paradise Lost* and other poems for himself, he will build his own Milton. He will also check their Milton and his against the basic evidence. The primary materials for the study of Milton's poems are the poems. The primary materials for the study of his life are Milton's works, the records of his life,[8] the early biographies,[9] and Milton's utterances about himself. His utterances about himself constitute this volume. It is not a biography, not an autobiography, but it is a means by which a student of Milton may enhance his understanding of the poet and his poems.

5 *Ibid.*, p. 38-39.
6 *Ibid.*, Introduction, p .x.
7 *Ibid.*, p. 29
8 Most easily available in J. Milton French, *Life Records of John Milton*, New Brunswick, New Jersey, 1949-1953.
9 Most easily available in Helen Darbishire's edition, to which reference has been made.

PREFACE

MY aim in this book has been to make available in a single volume
all of Milton's utterances upon himself and his work and to provide
the very slight apparatus necessary to understand and to judge what
he has to say. I have avoided interpretation because it has seemed to
me above all things desirable that Milton should be allowed to speak
for himself. The value of what he says I have tried to estimate in the
Introduction.

The classification of the extracts from Milton that are presented
here is necessarily somewhat arbitrary. To arrange Milton's words
into a coherent chronological account of his life is impossible, I
think; to present them in the order of their composition would result in chaos. Consequently the various extracts have been grouped
by subject and arranged within the groups with a few exceptions in
the order of composition. Thus the passages dealing chiefly with
Milton's aspirations as a poet are put in one group, those with his
blindness in another, and so on. But Milton sometimes speaks of his
blindness and of his ambitions as a poet in the same passage, even
in the same sentence, and I have not thought it desirable to break
such passages into bits. Consequently it is not possible to read all
that Milton has to say about his blindness, his poetic aspirations, his
achievements in prose, or upon any other personal subject, by reading a single section of this book, and frequent cross reference has
been necessary.

The text includes only those passages in Milton which are avowedly written of himself or his work. When Samson speaks, or Satan,
or Christ, like every other Milton student, I often hear Milton speak
also. But to let Satan or Christ speak for Milton is comparable, almost, to letting Iago or Othello speak for Shakespeare. It is letting
Satan speak for Milton, I think, that has led certain recent Milton
scholars into serious misunderstandings of the man they study, just

as I am sure some students are misled about Shakespeare who let Hamlet speak too literally for him. I have not excluded interesting parallels between autobiographical passages in Milton and speeches assigned in the poems to his various creations from my notes, however.

The work of preparing *Milton on Himself* has been greatly lightened by the existence after so long a need for it of a complete *Milton*. The text is taken from the Columbia *Milton* by permission of the Columbia University Press, and in Appendix A references to the Columbia *Milton* are given for all extracts.

In spite of convictions to the contrary, I have seen fit to modernize spelling and punctuation, the gain in clearness and ease of reading seeming to me to outweigh the loss in lack of fidelity to what Milton wrote. In punctuation I have often had to be satisfied with compromise, however, for the differences between seventeenth-century pointing and twentieth-century are as often as not reflections of differing conceptions of what constitutes a sentence. The result is a mixture of Milton's punctuation and mine; but in what I have changed and what I have left, I have been guided always by the desire for clarity. For the sake of uniformity I have normalized the spelling and punctuation even of the translations. By permission of Constable & Co. Ltd., publishers of Miss Helen Darbishire's *The Early Lives of Milton*, I have quoted in the course of my Introduction and notes various passages from the early biographies of Milton. These I have also modernized.

This book will be regarded by some, perhaps, as another contribution to what has been called 'the de-Massonizing' of Milton. Masson's *Life* is a work so overwhelming that all students of Milton since Masson have in some measure seen Milton through Masson's eyes. Here the attempt has been made to see Milton directly. But in the Introduction and notes I have nevertheless borrowed much more heavily from Masson than from anyone else, as must I think every student of Milton's life. By permission of the University of Michigan Press I have quoted at some length from Professor Hanford's 'The Youth of Milton' in *Studies in Shakespeare, Milton, and*

Donne. I have also depended frequently upon Professor Hanford's *A Milton Handbook,* upon Mr. Tillyard's *Milton* and upon his Introduction and notes to *Milton: Private Correspondence and Academic Exercises,* upon Miss Darbishire's *The Early Lives of Milton,* upon Smart's edition of *Milton's Sonnets,* and although largely in disagreement upon S.B.Liljegren's *Studies in Milton.* Other obligations are acknowledged in the notes.

I am under personal obligations to Mrs. Helen Senour of the Oberlin College Library, to Mrs. Henry Sams, to Mr. Charles G. Proffitt of the Columbia University Press, to Professor Howard F. Lowry of the College of Wooster, to Professor Andrew Bongiorno, especially, and to others of my colleagues at Oberlin College, to Professor James Holly Hanford of Western Reserve University, and to my wife, who has studied well the precept of *Paradise Lost, IX,* 232–234. It is her book as well as mine.

J.S.D.

Oberlin, Ohio
January 1, 1939

CONTENTS

INTRODUCTION

I

OF Milton's activities as a schoolmaster, of the attitude of his students toward him and of his attitude toward his students, of some of his friendships, of his personal mannerisms—his satirical wit and his strongly pronounced *r*'s—, of his habits of composition and dictation, of his three marriages, his treatment of his daughters, and his domestic life in general, we know from Milton himself but little, of some of these matters nothing, and are dependent upon the contributions of the early biographies. For other knowledge the early biographers themselves are dependent upon Milton's own utterances; for it is from Milton himself that we learn most of what we know of his education, of his travels, of his early and life-long devotion of himself to poetry, of his pride, his noble resignation, his consciousness of a high prophetic mission. From Milton himself, too, comes much of our knowledge of some of his friendships, of his particular aims in prose and in poetry, and (although largely by indirection) of his essential humanism and no less essential Puritanism. Nor do we know these things only because a poet always and unconsciously reveals himself in his writings to those who have wits enough to understand him, but rather because Milton wants us to know them, takes trouble that we may. And just as the perusal of the early lives of Milton as Miss Darbishire presents them to us gives a fresh, a clearer and more vivid picture of the man, so also does understanding acquaintance with Milton's own utterances upon himself add freshness and clarity. The result is an increase in the value to us of the mass of biographical and critical scholarship which may sometimes obscure the picture that it seeks to illuminate if we are not careful to refer to first sources.

Much of what we know of Milton we owe to the habit of periodic

self-examination which Professor Hanford has pointed out as characteristic of him.[1] At various mile-posts in his life, Milton paused to
take stock. Thus on the attainment of his majority, we find him
looking back over his past and ahead to his future, laying down for
himself, perhaps in part as a self-imposed course of training for the
vocation of epic poet, plans for a series of poems on religious themes,
plans from which come the *Nativity Ode*, *The Passion*, and possibly
Upon the Circumcision.[2] We see how he wrote of his beginning to
Diodati and how he poured out to Diodati his high hopes for the
future. The sonnet written upon the attainment of his twenty-third
year, 'How soon hath time . . .,' with the 'Letter to a Friend' in
which it is incorporated in the Trinity College Manuscript of Milton's minor poems, is another instance of his taking stock, of his
self-evaluation. So is the long account of his education in *An
Apology for Smectymnuus*, of the series of literary and moral in-
fluences to which he has been subject, and so are the passages in
the *Reason of Church Government* and the *Second Defence of the
People of England* in which he tells us not only who and whence he
is, but also what he has done and what he hopes to do. Perhaps the
publication of his collected poems in 1645 grew out of another self-
examination during which Milton decided that he was ready now to
turn from minor to major poetry.

The records that Milton has left of such moments of self-scrutiny
tell us what Milton thought of himself and what he wished others
to think. We shall not often find his judgements wrong. Much more
often than we shall find it necessary to make allowances for unreasonable bias in Milton, we shall find that we may accept what he
says with very little qualification indeed. We shall not agree with
Milton that he is infallible. We may not always believe that his
intellectual history was quite so orderly as it seemed to him in
retrospect, as in his account, for example, of the occasion for the
divorce pamphlets which we find in the *Second Defence* or in the
account of his reading and its effect upon his mind in *An Apology*

1 *Youth of Milton*, p.129.
2 Ibid. pp.126–127.

for Smectymnuus. We shall not be sure that Milton is as unconcerned as he thinks when he discusses his own personal appearance in reply to his enemies' descriptions of him. But in each of these matters as in others in which Milton seems either himself not to understand or else to obscure the issue, our problem is not so much one of correcting a misrepresentation as of correcting the perspective where the picture is badly drawn, and once or twice of filling in a blank in the canvas.

It is necessary, for example, to make a place for Mary Powell.

Milton says that he wrote his divorce pamphlets because, of the three types of liberty, he had himself written of the ecclesiastical, the magistrates were busy with the civil, and there was left for treatment the domestic. Nowhere in any of his works does he make direct mention of his marriage to Mary Powell. But as Professor Grierson observes, 'no one was ever, in one way, more susceptible to experience than Milton.'[3] The incidents of his own life lay behind his opinions no matter what his subject, and his unhappy marriage must have been the background for his divorce pamphlets just as the attacks upon those pamphlets lay behind his defence of free speech in the *Areopagitica.* But Professor Grierson further observes that Milton's personal motives became for him high ideals, that 'the cause for which he fought was always in his eyes the cause of humanity, the great cause of liberty.'[4]

It is necessary then that we add for ourselves, from the accounts in the early lives and from what we may read between the lines of *Paradise Lost* and *Samson Agonistes,* what Milton does not tell us directly, that his union with Mary Powell was the experience which impressed upon him the inadequacy of the marriage laws. 'But we need not therefore conclude,' says Mr. Tillyard, 'that what he did say was a mass of lies.'[5] There is no reason why an opinion based in some measure upon a personal experience should not be part of a coherent body of thought, such a body of thought as 'could

3 H.J.C.Grierson (Sir Herbert), *Cross Currents in English Literature of the Seventeenth Century,* p.237. London, 1929.
4 Ibid.
5 *Milton,* pp.109–110.

only have been formed in the meditative period before the Civil War.'⁶

But this does not quite end the matter. All critics agree that Milton's first marriage, or rather the shock of disillusionment that came with it, was one of the most significant experiences of Milton's life, that it was not merely the inciting cause of the divorce pamphlets, but that it changed the man and affected his entire work. Some, Saurat, for example, think it a crisis of such importance in Milton's existence that we must interpret almost every incident of his life and almost every line of his work in the light of it. And though we may disagree with Saurat in part, thinking it the danger of our age in biography that it tends to give more than due emphasis to such experiences, we must at least agree that in the series of great disappointments that make up the story of Milton's life, this was the one for which he was least prepared. Throughout his life, even through his subsequent marriages, Milton never recovered from the effects of his disappointment in Mary Powell. Thus, while none of *Samson Agonistes* is avowedly autobiographical, we cannot fail to find in it strong reminiscences of Milton's experience with Mary Powell—and of other events in his life. The parallels are too many. Like Samson, Milton is blind, disgraced, and has been captive. Like Samson, he has suffered in his marriage with a 'fell adversary,' and like Samson he has 'driven from the field of battle a boasting Harapha in the person of Salmasius.'⁷

Salmasius we need not fill in; Milton gives him pages enough, and to spare, but for Mary Powell we must go outside, to the early lives and to the hundreds of pages devoted to her in the later ones. But we must not forget that the omission of her name from the text of the present volume is an omission for which Milton himself is responsible, and an omission which has its own significance. 'A thousand miseries,' says Dr. Johnson, 'make silent and invisible

---

6 Ibid.
7 Sir Herbert J. C. Grierson, *Milton and Wordsworth*, pp. 136–137. Cambridge, 1937.

inroads on mankind, and the heart feels innumerable throbs which never break into complaint.'

But pages enough and to spare for Salmasius. And here is another necessary correction. It will seem that Milton gives far more than justly proportionate space in his writing about himself and his work to the explanation and justification of his part in the pamphlet warfare which accompanied the hardly more deadly military warfare of the Puritan revolution. At any rate, discussion of the prose controversies is given more space in that writing than Milton's friends, than his blindness, than his poetry, than his literary and prophetic ambitions.

For this fulness of treatment there are a number of reasons.

For one thing, Milton was apparently quite genuinely worried about the charges of indecency brought against him as a result of his use of the invective which was one of the conventions of pamphlet warfare. It is characteristic, however, that he makes his apologies and explanations of it the means of further insult by explaining that the nature of his antagonists makes savage, even indecent, treatment necessary, and once by protesting that he has for many pages employed no lewd word except the name of his opponent. His arguments in defence of his violence are hardly even specious, but their very presence (and even their weakness) is proof that he thought the charge a serious one.

Another reason for the apparent disproportion is that the longest and certainly the most active single period of Milton's life, in so far as a life so much of a piece as Milton's can be broken into periods, was devoted to the writing of controversial prose. Furthermore, most of the autobiographical passages are to be found in the prose, and hence come from the period of the prose, during which he was naturally preoccupied with it. And it was upon the basis of the prose pamphlets and in answer to them that personal attacks were made upon him.

Milton was not the man to leave himself undefended when he undertook the defence of the English people. We must not forget his habit of transmuting his personal into national needs, of identi-

fying himself with his cause and his cause with the nation's, of regarding himself 'as a member incorporate into that truth whereof'
he was persuaded.[8]

After the manner of the age, and of most ages, the attacks upon
Milton's pamphlets went far enough afield to pay violent disre-
spects to Milton's habits and person. His rejoinders therefore assert
his own righteousness and his opponents' vices. For the champion
is of a piece with his cause. Expanding himself, as it were, into his
cause, Milton expands his opponents into theirs. Consequently his
personal attacks upon his opponents, Bishop Hall, Salmasius, Alexander More, and even Vlaccus, More's printer, and the poor solicitor who is the subject matter of *Colasterion*, have a common justification with his defences of himself against their attacks. When the
reader learns what manner of men Milton's enemies are, he will
know what to think of their cause, and if the reader of scurrilous
and libellous attacks upon Milton is not disabused, Milton's, the
true cause, will suffer.

Of Salmasius and Alexander More, consequently, even when
Milton is talking about himself, we find more than we can wish, the
treatment of their real and imaginary vices which is mixed with
Milton's defences of himself being an accident of Milton's quarrels
with them. But the presence of disproportionate treatment of his
opponents within Milton's accounts of the controversies does not
mean that disproportionate emphasis is given controversy itself as
a part of his activity. The fulness of that treatment we cannot regret, in the first place because it is there that we find sandwiched in
most of our first-hand knowledge of Milton, and in the second
place because it reminds us of the great importance of those controversies to Milton. In the light of that importance, the appearance of disproportion will be seen to be illusory.

Milton early devoted himself to the cause of poetry. His life was
planned as few lives are to reach a predetermined goal: he was to be
a great poet. He was, moreover, to be a national poet, to write for
Englishmen an English epic to the glory of England. For the edifica-

8 *An Apology for Smectymnuus* (extract 105, below).

tion of England, too; for his was to be a poem 'doctrinal to the nation'while it embellished the heroic actions of an Englishman, probably King Arthur,[9] who could be made the pattern of a Christian
hero.

But Milton was turned aside from this, the first business of his
life, by the obligation which he felt (none more strongly) to throw
what strength he had into the struggle of Englishmen for what he
thought was their freedom. 'Always stronger in mind than in body,'
it was at once apparent that *his* pen, at least, was mightier than his
sword, and that it must be with his pen, even though it wrote prose
and hence was guided as it were but by his left hand, that he could
make his most valuable contribution. The hope of England and the
hope of the world were at stake, and Milton espoused the cause of
the Commonwealth, not because he was willing that his heart

> The lowliest duties on herself did lay,

but because what he undertook was

> . . . Liberty's defence, my noble task,
> Of which all Europe talks from side to side.

Milton, then, no doubt regarded the writing of his controversial
prose as an interruption of the progress of his plan of life, but it
was an interruption welcomed because at the time and in the circumstances it was the more important work.

Milton's satisfaction in that work is apparent when at one stage
it seems finished and he is able to declare in 1654, in the *Second
Defence*, that he has performed the service most valuable to the
commonwealth, defending liberty and the actions of his countrymen not only to England, but to the world, continuing that

> as the poet who is styled epic . . . undertakes to embellish not
> the whole life of the hero whom he proposes to celebrate in song,
> but usually one particular action of his life, . . . so likewise

9 But the plans for poems in the Trinity College Manuscript show that he at
one time also considered King Alfred a possible hero.

will it suffice for my duty and excuse that I have at least embellished one of the heroic actions of my countrymen.[10]

This is to say by implication at least, that in the performance of the duty which seemed to lead him away from the performance of the central function of his life, he has in part performed that function also. Professor Grierson interprets this passage to mean that Milton has come to think that he has in writing the defences achieved his ambition to write an epic on an historical subject for the edification of Englishmen.[11] Milton himself in his statement of his purpose in the *First Defence* says he is about

> to relate no common things, or mean; but how a most puissant king, when he had trampled upon the laws, and stricken down religion, and was ruling at his own lust and wantonness, was at last subdued in the field by his own people, who had served a long term of slavery; how he was thereupon put under guard, and when he gave no ground whatever, by either word or action, to hope better things of him, was finally by the highest council of the realm condemned to die, and beheaded before his very palace gate.[12]

This, the overthrow, the trial, and the execution of the King is the deed 'exemplary to the nations,' and the theme of his epic.

And if, Grierson points out, if the defences are the fulfilment of Milton's dream of writing a national epic, then *Paradise Lost* is not the fulfilment of that original intention, but something else 'to which he passed when that had been achieved in ways decreed by God and Destiny.'[13] And if this be so—indeed, whether it be literally so or not—the writing of the prose pamphlets is not to be considered as in Milton's eyes a comparatively unimportant task, unwillingly undertaken, but on the contrary a very significant and satisfying task, worthy of the attention it receives in the autobio-

10 Extract 129.
11 *Milton and Wordsworth*, pp.72–73.
12 Extract 91.
13 *Milton and Wordsworth*, p.73.

graphical passages and in Milton's judgement worthy of the years and the sacrifices devoted to it.

It is no new thing for us to be reminded that Milton's verse is in bulk far from the greater portion of his work, or that it was his fame as a writer of prose controversy, not his fame as a poet, which brought to his door distinguished visitors to England, so that Aubrey could observe that 'the only inducement of several foreigners that came over into England, was chiefly to see O. Protector & Mr. J. Milton.'[14] But the significance of the reminder is made clearer when we see that Milton also considered his prose, the *First Defence*, specifically, a memorial which would not easily perish and to speak in 1658 of the world's reception of it as 'my zealous labour's fruit—the highest that I for my part have set before me in this life,'[15] even though, with obvious reference to *Paradise Lost*, the same paragraph promises yet greater things. It shows us that in this respect no correction even of perspective is necessary.

But as it is necessary to make some allowance for the conventions of pamphlet warfare in our judgements of Milton's character and taste based on his prose (although less allowance than he asks of us, since he adopted the conventions even while he protested against them), so is it necessary to make allowances in our estimates of his friendships for the conventions of the Latin letter. Thus Mr. Tillyard observes that we must remember in reading the Latin correspondence that

> Milton treated the Latin letter as a serious set form of composition, on which a good deal of trouble had to be expended. It was something that served among other things to exhibit the writer's command over the Latin language.[16]

The result is that the Latin letters are deliberately, and to modern taste, extravagantly, rhetorical. If from them we are to learn what Milton's feelings are toward the friend to whom he writes, we must

14 Darbishire, *Early Lives*, p.7.
15 In the epilogue to the second edition of the *First Defence* (extract 120).
16 Tillyard, *Correspondence and Academic Exercises*, pp.ix–x.

tone down what he says. In the first letter, for example, to Thomas Young, his teacher, we cannot fail to find sure evidences of a genuine affection and of great respect for Young, but we cannot read quite literally when Milton calls

> God to witness how much in the light of a father I regard you, with what singular devotion I have always followed you in thought, and how I feared to trouble you with my writings,

nor can we quite accept his excuse for not writing oftener, whatever Young made of it:

> My first care, I suppose, is that since there is nothing else to commend my letters, their rarity may commend them.[17]

But once we have accepted the convention, the necessary corrections or qualifications make themselves, and even in translation there is no difficulty in recognizing the much more literal genuineness of such letters as those to Diodati and to Carlo Dati.

For the most part, then, there are very few difficulties in interpretation. As far as Milton's account of himself goes, the narrative is simple and straightforward. Despite the long defences of his personal morality, Milton tells us very little indeed of his genuinely personal life, and a great deal of his literary, his professional life, and of his intellectual development. What he tells us is about as trustworthy as autobiography can be.

II

In Milton's time and in our own there have been critics and biographers who have regarded Milton as far indeed from trustworthy, and although we need not here enter into a detailed discussion of the accusations brought against Milton by the Royalists of the seventeenth century and by Herr Mutschmann in the twentieth, we cannot avoid the question.

The whole of Milton's controversy with Alexander More, to which we have already made passing reference, one of the most

[17] Familiar Letter 1 (extract 15).

frequently urged instances of Milton's 'untrustworthiness,' arises from the false attribution to More of a book of which he was not the author. *Regii Sanguinis Clamor ad Coelum* . . ., 'The Cry of the Royal Blood to Heaven against the English Parricides,' is an anonymous pamphlet which, condemning the revolution in the most violent terms, praises Salmasius and attacks Milton, and after him some of his colleagues in the Commonwealth. The book was written by the younger Peter Du Moulin, but was in part sponsored by Alexander More, a French-born Scotch clergyman in Holland, who wrote the foreword in praise of Salmasius and abuse of Milton. On the basis of letters from friends on the continent, Milton attributed the whole work to More and after some delay prepared a *Second Defence of the People of England in Reply to an Infamous Book entitled 'Cry of the King's Blood to Heaven against the English Parricides,'* on his usual theory that the best defence is a strong attack. More's character is dissected by a very cruel scalpel. Pages of the book are devoted to his real and imaginary disgraces, especially to a story of his seduction of Pontia or Bontia, an English servant-girl in Salmasius' household. But attack is not Milton's only defence, and long passages provide us with valuable discussions of Milton's habits, training, achievements, and ambitions.

When Milton's book was ready for the press, word came to More of its imminent publication through Milton's friend, John Durie. More, who was, we have said, not really the author of the *Cry*, communicated his denial to Milton through Durie, two of whose letters upon the subject survive, and through the Dutch ambassador, Nieuport. But Milton's book was finished, and he was in no mood for unsupported denials.

Here Aubrey's note upon the subject is pertinent and amusing:

Memorandum. His sharp writing against Alexander More, of Holland, upon a mistake, notwithstanding he had given him by the Ambassador (Nieuport, the Dutch Ambassador) all satisfaction to the contrary, viz. that the book called *Clamor* was writ by Peter Du Moulin. Well, that was all one; he having writ it, it should go into the world. One of them was as bad as the other.[18]

So far we can follow Milton's argument. We do not know how conclusive the information given him by Nieuport was, but Milton's own statement that it was a mere denial communicated through Nieuport by More is circumstantial and quite convincing. Surely, if it were such, Milton could hardly be expected to accept a mere denial from a man to whom he had applied the epithet *liar* as one of the mildest of many epithets. Besides, More had sponsored the book and had written the foreword at least. One of them *was* as bad as the other. The reply was already written and ready for publication. And Milton was a stubborn man.

But the argument went further. Alexander More was a brave man, whatever else he may have been. He answered Milton's 'calumny' in a volume called *Fides Publica* . . ., the 'Public Faith of Alexander More,' in which he denies again and again the authorship of the *Cry*, insisting also that Milton knew even at the time of the publication of the *Second Defence* that he was not the author. He is generous, too, with further abuse of Milton.

The *Public Faith* Milton also undertook to answer, in the *Defence of Himself*, responding to the fresh attacks made upon him and undertaking to prove (addressing More)

> either that you were the author of that notorious libel against us [the *Cry*], or that you have given sufficient cause for being deservedly considered as the author . . .,[19]

on the double ground that More had assisted in the publication and is the kind of man who might have written the *Cry* even though perhaps he didn't. This is as near to a confession of error as Milton ever comes.

An account of the situation by the real author of the *Cry* appeared

18 Darbishire, *Early Lives*, pp.14–15.
19 Extract 93.

in 1670, for in that year a volume by Peter Du Moulin was published in which is a Latin poem, 'To the Bestial Blackguard John
Milton, Parricide and Advocate of the Parricide,' reprinted from
the *Cry* and equipped with a Latin prose account of its occasion.
Masson translates as follows:

> Into what danger I was thrown by the first appearance of this
> poem in the *Clamor Regii Sanguinis* would not seem to me
> worthy of public notice now, were it not that the miracle of di
> vine protection by which I was kept safe is most worthy of the
> common admiration of the good and the praise of the Supreme
> Deliverer. I had sent my manuscript sheets to the great Salma
> sius, who entrusted them to the care of that most learned man,
> Alexander Morus. This Morus delivered them to the printer,
> and prefixed to them an Epistle to the King, in the Printer's
> name, exceedingly eloquent and full of good matter. When that
> care of Morus over the business of printing the book had become
> known to Milton . . ., Milton held it as an ascertained fact that
> Morus was the author of the *Clamor*; whence that most virulent
> book of Milton's against Morus, entitled *Defensio Secunda pro
> Populo Anglicano*. . . . Meanwhile I looked on in silence, and
> not without a soft chuckle, at seeing my bantling laid at another
> man's door, and the blind and furious Milton fighting and slash
> ing the air, like the hoodwinked horse-combatants in the old
> circus, not knowing by whom he was struck and whom he struck
> in return. But Morus, unable to stand out against so much ill-
> will, began to cool in the King's cause, and gave Milton to know
> who the author of the *Clamor* really was. For, in fact, in his Re
> ply to Milton's attack he produced two witnesses, of the highest
> credit among the rebels, who might have well known the author,
> and could divulge him on being asked. Thus over me and my
> head there hung the most certain destruction. But that great
> Guardian of Justice, to whom I had willingly devoted both my
> labour and my life, wrought out my safety through Milton's
> own pride, as it is customary with His Wisdom to bring good

out of evil, and light out of darkness. For Milton, who had gone full tilt at Morus with his canine eloquence, and who had made it almost the sole object of his *Defensio Secunda* to cut up the life and reputation of Morus, never could be brought to confess that he had been so grossly mistaken. . . . And so, Milton persisting in his blundering charge against Morus for that dangerous service to the King, the other Rebels could not, without great damage to their good patron, proceed against any other than Morus as guilty of so great a crime. And, as Milton preferred my getting off scatheless to being found in a ridiculous position himself, I had this reward for my pains, that Milton, whom I had treated so roughly, turned out my patron and sedulous body-guard. Don't laugh, reader; but give thanks, with me, to God, the most good, the most great, and the most wise, deliverer.[20]

Though his reading of More's denial of authorship of the *Cry* as an evidence of More's cooling in the King's cause and his partial attribution of his escape to divine justice leave us unconvinced, Du Moulin is of course partly right in attributing that escape also to Milton's pride. But Milton himself gives another and better explanation of his refusal to make a full confession of error. More, he says, labours his one point, that he was not the author of the *Cry*, so hard and so long, giving little or no attention to other charges brought against him, because he hopes that by discrediting Milton upon this one point he will cast doubt over Milton's whole work and endanger Milton's cause itself. The danger is real. Confident of the justice of his own cause, and certain of More's attachment to the other, Milton needs no other justification for his injustice, especially since he does not undertake to assert More's authorship of the *Cry* without qualification, but merely that More deserves to be considered author of it if he wasn't actually. To be sure, having made the qualification, Milton does often repeat his charge without it.

Of this incident in Milton's career there are two current interpretations. Liljegren, writing of Milton's 'intense feeling of ma-

20 Masson, *Life*, Vol. V, pp.219–221.

jesty and elevation above the human race at large,' cites it as an instance of

> sentiments and a mode of reasoning toward fellow-creatures
> that seem as absolute and arbitrary as those which he censured
> so severely in Charles I,

and continues that Charles himself could hardly have punished one of his subjects for a crime 'proved to have been committed by another,' simply because he chose to consider him guilty. Milton's treatment of More Liljegren describes as 'majestically indifferent to truth or untruth, fact or gossip.'[21]

Mr. Tillyard, on the other hand, finds in the incident evidence that Milton in controversy was really impersonal, that Salmasius and More 'are hypotheses who have to be damaged by every possible means,'[22] that Milton's real concern is not with personalities, but with the abstract theme of dispute.

Although Mr. Tillyard, it may seem, is going farther than necessary to explain (not in any attempt to explain away, however) Milton's conduct, it is certain that Liljegren is too hard upon Milton. The assignment of the authorship of the *Cry* to Alexander More was only mistaken, not groundless and arbitrary. Nor even after that authorship had become doubtful was Milton meting out punishment to More for a crime in which he was not concerned. If the *Cry* were a crime, More was an accomplice in it and thus in Milton's eyes deserving of the punishment the crime merited. Nor could we ask, surely, as Liljegren seems to do, that Milton examine with much care the truth or untruth of the other charges brought against More by gossip, or fail to make the most of the Pontia episode and the quarrel between More and Salmasius that grew out of it. If the attacks made upon Milton were to be answered in kind, his opponents were indeed, as Mr. Tillyard says, 'to be damaged by every possible means,' even though we may not agree that Milton 'never envisages them as human beings.'[23]

21 Liljegren, *Studies in Milton*, pp.xx–xxi.
22 *Milton*, pp.131–132.
23 Ibid.

Another, perhaps more serious, charge of falsehood brought against Milton, also by Liljegren as it was earlier brought by the Royalists, is the charge that it was by Milton's contriving that the prayer of Pamela from the *Arcadia* was introduced into the *Eikon Basilike* in order that he might have a ground on which to attack that volume in his reply, the *Eikonoklastes*. This charge is not so serious as it may at first seem if we remember not only that Milton thought the *Eikon Basilike* a forgery, and not by the King at all, and therefore might again think of himself as fighting fire with fire, but also that it almost certainly was a forgery, written by Dr. John Gauden, Bishop of Exeter. But even though the charge is supported by Liljegren with his characteristic thoroughness and ingenuity, we are relieved of the task of explaining, apologizing, or justifying Milton's conduct in the matter by the refutation of Liljegren's argument in Smart's article, 'Milton and the King's Prayer,' where it is established

> that the King sometimes wrote out with his own hand a prayer which he thought suitable for his private devotions, and that one thus copied by him is included in the publication which contains Sir Philip Sidney's. The natural inference is that Charles had himself selected Sidney's prayer, as well as Bayly's, and used it in the same way and for the same purpose.[24]

Not only, then, is the prayer not a hoax engineered by Milton, it is not even part of Gauden's forgery. And while Milton's charges against the King's use of the Pamela prayer are indeed outrageous, they are not based upon a lie.

Whatever Milton's injustice, then, in his treatment of his opponents in pamphlet warfare, the charges of direct and deliberate falsehood brought against him on the basis of it are not well founded. In both instances that we have discussed, however, the charge is not that he lied about himself (although that is implied), but about others. Our concern is with his autobiographical writings. Their trustworthiness we must determine if we can, and it is

24 *Review of English Studies*, I (1925).

necessary therefore that we consider also charges of falsehood brought against Milton's accounts of his own actions and character.

In saying earlier that Milton's autobiographical utterances are as trustworthy as autobiography can be, we have implied a standard of honesty. It is taken from, of all English autobiographies, the most honest, Anthony Trollope's:

> That I, or any man, should tell everything of himself, I hold to be impossible. Who could endure to own the doing of a mean thing? Who is there that has done none? But this I protest:— that nothing that I say shall be untrue. I will set down naught in malice; nor will I give to myself, or others, honour which I do not believe to have been fairly won.

But we are assuming further what Trollope himself does not assume, and what he confirms by doing himself less than justice: that no man who writes much of himself can always know or always tell the literal truth in what he relates, whatever he may omit. Certainly, we must agree, Milton does not, although I think he can be cleared of charges of deliberate falsehood.

Milton is perhaps especially likely to mislead in passages in which he is replying to pamphlet attacks upon himself. In answer to the charges of Salmasius and Du Moulin that he was expelled from Cambridge and fled from his disgraces to Italy, for example, Milton replies in the *Second Defence* that he finished his full residence in Cambridge, obtaining his two degrees, and then returned home, leaving behind him the 'affectionate regret' of the Fellows of the College. It is, I think, as far as it goes, the exact truth. But it is not the whole truth, for Milton makes no mention of his quarrel with his tutor, Chappell, and the consequent rustication—which, indeed, Milton mentions only in Elegy I, to Diodati. Yet it seems probable that this rustication was the basis of the charge made in the *Cry* that he was expelled (although Hilaire Belloc thinks it refers instead to Milton's failure to secure a fellowship). There is of course no ground for the statement that Milton fled from his dis-

graces to Italy. But surely to demand of Milton that he provide his
opponents with information they apparently did not have of such an
incident (Aubrey says Chappell 'whipt him') is to expect more of
him than human nature can give. Nor can we in justice call such a
suppression dishonest.

Another passage in the *Second Defence* also comes into question.
In his account of his sojourn in Italy, Milton tells us that as he left
Naples for Rome,

> the merchants gave me an intimation . . . that, in case of my
> revisiting Rome, the English Jesuits had laid a plot for me be-
> cause I had spoken too freely on the subject of religion; for I had
> laid it down as a rule for myself never to begin a conversation on
> religion in those parts, but if interrogated concerning my faith
> to dissemble nothing. I therefore returned notwithstanding to
> Rome; I concealed from no one who asked the question, what I
> was; if anyone attacked me, I defended in the most open man-
> ner, as before, the orthodox faith, for nearly two months more,
> in the city even of the sovereign pontiff himself. By the will of
> God I arrived safe again at Florence. . . .[25]

This passage, Liljegren, again, discredits in large measure as
rising from Milton's desire to pose before the public. That the conduct of which he here gives an account is a source of pride for Milton we can hardly doubt. He was capable of taking pride in most
things he did, perhaps in all things of which he tells. But it does not
follow because he takes pride in telling of them that he did not do
them.

The grave danger of a Jesuit plot of which he speaks, Liljegren
observes, is hardly reconcilable with his acceptance of the hospi-
tality of the English Jesuit College at Rome. The register of guests
does show that Milton dined there in October 1638. But this was on
his first visit to Rome. Had Liljegren observed that fact and that
the warning of which Milton speaks is against his return to Rome
for a second visit, he would have found the reconciliation easier.

25 Extract 2.

We can well imagine Milton recalling things he said on his first visit—perhaps even at dinner at the college—and taking the warning seriously. Nor does Milton actually speak of any grave danger from a Jesuit plot: it is only that he was warned against one.

It is in this same passage that Milton tells us that when he left Naples Manso

> gravely apologized for showing me no more attention, alleging that . . . it was not in his power in that city, because I had not thought proper to be more guarded on the point of religion.

Of this the epigram that Manso sent to Milton with his gift of cups (or books) is confirmation. Masson translates as follows:

> Joannes Baptista Mansus, Marquis of Villa,
> Neapolitan, to John Milton, Englishman.
> Mind, form, grace, face, and morals are perfect; if but thy
> creed were,
> Then not Anglic alone, truly angelic thou'dst be.

In the autobiography of Lord Herbert of Cherbury we find an account of a visit to Rome and to the English Jesuit College in the year 1614. Lord Herbert also makes a second visit:

> . . . I returned to Rome, and saw the Pope in consistory, which being done, when the Pope being now ready to give his blessing, I departed thence suddenly, which gave such a suspicion of me, that some were sent to apprehend me, but I going a by-way escaped them, and went to my inn to take horse, where I had not been now half an hour, when the master or regent of the English college telling me that I was accused in the Inquisition, and that I could stay no longer with safety, I took this warning very kindly; howbeit I did only for the present change my lodging, and a day or two afterwards took horse and went out of Rome towards Siena. . . .

To the detail of Lord Herbert's account few who have read the autobiography will be inclined to give much credence. But however true or false it may be, the account itself is evidence that Protestants in Rome regarded Jesuit plots against them as serious realities and the Inquisition as a real danger.

'That Milton, as natural, freely discussed religion among the Svogliati at Florence,' Liljegren observes, 'does not nearly amount to the situation implied by his narrative.'[26] But it would be equally natural, surely, for a young Englishman travelling in seventeenth-century Italy with a Protestant chip on his shoulder to imagine a plot against him, especially since he might have been (and says he was) warned of the danger. Chief among the maxims 'of great use to one going abroad' for which Milton is indebted (and grateful) to Sir Henry Wotton was one advising him to 'keep his thoughts close and his countenance loose.' We may believe of Milton, however, that it was easier for him to keep his resolution to dissemble nothing than never to begin a conversation on religion. Even though he says himself, explaining his lack of fame at the beginning of the controversy with Salmasius, that he had 'learned to be long silent,' the gift of silence is not one which acquaintance inclines us to grant him. Finally, it is the biographers of Milton (those who admire him inordinately, and those like Liljegren who do not) that have made much of Milton's claim to courage in Rome. Milton himself only tells us that he was warned of a Jesuit plot, that he ignored the warning, and that by the will of God nothing came of it. We are meant, of course, to deduce his courage and his honesty, but we are left to make as much or as little of the plot as we will. That we may further deduce, from the account in the *Second Defence* and from the Manso epigram, that Milton's youthful brashness sometimes gave offence, Milton did not intend, but he nevertheless makes it a necessary deduction. That what he says of himself cannot be trusted still does not follow.

In *An Apology for Smectymnuus* Milton replies to the charges of Bishop Hall that he is an habitué of the playhouses and bordellos, on the evidence of acquaintance with them revealed in the *Animadversions* by Milton's mention of 'old cloaks, false beards, night-

26 *Studies in Milton,* p.16.

walkers, and salt lotion.' The charge that he haunts the bordellos Milton answers with the famous long account of his devotion to chastity as the most important of virtues. But the theatres are another thing. The argument follows:

> But since there is such necessity to the hearsay of a tire, a periwig, or a visard, that plays must have been seen, what difficulty was there in that, when in the colleges so many of the young divines, and those in next aptitude to divinity, have been seen so oft upon the stage, writhing and unboning their clergy limbs to all the antic and dishonest gestures of Trinculos, buffoons, and bawds, prostituting the shame of that ministry which either they had, or were nigh to having, to the eyes of courtiers and court ladies, with their grooms and mesdemoiselles? There while they acted, and overacted, among other young scholars, I was a spectator. They thought themselves gallant men, and I thought them fools; they made sport, and I laughed; they mispronounced, and I misliked; and to make up the atticism, they were out, and I hissed. Judge now whether so many good text-men were not sufficient to instruct me of false beards and visards without more expositors. And how can this confuter take the face to object to me the seeing of that which his reverent prelates allow, and incite their young disciples to act? For if it be unlawful to sit and behold a mercenary comedian personating that which is least unseemly for a hireling to do, how much more blameful is it to endure the sight of as vile things acted by persons either entered or presently to enter into the ministry, and how much more foul and ignominious for them to be the actors.[27]

Whether Milton attended the theatres up to their closing in September 1642, the year in which this was written, I do not know. But Elegy I, to Diodati, written during the period of Milton's rustication from Cambridge, shows clearly that Milton's knowledge of the theatre came not only from amateur theatricals at the university, but also from the 'splendour of the rounded theatre' in London.

27 Extract 41.

And it was in 1640 that Milton took the house in Aldersgate Street where 'first it was his academic erudition was put in practice' when he turned schoolmaster. It was at this time

> that once in three weeks or a month, he would drop into the society of some young sparks of his acquaintance, the chief whereof were Mr. Alphrey, and Mr. Miller, two gentlemen of Gray's Inn, the beaux of those times, but nothing near so bad as those nowadays; with these gentlemen he would so far make bold with his body as now and then to keep a gaudy-day.[28]

It is not impossible that such a gaudy-day included attendance at the theatre. Whether it did or not, the passage in *An Apology for Smectymnuus* is misleading in so far as it suggests that Milton gained all his knowledge of the theatre while he was in Cambridge, and of course this is its implication. But the last two sentences quoted from it above are almost an admission of theatre-going and are a partial defence of it on the ground that if it is proper for amateurs to take part in plays it is proper for Milton to watch professionals. At any rate we may search long and hard throughout the passage for a flat denial of attendance at the playhouses and not find it.

In the matter of theatre-going Milton no doubt intends to mislead us in the *Apology*, just as in his 'Letter to a Friend' he intends to mislead by writing of his preparation for a literary career in terms that make it possible for the friend to understand him to be writing of preparation for a career in the church. But in both instances, as in the *Second Defence* where he denies expulsion from Cambridge without mentioning his rustication, Milton is quite apparently taking great pains, even to the point of weakening his argument, to avoid a direct lie. And here, as in the other passage we found justification for his failure to supply his opponents with ammunition to be used against himself, we can find it again in the fact that Hall in his attack upon Milton combines the haunting of theatres and brothels into a single accusation. To defend theatre-going or to admit it might easily have been (under the prevailing standards of

28 Edward Phillips. Darbishire, *Early Lives*, p.62.

literary controversy almost certainly would have been) somehow interpreted to be an admission of guilt covering both halves of the charge.

Professor Hanford observes of the 'Letter to a Friend' that there is in it the 'misleading suppression of a part of his full mind, which we may regard as a characteristic manifestation of Miltonic strategy.'[29] Such a 'misleading suppression' is the response to Hall's charge here, and such another, perhaps, Milton's account of the occasion for the divorce pamphlets. But the care to avoid a direct lie discernible even in these unquestionably misleading passages makes it extremely doubtful that we ought ever to mistrust a direct statement of Milton about himself—even his statement in the *Areopagitica* that he met Galileo when he was in Italy. On this point Liljegren argues tellingly from the difficulties encountered by Benedetto Castelli when he visited Galileo in the fall of 1638, and from the general difficulties of access to Galileo because of the Inquisition and because of Galileo's ill health. But Miss Marjorie Nicolson points out that Liljegren 'lays his stress rather upon the difficulties which Castelli met than upon the fact that he succeeded in his request,'[30] and that he 'passes over too easily the visit of Padre Clement in January, 1639' and fails to mention at all other visitors to Galileo in 1639 and 1641. Miss Nicolson also observes that Signor Favaro, from whose edition of *Le Opere* Liljegren takes his information, and 'who has more intimate knowledge of this evidence than any other scholar, has found no reason to doubt Milton's statement.' Her argument that the 'Inquisition may have had reasons for suspicions of Castelli which did not exist in Milton's case, particularly if Milton's visit occurred during his first stay in Florence,' before he had made himself obnoxious by defending 'the orthodox faith' whenever he was interrogated, not only strengthens the probability of the visit to Galileo but gives us a tentative date for it. In any event, although perhaps the case against Milton here cannot be

29 *Youth of Milton*, p.130.
30 Marjorie Nicolson, 'Milton and the Telescope,' *English Literary History*, II (1935), pp.8–10 and note 36, p.8.

discredited as completely as that against him in the Pamela-prayer incident, it is still far from proved. Until it is, or until other instances of out and out falsehood are found in Milton, the presumption must remain in his favour.

We may conclude, then, that in order to arrive at a trustworthy conception of Milton's character and a knowledge of the events of his intellectual development by reading what he says of himself, we must be on our guard against 'misleading suppressions' of pertinent material, we must fill in gaps left deliberately or because of Milton's lack of proper perspective with information drawn from other sources, and we must, each of us in his own way, read between the lines not only of Milton's autobiography, but of his whole work, for that unconscious revelation of self which is quite as important and if we can but understand it quite as trustworthy as the conscious. Whatever allowances we make for error, omission, or intent to mislead in the writings of Milton on himself (and various readers will make varying allowances), those writings are the sole source of some of our knowledge of Milton and the chief source of other knowledge. As such they are interesting not only to the biographer or professional critic of Milton, but to every other student of Milton as well. It is in this conviction that they are collected in this volume.

MILTON ON HIMSELF

MILTON ON HIMSELF

I. A PLAN OF LIFE

All my mind was set
Serious to learn and know, and thence to do,
What might be public good; myself I thought
Born to that end, born to promote all truth,
All righteous things.

1. From the *Reason of Church Government*. 1642.

At the beginning of the second book of this, the most telling of his ecclesiastical pamphlets, Milton has spoken of the burden of knowledge and of the obligation of the men who bear it to speak what they know. In citing the lament of Jeremiah that he was born 'a man of strife and contention,' and the unhappiness of Sophocles' Tiresias that he knew more than other men, Milton implies that he himself shares the burden, and then in the present extract proceeds to explain the requirement that he speak, and his fitness for the particular task he has undertaken. He then goes further to explain his preparation for a literary life and something of his literary aspirations.

This extract may better belong with Milton's various utterances upon his poetic ambitions (section VIII), but it has been put here to serve as a general introduction to all Milton's comment upon himself because it is a statement of the plan of life by which he lived.

FOR surely to every good and peaceable man it must in nature needs be a hateful thing to be the displeaser and molester of thousands; much better would it like him doubtless to be the messenger of gladness and contentment, which is his chief intended business, to all mankind, but that they resist and oppose their own true happiness. But when God commands to take the trumpet and blow a dolorous or a jarring blast, it lies not in man's will what he shall say or what he shall conceal. If he shall think to be silent as Jeremiah did, because of the reproach and derision he met with daily, and 'all his familiar friends watched for his halting,' to be revenged on him for speaking the truth, he would be forced to confess as he confessed,

'His word was in my heart as a burning fire shut up in my bones; I was weary with forbearing, and could not stay.' Which might teach these times not suddenly to condemn all things that are sharply spoken or vehemently written as proceeding out of stomach, virulence, and ill nature, but to consider rather that if the prelates have leave to say the worst that can be said and do the worst that can be done, while they strive to keep to themselves, to their great pleasure and commodity, those things which they ought to render up, no man can be justly offended with him that shall endeavour to impart and bestow without any gain to himself those sharp but saving words which would be a terror and a torment in him to keep back. For me, I have determined to lay up as the best treasure and solace of a good old age, if God vouchsafe it me, the honest liberty of free speech from my youth, where I shall think it available in so dear a concernment as the church's good. For if I be either by disposition, or what other cause, too inquisitive or suspicious of myself and mine own doings, who can help it? But this I foresee, that should the church be brought under heavy oppression, and God have given me ability the while to reason against that man that should be the author of so foul a deed, or should she by blessing from above on the industry and courage of faithful men change this her distracted estate into better days without the least furtherance or contribution of those few talents which God at that present had lent me, I foresee what stories I should hear within myself, all my life after, of discourage and reproach. 'Timorous and ingrateful, the church of God is now again at the foot of her insulting enemies: and thou bewailest. What matters it for thee or thy bewailing? When time was, thou couldst not find a syllable of all that thou hadst read or studied to utter in her behalf. Yet ease and leisure was given thee for thy retired thoughts out of the sweat of other men. Thou hadst the diligence, the parts, the language of a man, if a vain subject were to be adorned or beautified; but when the cause of God and His church was to be pleaded, for which purpose that tongue was given thee which thou hast, God listened if He could hear thy voice among His zealous servants, but thou wert dumb as a beast; from hence forward be that which thine own brutish silence hath made thee.' Or else I should have heard on the other ear, 'Slothful, and ever to be set light by, the church hath now overcome her late distresses after the unwearied labours of many her true servants that stood up in her defence; thou also wouldst take upon thee to share amongst them of their joy: but wherefore thou? Where canst thou show any word or deed of thine which might have hastened her peace? Whatever thou dost now talk or write or look is the alms of other men's active prudence and zeal. Dare not now to say or do anything better than thy former sloth and infancy; or if thou darest, thou dost impudently to make a thrifty purchase of boldness to thyself out of the painful merits of other men. What before was thy sin, is now thy duty to be, abject, and worthless.' These and such like lessons as these, I know would have been my matins duly, and my evensong. But now by this little diligence, mark what a privilege I have gained: with good men and saints to claim my right of lamenting the tribulations of the church, if she should suffer, when others that have ventured nothing for her sake have not the honour to be admitted mourners. But if she lift up her drooping head and prosper, among those that have something more than wished her welfare I have my charter and freehold of rejoicing to me and my heirs. Concerning therefore this wayward subject against prelaty, the touching whereof is so distasteful and disquietous to a number of men, as by what hath been said I may deserve of charitable readers to be credited, that neither envy nor gall hath entered me upon this controversy, but the enforcement of conscience only, and a preventive fear lest the omitting of this duty should be against me when I would store up to myself the good provision of peaceful hours. So lest it should be still imputed to me, as I have found it hath been, that some self-pleasing humour of vainglory hath incited me to contest with men of high estimation, now while green years are upon my head,[1] from this needless surmisal I shall hope to dissuade the intelligent and equal auditor if I can but say successfully that which in this exigent behoves me,

1 Milton was thirty-three.

although I would be heard only, if it might be, by the elegant and learned reader, to whom principally for a while I shall beg leave I may address myself. To him it will be no new thing though I tell him that if I hunted after praise by the ostentation of wit and learning I should not write thus out of mine own season, when I have neither yet completed to my mind the full circle of my private studies, although I complain not of any insufficiency to the matter in hand; or were I ready to my wishes, it were a folly to commit anything elaborately composed to the careless and interrupted listening of these tumultuous times. Next, if I were wise only to mine own ends, I would certainly take such a subject as of itself might catch applause, whereas this hath all the disadvantages on the contrary, and such a subject as the publishing whereof might be delayed at pleasure, and time enough to pencil it over with all the curious touches of art, even to the perfection of a faultless picture, whenas in this argument the not deferring is of great moment to the good speeding, that if solidity have leisure to do her office, art cannot have much. Lastly, I should not choose this manner of writing, wherein knowing myself inferior to myself, led by the genial power of nature to another task, I have the use, as I may account it, but of my left hand. And though I shall be foolish in saying more to this purpose, yet since it will be such a folly as wisest men going about to commit have only confessed and so committed, I may trust with more reason, because with more folly, to have courteous pardon. For although a poet soaring in the high region of his fancies with his garland and singing robes about him might without apology speak more of himself than I mean to do, yet for me sitting here below in the cool element of prose, a mortal thing among many readers of no empyreal conceit, to venture and divulge unusual things of myself, I shall petition to the gentler sort, it may not be envy to me. I must say therefore that after I had from my first years by the ceaseless diligence and care of my father, whom God recompense, been exercised to the tongues and some sciences, as my age would suffer, by sundry masters and teachers both at home and at the schools, it was found that whether aught was imposed me by them that had the overlooking, or betaken to of mine own choice, in English or other tongue, prosing or versing, but chiefly this latter, the style by certain vital signs it had, was likely to live. But much latelier in the private academies of Italy, whither I was favoured to resort, perceiving that some trifles which I had in memory, composed at under twenty or thereabout (for the manner is that every one must give some proof of his wit and reading there), met with acceptance above what was looked for, and other things which I had shifted in scarcity of books and conveniences to patch up amongst them were received with written encomiums, which the Italian is not forward to bestow on men of this side the Alps, I began thus far to assent both to them and divers of my friends here at home, and not less to an inward prompting which now grew daily upon me, that by labour and intent study (which I take to be my portion in this life) joined with the strong propensity of nature, I might perhaps leave something so written to aftertimes, as they should not willingly let it die.[2] These thoughts at once possessed me, and these other: that if I were certain to write as men buy leases, for three lives and downward, there ought no regard be sooner had than to God's glory by the honour and instruction of my country. For which cause, and not only for that I knew it would be hard to arrive at the second rank among the Latins, I applied myself to that resolution which Ariosto followed against the persuasions of Bembo, to fix all the industry and art I could unite to the adorning of my native tongue; not to make verbal curiosities the

2 The various Latin elegies, especially those addressed to Diodati—indeed all the material to be found in section VIII below, upon Milton's poetic aspirations and achievements—, and the extended analysis of his poetic and moral development in *An Apology for Smectymnuus* (extract 41), provide interesting commentary upon this passage in showing that Milton's dedication of himself to poetry and his confidence in his ability as a poet came in fact much earlier than his sojourn in Italy. But even though Milton knew he was a poet long before the Italian journey, the enthusiasm of his Italian friends for his work was a great stimulus to him. And while some of the young men whom he met in Italy may have found Milton a little prudish, as Mr. Liljegren suggests, and Manso at least of the older a little opinionated, as we have seen in our Introduction, there can be no doubt of their appreciation of his genius nor that his account of it here is on the whole a modest one.

end[3] (that were a toilsome vanity), but to be an interpreter and relater of the best and sagest things among mine own citizens
throughout this island, in the mother dialect.[4] That what the
greatest and choicest wits of Athens, Rome, or modern Italy, and
those Hebrews of old, did for their country, I in my proportion
with this over and above of being a Christian, might do for mine:
not caring to be once named abroad, though perhaps I could attain
to that, but content with these British Islands as my world, whose
fortune hath hitherto been, that if the Athenians, as some say, made
their small deeds great and renowned by their eloquent writers,
England hath had her noble achievements made small by the unskilful handling of monks and mechanics.[5]

Time serves not now, and perhaps I might seem too profuse to
give any certain account of what the mind at home in the spacious
circuits of her musing hath liberty to propose to herself, though of
highest hope and hardest attempting: whether that epic form
whereof the two poems of Homer and those other two of Virgil and
Tasso are a diffuse, and the book of Job a brief model: or whether
the rules of Aristotle herein are strictly to be kept, or nature to be
followed, which in them that know art and use judgement is no

3 Cf. *At a Vacation Exercise* (extract 50):
  Not those new-fangled toys and trimming slight
  Which takes our late fantastics with delight.
4 Other equally clear evidences of Milton's interest in Italian Renaissance
  humanism are frequent; e.g. in the Foreword to *Samson Agonistes* (extract
  68), upon the nature of tragedy, and in the translation from Horace in the
  Latin measure 'as near as the language will permit.' For him, as for Spenser, the use of the vernacular for patriotic reasons after the precedent of
  Ariosto is a part of this interest. And Professor Hanford finds even in Elegy
  I (extract 147) 'the typical Renaissance ambition to "overgo" some reputed
  classic name in his own tongue and upon a kindred theme.' (*Youth of
  Milton*, p.114.) The same ambition is discernible in what follows in this
  passage.
    Utterances like this to show how highly Milton valued the epic gift are
  frequent. See section VI, note 12 and section X, note 18.
5 Milton repeats his disdainful treatment of monkish history in the *History
  of Britain*: 'This we must expect: in civil matters to find them dubious re-
  laters and still to the best advantage of what they term Holy Church,
  meaning indeed themselves; in most other matters of religion, blind, as-
  tonished, and struck with superstition as with a planet; in one word,
  monks.'—Columbia *Milton*, Vol. X, p.102.

transgression, but an enriching of art: and lastly what king or knight before the conquest might be chosen in whom to lay the pattern of a Christian hero. And as Tasso gave to a prince of Italy his choice whether he would command him to write of Godfrey's expedition against the infidels, or Belisarius against the Goths, or Charlemagne against the Lombards, if to the instinct of nature and the emboldening of art aught may be trusted, and that there be nothing adverse in our climate[6] or the fate of this age, it haply would be no rashness from an equal diligence and inclination to present the like offer in our own ancient stories. Or whether those dramatic constitutions wherein Sophocles and Euripides reign shall be found more doctrinal and exemplary to a nation, the Scripture also affords us a divine pastoral drama in the Song of Solomon, consisting of two persons and a double chorus, as Origen rightly judges. And the Apocalypse of Saint John is the majestic image of a high and stately tragedy, shutting up and intermingling her solemn scenes and acts with a sevenfold chorus of hallelujahs and harping symphonies: and this my opinion the grave authority of Pareus commenting that book is sufficient to confirm.[7] Or if occasion shall lead to imitate those magnific odes and hymns wherein Pindarus and Callimachus are in most things worthy, some others in their frame judicious, in their matter most an end faulty. But those frequent songs throughout the law and prophets beyond all these, not in their divine argument alone, but in the very critical art of composition, may be easily made appear over all the kinds of lyric poesy to be incomparable.[8] These abilities, wheresoever they be found, are the inspired gift of God rarely bestowed, but yet to some (though most abuse) in every nation, and are of power beside the office of a pulpit to inbreed and cherish in a great people the seeds

6 See section IX, note 8.

7 In the Foreword to *Samson Agonistes* (extract 68) Milton urges the respectability of the dramatic form in part upon the precedent of Scripture, perhaps in apology to his Puritan allies, but also, of course, because Scriptural precedent, like classical, was important to him in literary practice.

8 In the anonymous *Life* we find the following sentence: 'And David's Psalms were in esteem with him above all poetry.'—Darbishire, *Early Lives*, p.33.

of virtue and public civility, to allay the perturbations of the mind
and set the affections in right tune, to celebrate in glorious and
lofty hymns the throne and equipage of God's almightiness and
what He works and what He suffers to be wrought with high providence in His church, to sing the victorious agonies of martyrs and
saints, the deeds and triumphs of just and pious nations doing valiantly through faith against the enemies of Christ, to deplore the
general relapses of kingdoms and states from justice and God's
true worship. Lastly, whatsoever in religion is holy and sublime, in
virtue amiable or grave, whatsoever hath passion or admiration in
all the changes of that which is called fortune from without or the
wily subtleties and refluxes of man's thoughts from within, all these
things with a solid and treatable smoothness to paint out and describe, teaching over the whole book of sanctity and virtue through
all the instances of example with such delight, to those especially
of soft and delicious temper who will not so much as look upon
Truth herself unless they see her elegantly dressed, that whereas
the paths of honesty and good life appear now rugged and difficult,
though they be indeed easy and pleasant, they would then appear to
all men both easy and pleasant, though they were rugged and difficult indeed. And what a benefit this would be to our youth and
gentry may be soon guessed by what we know of the corruption
and bane which they suck in daily from the writings and interludes
of libidinous and ignorant poetasters, who having scarce ever heard
of that which is the main consistence of a true poem, the choice of
such persons as they ought to introduce, and what is moral and de-
cent to each one, do for the most part lap up vicious principles in
sweet pills to be swallowed down, and make the taste of virtuous
documents harsh and sour. But because the spirit of man cannot
demean itself lively in this body without some re-creating inter-
mission of labour and serious things, it were happy for the commonwealth if our magistrates, as in those famous governments of old,
would take into their care, not only the deciding of our contentious
law cases and brawls, but the managing of our public sports and
festival pastimes, that they might be, not such as were authorized

a while since, the provocations of drunkenness and lust, but such as may inure and harden our bodies by martial exercises to all warlike skill and performance, and may civilize, adorn, and make discreet our minds by the learned and affable meeting of frequent academies and the procurement of wise and artful recitations sweetened with eloquent and graceful enticements to the love and practice of justice, temperance, and fortitude, instructing and bettering the nation at all opportunities, that the call of wisdom and virtue may be heard everywhere—as Solomon saith, 'She crieth without, she uttereth her voice in the streets, in the top of high places, in the chief concourse, and in the openings of the gates.' Whether this may not be not only in pulpits, but after another persuasive method, at set and solemn panegyries, in theatres, porches, or what other place or way may win most upon the people to receive at once both recreation and instruction, let them in authority consult. The thing which I had to say, and those intentions which have lived within me ever since I could conceive myself anything worth to my country, I return to crave excuse that urgent reason hath plucked from me by an abortive and foredated discovery. And the accomplishment of them lies not but in a power above man's to promise; but that none hath by more studious ways endeavoured, and with more unwearied spirit that none shall, that I dare almost aver of myself, as far as life and free leisure will extend, and that the land had once enfranchised herself from this impertinent yoke of prelaty, under whose inquisitorious and tyrannical duncery no free and splendid wit can flourish. Neither do I think it shame to covenant with any knowing reader that for some few years yet I may go on trust with him toward the payment of what I am now indebted, as being a work not to be raised from the heat of youth or the vapours of wine, like that which flows at waste from the pen of some vulgar amorist or the trencher fury of a rhyming parasite, nor to be obtained by the invocation of Dame Memory and her siren daughters, but by devout prayer to that eternal Spirit who can enrich with all utterance and knowledge, and sends out His seraphim with the hallowed fire of His altar to touch and purify the lips of

whom He pleases: to this must be added industrious and select
reading, steady observation, insight into all seemly and generous
arts and affairs,[9] till which in some measure be compassed, at mine
own peril and cost I refuse not to sustain this expectation from as
many as are not loath to hazard so much credulity upon the best
pledges that I can give them. Although it nothing content me to
have disclosed thus much beforehand, but that I trust hereby to
make it manifest with what small willingness I endure to interrupt
the pursuit of no less hopes than these, and leave a calm and pleasing solitariness fed with cheerful and confident thoughts to embark
in a troubled sea of noises and hoarse disputes, put from beholding
the bright countenance of truth in the quiet and still air of delightful studies to come into the dim reflection of hollow antiquities sold
by the seeming bulk, and there be fain to club quotations with men
whose learning and belief lies in marginal stuffings, who when they
have like good sumpters laid ye down their horseload of citations
and fathers at your door, with a rhapsody of who and who were
bishops here or there, ye may take off their packsaddles, their day's
work is done, and episcopacy, as they think, stoutly vindicated. Let
any gentle apprehension that can distinguish learned pains from
unlearned drudgery imagine what pleasure or profoundness can be
in this, or what honour to deal against such adversaries. But were it
the meanest underservice, if God by His secretary conscience en-
join it, it were sad for me if I should draw back, for me especially,
now when all men offer their aid to help ease and lighten the difficult labours of the church, to whose service by the intentions of my
parents and friends I was destined of a child, and in mine own resolutions, till coming to some maturity of years and perceiving what
tyranny had invaded the church, that he who would take orders
must subscribe slave, and take an oath withal, which unless he took
with a conscience that would retch, he must either straight perjure
or split his faith, I thought it better to prefer a blameless silence
before the sacred office of speaking bought, and begun with servi-

9 Cf. the description of the poet's lot in *Lycidas*, l.72:
        To scorn delights and live laborious days.

tude and forswearing. Howsoever thus church-outed by the prelates,[10] hence may appear the right I have to meddle in these matters, as before the necessity and constraint appeared.

10 Mr. Liljegren points out that although Milton was 'church-outed' by the
prelates because he could not subscribe the articles of the church, he must
have signed them to secure his degree from Cambridge (*Studies in Milton*,
p.xxx). In making this another instance of Milton's dishonesty, Liljegren,
I think, again sets up for Milton standards of slavish honesty above the
lot of all but fanatics and martyrs and then condemns him because he does
not live in accordance with such standards. Had Milton been John Knox,
he would no doubt have failed to secure his degree. But Milton, Puritan
though he was, was not cursed with the literal-mindedness of the fanatical
Roundhead. Surely it is one thing to subscribe the articles of the established church as a requirement for graduation from the university and
another to accept a ministry in the church based upon them. Of course it
is true, too, that Milton's literary ambitions had perhaps as much to do
with his failure to enter the church as his hatred of prelaty.

II. 1608–1654

Who, then, and whence I am.

2. From the *Second Defence*. 1654.

From the Latin.

Milton is here refuting charges of immorality brought against him in the *Cry of the Royal Blood to Heaven against the English Parricides*, Du Moulin's reply to the *First Defence*. He is responding to the reproach of the *Cry* that an unknown writer should dare do battle with Salmasius as Milton in the *First Defence* had done. In telling 'who and whence' he is, Milton is led into the fullest account of his life that he gives anywhere.

'ONE John Milton, a great hero doubtless, was found, to be opposed to Salmasius.' I did not know that I was a hero, though you,[1] for aught I know, may be the son of some frail heroine; for you are one entire mass of corruption. That I was the only one who was found to defend the cause of the people of England, if I consider the interests of the commonwealth, is a subject of real concern to me; if I consider the glory, it is not willingly that I suffer anyone to share it with me. Who and whence I am, say you, is doubtful. So also was it doubtful, in ancient times, who Homer was, who Demosthenes. The truth is, I had learned to be long silent, to be able to forbear writing, which Salmasius never could, and carried silently in my own breast what if I had chosen then, as well as now, to bring forth, I could long since have gained a name. But I was not eager for fame, who is slow of pace; indeed, if the fit opportunity had not been given me, even these things would never have seen the light, little concerned though others were ignorant that I knew what I did. It was not the fame of everything that I was waiting for, but the oppor-

---

1 Milton is addressing Alexander More, whom he erroneously thought to be author of the *Cry of the Royal Blood*. See Introduction, pp.xxii–xxvii.

tunity. Hence it happened that I was known to no small number of persons before Salmasius was known to himself; now he is more known than the pack-horse Andremon.—'Whether he is a man or a worm.' In very truth, I had rather be a worm, a confession which King David also makes of himself, than conceal within my breast that worm of yours that shall never die.—You proceed—'It is said that the man was expelled from the University of Cambridge for his debaucheries, and that, flying from his disgrace and his country, he shifted his quarters to Italy.' It may be conjectured even from this what credit is due to those from whom you received your information of our affairs: for, that both you and they are guilty of a most impudent falsehood in this particular is well known to all who know me, and shall presently be shown more at large. Now, after being expelled from Cambridge, why should I shift my quarters to Italy rather than to France or Holland? where you, who are covered with debaucheries out of number, and a minister of the gospel, not only live with impunity, but preach; but, to the utter disgrace of that church, defile with your filthy hands even the holy ministries. Why then to Italy, More? Like another Saturn, I suppose, I fled to Latium to find a hiding place! But I fled to Italy, not, as you imagine, as to the skulking corner or the place of refuge to the profligate, but because I knew, and had found before, that it is the retreat of civility and of all polite learning.—'On his return, he wrote his book on divorce.' I wrote nothing more than what Bucer before me wrote at large on the kingdom of Christ, than what Fagius on Deuteronomy, Erasmus on the first epistle to the Corinthians—works intended for the particular benefit of Englishmen— than what many other very celebrated men have written for the good of mankind in general. Why that should be charged upon me in particular as a fault which nobody finds fault with in them, I cannot comprehend. I could wish only that I had not written in the vernacular tongue, for I had not fallen upon vernacular readers,[2] with whom it is usual to be unconscious of their own good fortune and to ridicule the misfortune of others. And is it for you, base se-

2 Cf. Familiar Letter 16 (extract 130).

ducer, to make a clamour about divorce, who have been guilty of the most cruel of all divorces with Pontia, the waiting maid, whom you engaged in marriage, and with this lure debauched her? And yet this servant of Salmasius was an Englishwoman, as it is said, attached the most warmly to the royal party; in short, miscreant, you loved her as a royal thing and left her as a public thing; but take care you are not found to be the author of her conversion, the thought of which you seem so unable to endure; take care, I say, lest by utterly overturning Salmasia's sovereignty, you do not convert Pontia into a republic. In this way, indeed, you are said to have founded, though yourself a royalist, many republics in the same city, or to administer them as public minister after they have been founded by others. Such are your divorces, or as you would rather have it, your diversions, from which you have come out against me, a very Curius.—You now return to your lies. 'When the decapitation of the King was agitated by the conspirators, he wrote to them, while yet wavering, and urged them to the horrid deed.'[3] Now I neither wrote to them, nor was it possible that I should urge those who had already resolved upon the thing without even an intention of consulting me. But I shall speak of what I wrote upon that subject hereafter, as also of the *Eikonoklastes*.

Since this man (though I am in doubt whether I should call him a man, or merely the refuse of a man) from his corruption of maid-servants has proceeded to corrupt all truth, and by heaping upon me lies without number has endeavoured to render my name infamous among foreigners, let me entreat that I may not be misinterpreted, that I may not excite ill will, that I may not give of-

---

3 Milton describes the *Tenure of Kings and Magistrates* below in the present extract. It was apparently written during the captivity and trial of King Charles and was published two weeks after his death. The pamphlet is an unimpassioned study in abstract and philosophical terms of the question of sovereignty. In it Milton defends the 'right' of men to call to account, depose, and put to death 'a tyrant or wicked king.' The pamphlet contains no mention of Charles, but of course its bearing was unmistakable. It is addressed to no person or group. Perhaps it is not to the *Tenure of Kings* at all but to some supposed private, unpublished communication that Du Moulin refers.

fence, if I have spoken before, and if I shall speak again, more of myself than I could wish; that, if I cannot rescue my eyes from blindness, my name from oblivion or calumny, I may at least be able, in open day, to redeem my life from that dimness which is produced by a stain. This will be necessary for me on more accounts than one. And first, that so many excellent and learned men throughout the neighbouring nations, who are now reading my writings and are disposed to think favourably of me, may not feel regret and shame on my account, but may be convinced that I am not such a one who has ever disgraced fair words by foul deeds or the language of a free man by the actions of a slave, and that my life, by God's help, has been ever far removed from all baseness and loose behaviour. Secondly, that those praiseworthy and illustrious men whose eulogies I undertake to pronounce may know it to be my opinion that there could be no greater cause for shame, while myself was vicious and deserving of reproof—in fine, that the people of England, to whose defence, whether it was my destiny or my duty, I was impelled by their own virtue, may know, that if I have ever led a life free from shame and dishonour, my defence (whether it may redound to their honour and ornament I know not) can certainly never prove to them a cause of shame or disgrace.[4] Who, then, and whence I am I will now make known.

I was born at London of respectable parents. My father was a man of the highest integrity; my mother, an excellent woman, was particularly known throughout the neighbourhood for her charitable donations. My father destined me from a child for the pursuits of polite learning, which I prosecuted with such eagerness that after I was twelve years old I rarely retired to bed from my lucubrations till midnight. This was the first thing which proved pernicious to my eyes, to the natural weakness of which were added frequent headaches. But as all this could not abate my instinctive ardour for learning, he provided me, in addition to the ordinary instructions of the grammar school, masters to give me daily lessons at home. Being thus instructed in various languages, and having

4 See Introduction, pp.xvii–xviii.

gotten no slight taste of the sweetness of philosophy, he sent me to Cambridge, one of our two national colleges.[5] There, aloof from all profligate conduct, and with the approbation of all good men, I studied seven years, according to the usual course of discipline and of scientific instruction—till I obtained, and with applause, the degree of master, as it is called; when I fled not into Italy, as this foul miscreant falsely asserts, but of my own free will returned home, leaving behind me among most of the Fellows of the College, who had shown me no ordinary attention, even an affectionate regret.[6] At my father's country house, to which he had retired to pass the remainder of his days, being perfectly at my ease, I gave myself up entirely to reading the Greek and Latin writers, exchanging, however, sometimes, the country for the town, either for the purchase of books or to learn something new in mathematics or in music, which at that time furnished the sources of my amusement. After passing five years in this way, I had the curiosity, after the death of my mother, to see foreign countries, and above all, Italy; and having obtained permission of my father, I set out, attended by one servant.[7] On my departure I was treated in the most friendly manner by Sir Henry Wotton, who was long ambassador from King James to Venice, and who not only followed me with his good wishes, but communicated in an elegant letter some maxims of the greatest use to one who is going abroad.[8] From the recommendation of others, I was received at Paris with the utmost courtesy by the noble Thomas Scudamore, Viscount of Sligo, who of his own accord introduced me, accompanied by several of his suite, to the learned Hugo Grotius, at that time ambassador from the

5 Milton, it must be remembered, if this identification of Cambridge is to be understood, is writing in Latin, for the world.

6 See Introduction, pp.xxix–xxx.

7 Cf. the *Defence of Himself* (extract 43): 'I am now come to my third crime; namely, that I said I went abroad with one servant.' We can hardly ask better commentary than this upon the conventions of seventeenth-century pamphlet warfare, that More in his answer to the *Second Defence* lights upon this passage for ridicule and that Milton found it necessary to refute a charge of beggarliness based upon the 'one servant.'

8 This letter was published in the 1645 edition of Milton's *Poems, Both English and Latin.*

Queen of Sweden to the King of France, and whom I was very de-
sirous of seeing. On my setting out for Italy some days after, he
gave me letters to the English merchants on my route, that they
might be ready to do me any service in their power. Taking ship at
Nice, I arrived at Genoa, and soon after at Leghorn and Pisa;
thence to Florence. In this last city, which I have always valued
above the rest for the elegance of its dialect and of its genius, I continued about two months. Here I soon contracted a familiar acquaintance with many persons eminent for their rank and learning,
and regularly frequented also their private academies—an institu-
tion which deserves the highest commendation, as calculated to
preserve at once polite letters and friendly intercourse:[9] for, the
pleasing, the delightful recollection I still retain of you Jacobo
Gaddi, of you Carolo Dati, Frescobaldi, Coltellino, Bonmattei,
Clementillo, Francini, and many others, no time will efface.[10] From
Florence I pursued my route to Siena, and then to Rome; and

9 Comparison of this passage with the corresponding account in the anonymous *Life* of Milton shows how dependent even Milton's contemporary
biographers were upon Milton's autobiographical passages:
 'Being now become master of what useful knowledge was to be had in
books, and competently skilled amongst others in the Italian language, he
made choice of that country to travel into, in order to polish his conversation and learn to know men. And having received instructions how to demean himself with that wise observing nation, as well as how to shape his
journey, from Sir Henry Wotton, whose esteem of him appears in an elegant
letter to him upon that subject, he took his way through France. In this
kingdom, the manners and genius of which he had in no admiration, he
made small stay, nor contracted any acquaintance, save that, with the
recommendation of Lord Scudamore, our King's ambassador at Paris, he
waited on Hugo Grotius, who was there under that character from the
Crown of Sweden.
 'Hasting to Italy by way of Nice, and passing through Genoa, Leghorn,
and Pisa, he arrived at Florence. Here he lived two months in familiar and
elegant conversation with the choice wits of that city, and was admitted by
them to their private academies, an economy much practised among the
virtuosi of those parts for the communication of polite literature as well as
for the cementing of friendships.'—Darbishire, *Early Lives*, pp.19–20.
 Other passages in this and the other lives are equally dependent, although they also contain much invaluable material not available from Milton himself.
10 Cf. extract 1. These are the members of the 'private academy' to which
Milton was 'favoured to resort.'

having been detained about two months in this city by its antiquities and ancient renown (where I enjoyed the accomplished society
of Lucas Holstenius and of many other learned and superior men),
I proceeded to Naples. Here I was introduced by a certain hermit
with whom I had travelled from Rome to John Baptista Manso,
Marquis of Villa, a man of the first rank and authority, to whom
the illustrious Italian poet, Torquato Tasso, addressed his book on
friendship. By him I was treated while I stayed there with all the
warmth of friendship, for he conducted me himself over the city
and the Vice-regent's court, and more than once came to visit me
at my own lodgings. On my leaving Naples, he gravely apologized
for showing me no more attention, alleging that although it was
what he wished above all things, it was not in his power in that city
because I had not thought proper to be more guarded on the point
of religion. As I was preparing to pass over also into Sicily and
Greece, I was restrained by the melancholy tidings from England
of the civil war: for I thought it base that I should be travelling at
my ease, even for the improvement of my mind abroad, while my
fellow citizens were fighting for their liberty at home. As I was
about to return to Rome, the merchants gave me an intimation that
they had learned from their letters that, in case of my revisiting
Rome, the English Jesuits had laid a plot for me because I had
spoken too freely on the subject of religion; for I had laid it down
as a rule for myself never to begin a conversation on religion in
those parts, but if interrogated concerning my faith, whatever might
be the consequence, to dissemble nothing. I therefore returned
notwithstanding to Rome; I concealed from no one who asked the
question, what I was; if anyone attacked me, I defended in the most
open manner, as before, the orthodox faith, for nearly two months
more, in the city even of the sovereign pontiff himself.[11] By the will
of God I arrived safe again at Florence, revisiting those who longed
no less to see me than if I had returned to my own country. There I
willingly stopped as many months as before (except that I made an

---

11 See Introduction, pp.xxx–xxxii.

excursion for a few days to Lucca[12]), when, crossing the Apennine, I made the best of my way through Bononia and Ferrara to Venice. Having spent a month in getting a survey of this city, and seen the books shipped which I had collected in Italy, I was brought by way of Verona, Milan, and the Pennine Alps, and along the lake Lemano, to Geneva. This city, as it brings to my recollection the slanderer More, makes me again call God to witness that in all these places where so much licence is given I lived free and untouched of all defilement and profligate behaviour, having it ever in my thought that if I could escape the eyes of men, I certainly could not escape the eyes of God.[13] At Geneva I had daily intercourse with John Deodati,[14] the very learned professor of divinity. Then, by the same route as before, I returned through France to my own country, after an absence of a year and about three months. I arrived nearly at the time that Charles, breaking the pacification, renewed the war, called the episcopal war, with the Scots, in which the royal forces were routed in the first engagement; and Charles, now finding the whole English nation enraged, and justly, to the last degree against him, not long after called a parliament, though not by his own will, but as compelled by his necessities. Looking about me for some place in which I might take up my abode, if any was to be found in this troubled and fluctuating state of affairs, I hired for me and my books a sufficiently spacious house in the city.[15] Here I returned with no little delight to my interrupted studies, leaving without difficulty the issue of things more especially to God and to those to whom the people had assigned that department of duty. Meanwhile, as the parliament acted with great vigour, the pride of the bishops began to lose its swell. No sooner did liberty of speech begin to be allowed than every mouth was open against the bishops.

12 The home of the Diodati family.
13 Alexander More in the *Public Faith of Alexander More* calls this a 'too anxious protestation.' Milton repeats it in the same words in the *Defence of Himself* (extract 43).
14 The uncle of Milton's school friend, Charles.
15 In Aldersgate Street. According to Edward Phillips, Milton first established himself in lodgings, however, at the house of Russell, a tailor, in St. Bride's Churchyard.—Darbishire, *Early Lives*, p.60.

Some complained of their personal vices, others of the vice of the order itself. It was wrong, they said, that they alone should differ from all other reformed churches; that it was expedient the church should be governed by the example of the brethren, and above all by the word of God. I became perfectly awake to these things; and perceiving that men were in the right way to liberty: that, if discipline originating in religion continued its course to the morals and institutions of the commonwealth, they were proceeding in a direct line from such beginnings, from such steps, to the deliverance of the whole life of mortal man from slavery—moreover, as I had endeavoured from my youth before all things not to be ignorant of what was law, whether divine or human; as I had considered whether I could ever be of use, should I now be wanting to my country, to the church, and to such multitudes of the brethren who were exposing themselves to danger for the gospel's sake—I resolved, though my thoughts were then employed upon other subjects, to transfer to these the whole force of my mind and industry. Accordingly, I first wrote *Of the Reformation of the English Church*, in two books, to a friend. Next, as there were two bishops of reputation above the rest[16] who maintained their own cause against certain leading ministers, and as I had the persuasion that on a subject which I had studied solely for the love of truth and from a regard to Christian duty I should not write worse than those who contended for their own lucre and most iniquitous domination, to one of them I replied in two books, of which one was entitled *Of Prelatical Episcopacy*, the other *Of the Reason of Church Government*; to the other, in some *Animadversions*, and soon after, in an *Apology*; and thus, as was said, brought timely succour to those ministers, who had some difficulty in maintaining their ground

16 Joseph Hall, Bishop of Exeter, and James Ussher, Archbishop of Armagh. It was in reply to a pamphlet by Hall, *An Humble Remonstrance to the High Court of Parliament,* that the original Smectymnuus pamphlet was written by Young and his collaborators. Both Hall and Ussher wrote replies to 'Smectymnuus,' and it was in response to them that Milton entered the controversy, writing *Of Prelatical Episcopacy* and the *Reason of Church Government* in reply to Bishop Ussher, and the *Animadversions* and the *Apology* in direct controversy with Bishop Hall.

against the bishops' eloquence: from this time too, I held myself ready, should they thenceforward make any reply. When the bishops, at whom every man aimed his arrow, had at length fallen, and we were now at leisure as far as they were concerned, I began to turn my thoughts to other subjects; to consider in what way I could contribute to the progress of real and substantial liberty, which is to be sought for not from without, but within, and is to be obtained principally not by fighting, but by the just regulation and by the proper conduct of life. Reflecting, therefore, that there are in all three species of liberty, without which it is scarcely possible to pass any life with comfort, namely, ecclesiastical, domestic or private, and civil; that I had already written on the first species and saw the magistrate diligently employed about the third, I undertook the domestic, which was the one that remained.[17] But as this also appeared to be threefold, namely, whether the affair of marriage was rightly managed; whether the education of children was properly conducted; whether, lastly, we were to be allowed freedom of opinion, I explained my sentiments not only on the proper mode of

17 A discussion of the account here given of the occasion for the divorce pamphlets will be found in the Introduction, pp.xv–xvii. It is perhaps well to add to that discussion a reminder that Milton was, throughout his life, concerned with the cause of liberty and passionately devoted to it, and that his writings on divorce are in harmony with the tenor of his whole philosophy. Even though his disappointment in his first marriage may well have led him to think of divorce, even though his thought on the subject may be to some indeterminable extent the generalization of his personal experience in marriage and of his desire to escape from an unhappy marriage, the threefold division of liberty here is useful in the abstract and in the classification of his writings, even though he first undertook the defence of domestic liberty and then fitted the undertaking into his scheme of life. The further division of domestic liberty into three classifications represented by the four divorce pamphlets, *Of Education*, and the *Areopagitica* makes a satisfactory and convincing pattern. That the six works (and the second edition of the *Doctrine and Discipline of Divorce*) were all published between August 1, 1643 and the end of March, 1645 suggests that Milton was not even at the time unaware of the relationship between them. Professor Hanford points out that although Milton was apparently ignorant, when he began to write on the subject, of the body of Reformation literature on divorce, he 'had interested himself in the general philosophy of marriage as early as the Horton period, and . . . his mind was already set toward liberal thought regarding it.' —*Handbook*, p.81.

contracting marriage, but also of dissolving it, should that be found
necessary: and this I did according to the divine law which Christ
has never abrogated; and much less has he given a civil sanction to
any other that should be of higher authority than the whole law of
Moses. In like manner I delivered my own opinion and the opinion of others concerning what was to be thought of the single exception of fornication—a question which has been also copiously
elucidated by our celebrated Selden in his *Hebrew Wife,* published
some two years after. Again, it is to little purpose for him to make a
noise about liberty in the legislative assemblies, and in the courts of
justice, who is in bondage to an inferior at home—a species of bondage of all others the most degrading to a man. On this point, therefore, I published some books, and at that particular time, when man
and wife were often the fiercest enemies, he being at home with his
children, while she, the mother of the family, was in the camp of
the enemy, threatening slaughter and destruction to her husband.[18]
I next treated, in one little work, of the education of children, briefly
it is true, but at sufficient length, I conceived, for those who apply
themselves to the subject with all that earnestness and diligence
which it demands—a subject than which there can be none of
greater moment to imbue the minds of men with virtue, from which
springs that true liberty which is felt within; none for the wise ad-

18 This has been frequently noted as an obvious reference to the Cavalier
    affiliations of the Powells. Cf. *P.L.* Bk. X, ll.899–908.

> He never shall find out fit mate, but such
> As some misfortune brings him, or mistake;
> Or whom he wishes most shall seldom gain,
> Through her perverseness, but shall see her gained
> By a far worse, or if she love, withheld
> By parents; or his happiest choice too late
> Shall meet, already linked and wedlock-bound
> To a fell adversary, his hate or shame:
> Which infinite calamity shall cause
> To human life, and household peace confound.

The 'happiest choice' in this passage, met too late because of his marriage
to a 'fell adversary' (Mary Powell?) has been thought a reference to Milton's desire to marry, during Mary Powell's absence from him, 'one of
Dr. Davis's daughters, a very handsome and witty gentlewoman, but
averse, as it is said, to this motion,' of which Edward Phillips tells us.
—Darbishire, *Early Lives,* p. 66.

ministration of a commonwealth and for giving it its utmost possible duration. Lastly, I wrote, after the model of a regular speech, *Areopagitica*, on the liberty of printing, that the determination of true and false, of what ought to be published and what suppressed, might not be in the hands of the few who may be charged with the inspection of books, men commonly without learning and of vulgar judgement, and by whose licence and pleasure no one is suffered to publish anything which may be above vulgar apprehension. The civil species of liberty, the last which remained, I had not touched, as I perceived it drew sufficient attention from the magistrate. Nor did I write anything on the right of kings till the King, pronounced an enemy by the parliament, and vanquished in war, was arraigned as a captive before judges and condemned to lose his head. But when certain Presbyterian ministers at first the bitterest foes to Charles, unable to endure that the independent party should now be preferred to them, and that it should have greater influence in the senate, began to clamour against the sentence which the parliament had pronounced upon the King (though in no wise angry at the deed, but only that themselves had not the execution of it) and tried to their utmost to raise a tumult, having the assurance to affirm that the doctrine of Protestants, that all the reformed churches shrunk with horror from the atrocity of such a sentence against kings—then indeed, I thought it behoved me openly to oppose so barefaced a falsehood. Yet even then I neither wrote nor advised anything concerning Charles, but simply showed in general what may be lawfully done against tyrants, adducing in confirmation the authorities of no small number of the most eminent divines, inveighing at the same time almost with the zeal of a preacher against the egregious ignorance or impudence of those men, who had promised better things. This book was not published till after the death of the King, being intended rather to compose the minds of men than to settle anything relating to Charles, that being the business of the magistrates instead of mine—and which, at the time I speak of, had been already done. These services of mine, which were performed within private walls, I gratuitously bestowed at one time

upon the church, at another upon the commonwealth, while neither
the commonwealth nor the church bestowed upon me in return
anything beyond security. It is true that I gained a good conscience,
a fair repute among good men, and that the deeds themselves rendered this freedom of speech honourable to me. Some men however gained advantages, others honours, for doing nothing; but no
man ever saw me canvassing for preferment, no man ever saw me in
quest of anything through the medium of friends, fixed with suppli-
catory look to the doors of the parliament, or clung to the vestibules
of lower assemblies. I kept myself commonly at home, and supported myself, however frugally, upon my own fortune, though in
this civil broil a great part was often detained and an assessment
rather disproportionate imposed upon me. Having dispatched these
things, and thinking that for the future I should now have abundance of leisure, I undertook a history of the nation from its remotest origin, intending to bring it down, if I could, in one un-
broken thread to our own times. I had already finished four books,
when lo! (Charles' kingdom being reduced to a commonwealth)
the Council of State, as it is called, now first constituted by authority of Parliament, invited me to lend them my services in the department more particularly of foreign affairs—an event which had
never entered my thoughts![19] Not long after, the book which was
attributed to the King made its appearance,[20] written certainly with
the bitterest malice against the parliament. Being ordered to prepare an answer to it, I opposed the *Eikonoklast* to the *Eikon*, not,
as is pretended, 'in insult to the departed spirit of the King,' but in
the persuasion that Queen Truth ought to be preferred to King
Charles; and as I foresaw that some reviler would be ready with
this slander, I endeavoured in the introduction, and in other places

19 This account, which has been questioned, is confirmed by a passage in the
    anonymous *Life*, a passage not based on this since it adds particulars not
    here: 'Upon the change of government which succeeded the King's
    death, he was, without any seeking of his, by the means of a private ac-
    quaintance who was then a member of the new Council of State, chosen
    Latin Secretary.'—Darbishire, *Early Lives*, p.26.
20 Milton is obviously doubtful of the King's authorship of *Eikon Basilike*.

as far as it was proper, to ward off the reproach. Next came forward
Salmasius; and no long time, as More reports, was lost in looking
about for some person to answer him, so that all of their own accord instantly nominated me, who was then present in the Council.
—It is chiefly, More, for the sake of those good men, who have
otherwise no knowledge of me, that, to stop your mouth and to
confound your lies, I have so far given an account of myself. I tell
you, then, foul priest, hold your peace, I say: for the more you revile
me, the more fully will you compel me to explain my own conduct
—from which you could gain nothing yourself but the reproach,
already too heavy, of being a liar, and would lay open for me a still
wider field for the commendation of my own integrity.

III. PERSONAL APPEARANCE

I certainly never thought I should have to contend with the cyclops for the point of beauty.

3. *On the Man Who Had Engraved Milton's Likeness.* 1645.

From the Greek.

This epigram composed to be engraved under the portrait prefixed to the 1645 *Poems* is written with more humour than we expect of Milton. The humour is perhaps less surprising than Milton's willingness to let so bad a portrait appear. The engraver, we may be sure, if he engraved the epigram as well as the portrait, read no Greek.

THIS likeness you would perchance say had been graven by an unskilful man, were you to look at the genuine shape and appearance [i.e. its original].[1] But since, good friends, you know not him whose face is modelled here, you laugh at this misfit imitation by a worthless sculptor.

4. From the *Second Defence.* 1654.

From the Latin.

Let us come now to the charges against me. Can he [2] find anything to blame in my life or manners? Clearly nothing. What does he do then? He does what none but a brute and barbarian would have done; he upbraids me with my person and with my blindness.

A monster horrid, ugly, huge, and blind.

I certainly never thought I should have to contend with the cyclops for the point of beauty! But he immediately corrects himself. 'He is not huge, it is true: for nothing can be more lean, bloodless,

1 Bracket notes throughout the text are the translator's.
2 The author of the *Cry*.

and shrivelled.' Though it is to little purpose for a man to speak of his beauty, yet at last, as I have reason in this particular also for giving thanks to God, and am able to confound liars, lest anyone should haply think me some monster with a dog's head, or a rhinoceros (as the Spanish vulgar, trusting but too much to their priest, imagine of heretics), I will say a few words.

No one who has only seen me has ever to my knowledge thought me ugly: whether handsome or not, is a point I shall not determine. My stature, I own, is not tall, but may approach nearer to the middle than to the small size.[3] And what if small, as many men have been who were of the very first rank both in peace and war? And why should that stature be called small which is large enough for every virtuous purpose? But it is not true that I am thus lean beyond example; on the contrary, I possess that spirit and strength, that when my age and manner of life so inclined me I was neither unskilled in handling my sword nor unpractised in its daily use. Armed with this weapon, as I commonly was, I thought myself a match for any man, though far my superior in strength, and secure from any insult which one man could offer to another. At this day, I have the same spirit, the same strength, my eyes only are not the same; yet, to external appearance they are as completely without injury, as clear and bright, without the semblance of a cloud, as the eyes of those whose sight is most perfect. In this respect only am I a dissembler; and here it is against my will. In my countenance, than which, as he has said, there is 'nothing more bloodless,' there still remains a colour so very opposite to the bloodless and pale, that, though turned of forty, there is scarcely anyone who would not think me younger by nearly ten years. It is equally untrue that either my body or my skin is shrivelled. In these particulars, were

3 Aubrey's note is amusing: 'He was scarce so tall as I am. Quaere, Quot feet I am high? Resp. Of middle stature.' Aubrey also observes more elegantly that 'he was a spare man,' but 'his harmonical and ingenious soul dwelt in a beautiful and well proportioned body.' (Darbishire, *Early Lives*, pp.3–4.) The anonymous *Life* which Miss Darbishire attributes to John Phillips describes Milton as 'of a moderate stature and well proportioned, of a ruddy complexion, light brown hair, and handsome features; save that his eyes were none of the quickest.'—Ibid. p.32.

I guilty of any falsehood, I should deservedly expose myself to the ridicule of many thousands of my countrymen who know me personally, and even of foreigners not a few. Now if this man be detected of telling such impudent and unfounded falsehoods on a subject it was not at all necessary for him to meddle with, you may form a correspondent conjecture as to the rest.

Thus much have I been even constrained to say of my person.

5. From the *Defence of Himself*. 1655.

From the Latin.

The *Defence of Himself* is in answer to the *Public Faith of Alexander More*. It is More that Milton addresses.

You upbraid me however with the blindness of the cyclops; and to mend your impudence, you repeat the insult at the very moment that you deny you have given it. The eyes which before were no eyes are now removable and like those of a witch. Now I am a Narcissus, because I did not choose by your limning to be made a cyclops, and because you have seen a picture of me totally without likeness 'prefixed to my poems!' Now, my having consented, at the instance and from the importunity of the bookseller, to employ an unskilful engraver, because at that period of the war there was no other to be found in the city, argues not that I was over-solicitous, as you charge me, but that I was indifferent about the matter.[4]

Other of Milton's comments upon his personal appearance are in extracts 39, 46, *and* 48.

4 It was the portrait referred to here that was the occasion for Milton's Greek epigram about the engraver (extract 3).

Aubrey: 'The pictures before his books are not *at all* like him.' —Darbishire, *Early Lives*, p.3.

IV. LOVE

Whether the Muse or Love call thee his mate,
Both them I serve, and of their train am I.

6. Elegy VII. 1628.

From the Latin.

The frequent assumption that this elegy and the Italian sonnets are mere conventional poetic exercises robbed us for a long time of the understanding of valuable biographical material. The epilogue to the poem (extract 7) is our best commentary on the genuineness of the experience recorded.

I DID not yet know your ordinances, seductive Amathusia, and my breast was still empty of Paphian fire. O'er and o'er I spurned Cupid's shafts, as darts of a mere boy, I spurned your power divine, O mighty Cupid. 'Go, boy,' said I, 'pierce doves, that know naught of fighting—only unmanly wars befit an unmanly captain— or else, tiny lad, lead a proud triumph over sparrows: such trophies are worthy of warfare such as yours. Why guide your idle missiles 'gainst the sons of men? Not one jot of strength has *your* quiver against sturdy heroes.' The lad of Cyprus brooked not my words— no other god is more prompt to anger—, and so this savage [god] was hot now with double fires.

It was the springtime, and the light, shining o'er the roof-trees of the houses, had brought to you, May-month, your first day. But mine eyes were seeking still the vanishing night, and brooked not the early morning brightness. Lo, Love stood at my bed, tireless Love, with spangled wings. The rattling of his quiver betrayed the god as he stood beside me; his face, too, betrayed him and his lovely eyes with their sweet threats, and whatever else was worthy of a lad, worthy e'en of Love. Such is the lad of Sigeum, as, on everlasting Olympus, he mixes the brimming goblets for amorous Jove, or the lad who lured the lovely nymphs to his kisses, Thiodamas' son, Hylas, stolen by a Naiad. He had added wrath—and yet this, too, one would have thought, became him—and he had added wild threats, full of gall and bitterness. Thus then he spoke: 'Wretch, you had grown wise [in matters of love] more safely through [others'] example: now, you will testify yourself to the power of my right arm. You will be numbered among men who have tried and tested my strength; by your sufferings I shall fashion credence for the truth. It was I myself, yes I, that, if you know it not, tamed to the full, Phœbus, even when he was exulting in the Python's over-throw, to me even that glorious [god] yielded; as oft as he recalls Peneüs' daughter, he confesses, himself, that *my* darts work surer and deadlier havoc. Not more skilfully than I can the Parthian horseman draw home and bend his bow, the horseman whose wont it is to win his fight [by shooting his darts] behind his back. The Cydonian hunter, too, yields to me; so, too, did he who, all unwill-ing, was cause to his wife of a violent death. Mighty Orion, too, was o'ermastered by me, and Hercules' hands, and Hercules' comrade, too. Let Jupiter himself try to whirl his thunderbolts 'gainst me: my darts will be lodged [first] in the side of Jove. Whatever else you doubt, my shafts will teach you better [than words], and your own heart, to be assailed by me with no light stroke. Fool, fool, neither will the Muses you love have power to defend you, nor will Phœbus' snake proffer you aid.'

So he spake. Then, brandishing his arrow with the golden tip, he flew away, into the warm bosom of Cypris. But savagely, with threatening lips, he thundered against me, whose one thought was of laughter, and who had no fear of the lad.

Sometimes I found delight in the parts of the city where our citizens promenade, sometimes in the neighbouring countryside adjoining country houses. Crowds close compacted, crowds like in faces to goddesses, moved in brilliance to and fro through the midst of the streets and roads. And so the day flashed bright, glori-fied by a double brightness. Am I beguiling myself? or has Phœbus rays won from this source too? Not grimly did I flee visions so charming; no, I let myself be driven whithersoever youthful impulse bore me. Lacking all prescience, I sent my glances to meet their glances, nor could I withhold my eyes. One by chance I marked, towering [in beauty] over others: that radiance was the beginning of all my woe. So might Venus have wished herself to look to mortals, such the beauty in which the Queen of the Gods herself should have been seen. This lass Cupid, sly rogue, remembering, flung across my path; single-handed, he had before to my hurt woven these wiles. Hard by, too, the sly rogue was in hiding; many a shaft, and a huge load of torches hung from his back. Without delay, he clung now to the maiden's eyelids, now to her face, then settled on her lips, then was seated on her cheeks: whatever part the agile archer traverses, thence—ah me!—in a thousand places he smites my defenceless breast. Straightway unwonted frenzies entered my heart: I burned within with love, aye, all my being was afire.

Meanwhile, the lass who alone of lasses pleased now my tortured soul, was withdrawn from my gaze, ne'er again to return to mine eyes. But I went onward, voicelessly complaining, empty of wit, and, often irresolute, I was minded to retrace my steps. I am cleft asunder: one half of me tarries behind, the other follows my heart's desire; I find pleasure in weeping for the joys so suddenly wrested from me. So Juno's son wept for his lost heaven, after he was flung downward, among the hearths of Lemnos. So Amphiaraüs, when he was carried to Orcus by his panic-stricken steeds, looked back at the sun that had been wrested [from his eyes]. What am I to do, a poor unfortunate, by grief o'ermastered? I am not privileged either to lay aside the love I have welcomed, or to pursue it. O may it be vouchsafed to me to look once again on her beloved face, and in her presence to speak words, if only words of sadness! Mayhap she was not fashioned of unyielding adamant, mayhap she would not be deaf to my prayers. Believe me, no other man has e'er burned thus haplessly: I shall be set down as a pattern [of love's woes], yes, I first and alone. Spare me, Cupid, I pray, since you are the winged god of soft love. Let not your deeds be at odds with your gracious office. Now, now at least, your bow is full of terrors for me, O child of a goddess, child not less potent by your fires than by your darts. Your altars shall smoke with my gifts, you shall be for me very god, god supreme among the powers above. Take away, at last, my frenzies—no, take them not away. I know not why, but the lover, every lover, is so sweetly wretched. Only be gracious, and grant that if in days to come any lass is destined to be mine, a single shaft-point shall pierce two hearts destined to love.

7. Epilogue to Elegy VII. 1645.

From the Latin.

> The following extract, the epilogue to Elegy VII, the previous extract, has sometimes been considered an epilogue to the whole volume of Latin poems. Regarded, I think properly, as an epilogue to Elegy VII, Milton's protestation that he has outgrown his infatuation and is now proof against Cupid gives us a strong presumption that Elegy VII itself is not a mere Ovidian exercise but is in addition a record of a genuine experience. Young men are likely to fall in love when they wish to, and falling into hopeless love as Milton says he does in Elegy VII might even be a part of his imitation of his Latin and Italian forbears—a possibility which, if also a fact, would not make the experience any less real.

All this once on a time, with warped and twisted mind, and with all true zeal laid prostrate, I wrote, setting up idle trophies of my worthlessness. So utterly, forsooth, mischievous error wrenched me astray and drove me onward, and my untaught youth proved but misguided teacher, until the shades of Academe[1] proffered to me the Socratic streams, and untaught me, [and loosed] the yoke I had let fall [upon my neck]. Straightway, from that moment, the fires were quenched, my heart has been unyielding, belted with deep ice. Hence the lad fears the cold for his beloved shafts, and Venus herself dreads might that matches the might of Diomedes.

1 The reference is to Platonic philosophy, not to Cambridge. Dr. MacKellar points out the parallel with the passage in *An Apology for Smectymnuus* (extract 41), 'riper years and the ceaseless round of study and reading led me to the shady spaces of philosophy, but chiefly to the divine volumes of Plato and his equal, Xenophon.'—*Latin Poems*, p.241.

8. Sonnet I. 1630?

This, the nightingale sonnet, is Milton's only English poem which
may be thought to reflect with any directness an experience of
Milton in love. Only the Italian poems of Milton's other works
are like it in tone and substance. It is much less particular than
they, however, and less certainly than they an expression of a
genuine experience in love.

> O Nightingale, that on yon bloomy spray
>> Warbl'st at eve, when all the woods are still,
>> Thou with fresh hope the lover's heart dost fill,
>> While the jolly hours lead on propitious May.
> Thy liquid notes that close the eye of day,
>> First heard before the shallow Cuckoo's bill,
>> Portend success in love. O if Jove's will
>> Have linked that amorous power to thy soft lay,
> Now timely sing, ere the rude bird of hate
>> Foretell my hopeless doom in some grove nigh:
>> As thou from year to year hast sung too late
> For my relief, yet hadst no reason why.
>> Whether the Muse or Love call thee his mate,
>> Both them I serve, and of their train am I.

9. Sonnet II. 1630?

From the Italian.
  The biographical significance of this and the other Italian sonnets, Milton's 'love poems,' (extracts 9–14) has sometimes been
ignored and sometimes mistaken because of the erroneous belief,
furthered by Cowper's translation, that the poems were written in
Italy, and were a conventional literary exercise written in competi-
tion with Milton's Italian friends. They are, instead, a quite personal record of an early experience, written in England long before
the Italian journey.

Beauteous lady, whose fair name honoureth the grassy vale and the
noble gorge of the Reno,[2] lightened of all burden of worth must be
he who is not enamoured of thy gentle spirit:

2 *Emilia*, the name of the district through which the Reno flows, is then

Which sweetly revealeth itself in ever bounteous dispensations of its graciousness and of those charms—the shafts and the bow of Love—which engarland thine exalted virtue.

When, beautiful, thou speakest, or, in mood of happiness, sing in such guise that the hardest and wildest oak is moved to feeling, one must guard the gateways to ear and eye;

For if a man be unworthy of thy favour, may the grace of Heaven alone avail him, before love of thee hath aged in his heart.

10. Sonnet III. 1630?

From the Italian.

At eventide, on the rugged mountain slope, the practised shepherd girl carefully watereth the tender, beauteous flower exotical, so loath to grow in that high altitude far from the warm vale where it first sprouted.

So, Love, in my case, on my nimble tongue nurseth the first bud of a strange speech that I, deserting Thames for Arno,[3] may sing of thee, winsomely haughty one, in words uncomprehended of my own good people.

Such the behest of Love—[4] and from the fate of others I have learned that Love never yet hath bidden in vain:

Oh, would that my heart were less fertile, my breast more stony, toward one who findeth such fecund soil for the seed she soweth from Heaven!

apparently the lady's name. Smart by analysis of the sonnets discovers her to be of Italian descent, with dark complexion and dark eyes, a kind of beauty new to Milton. She spoke English, Italian, and other languages, sang well, and was familiar with Italian poetry. And since the sonnets are written in Italian at her request, because it is 'the language Love boasteth as his own,' Smart supposes 'that she was aware of his feeling, and was not unwilling to make some response.'—*Sonnets*, pp.133–134.

3 The desertion of the Thames for the Arno is not a desertion of England for Italy, a reference to an Italian journey, but rather the desertion of English for Italian speech.

4 'The behest of Love' is an anticipation of the whole of the *Canzone* which is the next extract. The lady herself commands him to write in Italian.

11. Canzone. 1630?

From the Italian.

Swains and maidens—all liege to Love—crowd laughingly about me: 'Why, O why, dost thou write of thy love in a strange and unknown tongue? How darest thou? Tell us' (so they chaff me) 'as thou hopest some day to win thy love and to attain the greatest of thy desires. Other shores, other waters, the banks of another stream, await thee—a fertile soil whereon an immortal guerdon of never-withering green is even now sprouting for thy brow! Why, then, a burden too heavy for thy shoulders?'

To thee, my song, will I tell my secret—and do thou make answer for me: my lady saith—and her words are my law—that this is the language Love boasteth as his own!

12. Sonnet IV. 1630?

From the Italian.

Diodati—[5] and I tell thee in amazement at myself—that same scornful I, who have always shown contempt for Love and have been wont to ridicule his wiles, have fallen into that trap which ensnareth on occasion the best of men.

Not golden tresses nor rosy cheeks have thus dazzled my eyes, but rather a fascinating Beauty exemplifying an Idea unknown, which filleth the heart with beatitude—a bearing fraught with virtue's dignity, the winning sparkle of clear black eyes, a speech adorned with divers languages, and a song such as to send the Moon astray as she followeth her laborious course in the high heavens; fain would I wax my ears against it, but the fire that darteth from her eyes maketh such remedy of little avail.[6]

5 Charles Diodati, an Italian Protestant resident in England, was the most intimate friend of Milton's youth.

6 Smart observes (*Sonnets*, p.150) what Diodati must also have noticed, and with pleasure, that this sonnet constitutes a retraction of Milton's earlier opinion, expressed in Elegy I (extract 147), also addressed to Diodati, that the blond beauty of English girls is preferable to that of any foreign type.

13. Sonnet V. 1630?

From the Italian.

Assuredly, my lady, thy beautiful eyes can be naught else but a Sun
to me. They beat upon me as he doth upon the wayfarer through the
sands of Lybia:

And from that part of my body wherein dwelleth my woe there
rusheth a hot vapour, the like whereof I have never known—in
lovers' parlance 'twould perchance be called a sigh, though truly I
know not what it be!

Part of it compressed and turbulent hideth in my heaving breast:
then a little of it, escaping, doth cool and freeze, thereabout:

But such of it as findeth its way to mine eyes, doth make all my
nights of rain until my Dawn returneth, her arms filled with roses.

14. Sonnet VI. 1630?

From the Italian.

Ingenuous youth and guileless lover I, certain I cannot be of being
ever other than I am. Devotedly, therefore, my Lady, I make thee
humble gift of my heart.

That heart, as I can vow after tests innumerable, I have found
faithful, fearless, steadfast—in all its thoughts, kindly, tactful, genial. In the face of the roar and thunder of the great world, it girdeth
itself with the impenetrable adamant of self-confidence as safe from
the doubts and envies, the fears and hopes, of the vulgar, as it is
enamoured of talent and noble worth, of poetry and the Muses.

One weakness in it wilt thou find; the spot wherein Love hath
implanted his incurable dart![7]

Milton also speaks of love in extracts 41, 42, 49, and 147.

7 Smart observes that after the conventional opening of this sonnet 'there
follows a portrait of Milton which would have been familiar to all, had it
been written in English.' (*Sonnets*, p.155.) It is for us an early instance of
Milton's periodic self-examination, one which represents well his satisfaction in what he found on such occasions.

V. FRIENDSHIPS

Shepherds of the same neighbourhood, devoted to the same pursuits.

15. Familiar Letter 1, to Thomas Young. 1627.[1]

From the Latin.

Thomas Young was Milton's early tutor. From 1620 to 1628 chaplain to the English merchants in Hamburg, he returned to an English pastorate in 1628 and later became the leader of the Smectymnuans, to whose name he contributed his initials. Although he left England when Milton was eleven years old, Young made a considerable impression upon Milton's mind.

ALTHOUGH I had resolved with myself, most excellent preceptor, to send you a certain small epistle composed in metrical numbers, yet I did not consider that I had done enough unless I wrote also another in prose; for the boundless and singular gratitude of mind which your deserts justly claim from me was not to be expressed in that cramped mode of speech, straitened by fixed feet and syllables, but in a free oration, or rather, were it possible, in an Asiatic exuberance of words. Albeit, in truth, to express sufficiently how much I owe you were a work far greater than my strength, even if I should ransack all those hoards of arguments which Aristotle or which that dialectician of Paris[2] has amassed, or even if I should exhaust all the fountains of oratory. You complain, indeed, as justly you may, that my letters to you have been as yet few and very short; but I, on the other hand, do not so much grieve that I have been remiss in a duty so pleasant and so enviable as I rejoice, and all but exult, at holding such a place in your friendship that you should care to ask for frequent letters from me. That I should never have written to you for

1 The date assigned is that given the letter by Mr. W. R. Parker: 'Milton and Thomas Young, 1620–1628,' *Modern Language Notes*, LIII (1938). There is no manuscript of the letter to confirm the dating assigned it in the badly printed edition of 1674. Mr. Parker's arguments are cogent.
2 Peter Ramus.

now more than three years, however, I pray you will not interpret to my discredit, but, in accordance with your wonderful indulgence and candour, view with a charitable construction. For I call God to witness how much in the light of a father I regard you, with what singular devotion I have always followed you in thought, and how I feared to trouble you with my writings. My first care, I suppose, is that, since there is nothing else to commend my letters, their rarity may commend them. Next, as that most vehement desire after you which I feel makes me always fancy you with me, and speak to you and behold you as if you were present, and so (as generally happens in love) soothe my grief by a certain vain imagination of your presence, it is in truth my fear that, as soon as I should meditate a letter to be sent you, it should suddenly come into my mind by what an interval of earth you are distant from me, and so the grief of your absence, already nearly lulled, should grow fresh, and break up my sweet dream. The Hebrew Bible, your truly most acceptable gift, I received some time since. These lines I have written in London amid city distractions, and not, as usual, surrounded by books: if, therefore, anything in this epistle shall please you less than might be, and disappoint your expectation, it shall be made up for by another more elaborate one as soon as I have returned to the haunts of the Muses.[3]

London: March 26, 1625.

16. From Elegy IV. 1627.

From the Latin.
    Addressed to Thomas Young, in Hamburg.

There [4] dwells a priest renowned, honoured from days of old for piety, well trained to feed the sheep that follow Christ. He, verily, is more than the half of my life; I live, perforce, with but half a life. Ah me! How many wide-spread seas, how many mountains inter-

3 Whatever the date, the reference is to Cambridge. If the letter was written in 1625, Milton has just been entered in the college books, but has not yet gone into residence (Masson, *Life*, Vol. I, p.148). If 1627 is the correct date, Milton is in London for the vacation.—Parker, op.cit.
4 In Hamburg.

posed coerce me to forego the very half of my self! Dearer to me is
he than were you, most learned of the Greeks, to Clinias' son, who
was of Telamon's line, and dearer than the mighty Stagirite to his
high-born pupil, whom the gracious maid of Chaonia bore as son to
Lybian Jove. What Amyntor's son, what Philyra's hero-son were
to the king of the Myrmidons, that was this priest to me. He led the
way for me, when first I traversed Aonia's retreats and the holy
greensward of the twice-cleft ridge,[5] [he led the way for me] when I
drank Pieria's waters, and, favoured by Clio, I thrice sprinkled my
happy lips with Castalia's wine. But flaming Æthon thrice saw the
Sign of the Ram, and thrice clothed with new gold the fleecy back
of the Ram, and twice you, Chloris, sprinkled the age-worn earth
with new verdure, and twice Auster stole away your riches: yet it
was not my privilege to feast mine eyes on his face, or to drink in
with mine ears the sweet strains of his voice. . . .

These words—if there is leisure, amid battles, for the Muses—
these words a loyal hand sends to you from England's shores. Accept a greeting heart-felt, however late it be; let it, by its very late-
ness, be to you all the more welcome. Late, yes, but genuine was the
greeting that chaste Penelope, daughter of Icarius, received from
her laggard lord. But oh, why was *I* minded to seek to purge away
guilt, guilt clear to all men's eyes, which he himself is utterly unable to extenuate? He is convicted laggard, rightly convicted, too,
and he himself admits his guilt, and is full of shame that he was
traitor to his friendly office, his duty. Do you only grant forgiveness
to him, now that he has confessed and is begging for forgiveness:
sins ever are made less when they lie open wide to view.

17. From the First Prolusion. 1627?

From the Latin.

This exercise more clearly even than the Sixth Prolusion, where
Milton begins to feel the jealousies of his fellow students subsid-
ing, shows that Milton must indeed have been unpopular in his

5 Mr. W. R. Parker thinks this, the conventional interpretation, a mistransla-
tion, that Milton is not saying Young was his first tutor but that Milton
was Young's first (or foremost) pupil.—Ibid.

early years as an undergraduate. What period of Milton's academic
life it represents we cannot be sure; certainly it is earlier than the
Sixth Prolusion.

All of the most distinguished teachers of rhetoric far and wide have
left behind the opinion—a fact which has not escaped your notice,
my fellow students—that in every kind of speaking, whether demonstrative or deliberative or judicial, the exordium ought to be
occupied with securing the good will of the listeners; otherwise the
minds of the audience could not be persuaded nor could the cause
be triumphant as one might wish. But if such is the fact, which—
may I not depart from the truth—I know is surely fixed and established by the agreement of all scholars, have mercy on me! To what
desperate straits am I reduced this day! I, who at the very beginning
of my speech fear lest I may advance something not at all worthy of
orators and lest I should have deviated unavoidably from the primary duty of a speaker; indeed, how can I expect your good will,
when, in this great assembly, I perceive almost as many persons
hostile to me as I behold with my eyes? Hence it is that I seem to
come as an orator to those who are inexorable. Great can be the
rivalry even in schools for the production of hatreds, either among
those pursuing different subjects, or among those following different methods in the same studies.[6] I really am not disturbed

> Lest Polydamas and the Trojan women
> Prefer Labeo to me; that is a trifle.

Truly, however, my soul cannot wholly despair, for I see here
and there, unless I am deluded, those who signify, not at all secretly, by the very quietness of their countenances, that they wish
me well. By these indeed, however few, for my part, I would prefer
to be approved, than by innumerable companies of the ignorant,
who have no brains, no power to reason correctly, no sound judgement, men who betray themselves by a certain boasting and quite

6 Cf. the Sixth Prolusion (extracts 18 and 39). Milton took active part in the
revolt against scholastic education when he was at Cambridge, no doubt
involving himself in some of the rivalries and hatreds referred to here.—
See Tillyard, *Correspondence and Academic Exercises*, pp.xix–xxiv.

laughable froth of words, from whom if you take away the medley begged from modern authors, immortal God! you will find them even more empty than a bean pod, and when they have exhausted their meagre supply of words and little maxims, they utter not even a grunt, being just as speechless as the little Seriphian frogs. But O with what difficulty would even Heraclitus himself, if he were alive, restrain his laughter, if by chance, the gods being willing, he could perceive these little speakers here, whom a short time ago he might have heard spouting in the buskined Orestes of Euripides, or more bombastically in the Hercules raging toward his death; at length their very slender supply of some little words being exhausted, parade in measured step with haughtiness laid aside, or crawl slowly off like certain little animals with their horns drawn in.

But I recover myself, having digressed a very little. If then there is anyone who, spurning the conditions of peace, would impose upon me 'truceless war,' him at the present moment I will not disdain to address and to ask that he put aside for a little while his animosity and that he be present as an impartial judge of this debate, nor that, on account of the fault of the orator, if there is any, he speak disparagingly of such a splendid and most noble subject. But if you should think these remarks a little too biting and steeped too much in vinegar, I acknowledge that I have done this very thing intentionally; for I wish that the beginning of my oration should resemble the very early dawn from whose gloomy clouds the clearest day is usually born.

18. From the Sixth Prolusion. 1628.

From the Latin.

It is in this passage that we have the record of Milton's decreasing unpopularity among his fellows at Cambridge. Indeed, that he was chosen to deliver this oration is proof that he had achieved some position at the university. With all due allowance for flattery in what Milton says of his hearers, it is apparent that he found genuine satisfaction in the reputation he had achieved and was genuinely concerned to please his audience in a task for which he was not, and knew he was not, well fitted.

When I came back hither recently, fellow students, from that city which is the capital of cities, stuffed, I might almost say, to corpulence with all the pleasures in which that place overflows beyond measure, I hoped I might have again hereafter that literary leisure, a kind of life in which I believe the heavenly spirits rejoice; and there was deeply in my mind a desire now at last to bury myself in literature and to besiege by day and by night most gracious Philosophy: thus always the alternation of labour and pleasure is wont to banish the weariness of satiety and to bring it to pass that things neglected for a while are taken up again more eagerly. Me, on fire with these desires, the almost annual observance of a very old custom has suddenly summoned and dragged away; and that leisure which I had primarily designed for the acquisition of wisdom I have been ordered to transfer to foolish trifles and to the invention of novel absurdities, as if there were not already quite enough fools, as if that famous ship of fools, celebrated not less than the Argo, had met with shipwreck, and finally as if matter for jesting were wanting at this time to Democritus himself.

But grant me pardon, I beseech you, my hearers; for this exercise, which we are celebrating today, although I have been a little too free-spoken about it, is in truth really not senseless, but rather exceedingly praiseworthy; which fact indeed I have proposed to myself at this time to set forth at once more clearly. Wherefore if Junius Brutus, that second founder of the Roman state, that great punisher of royal lust, dared suppress by feigning idiocy a soul almost equal to the immortal gods, and a wondrous natural ability; surely there is no reason why I should be ashamed to play the fool for a while with silly wisdom, especially by order of him whose business it is, like an aedile, to preside over these presumably solemn diversions. Besides, to no small degree, your courteousness, very lately made known to me—you who are members of the same college with me—has allured and enticed me to undertake these duties; for, when I was about to perform an oratorical function before you, some months gone by,[7] and I thought that any lucubrations what-

7 Probably the First Prolusion.

soever of mine would certainly be quite disagreeable, and that
Æacus and Minos would be more lenient judges than almost any
of you; truly, beyond my belief, beyond whatever slight hope I had,
they were received, as I noted, nay rather, I myself felt, with unusual applause from all, yea even from those who at other times, on
account of disagreements over our studies, possessed an absolutely
hostile and unfriendly spirit:[8] truly a magnanimous way of exer-
cising rivalry and one not unworthy of a royal heart; since indeed,
when friendship itself very frequently is wont to misrepresent many
things done without bad intent, then truly bitter and hostile enmity
did not unwillingly interpret in a kindly way and more indulgently
than was my desert many things spoken perhaps erroneously and
not a few doubtless unskilfully. Now, in a word, by this unparalleled example even foolish rage itself was seen to be sane of
mind and by this circumstance had washed away the disgrace of
madness.

But in truth I am highly delighted and in wonderful fashion I am
filled with pleasure when I behold myself surrounded and encompassed on every side by so great a concourse of most learned men.
Yet on the other hand, however, when I descend into myself, and,
as it were with my eyes turned inwardly, I secretly look upon my
weakness, of which I alone am often conscious, I blush, while a
certain unexpected sadness, rushing in, presses down and chokes
my leaping joy. But do not thus, fellow students, I beseech you, do
not thus leave me in the lurch, me prostrate and dismayed, struck
by the keenness of your eyes as though by lightning. May the breath
of your good will stimulate me, half dead, as it can, and revive me.
May it so happen, by your commands, that this torment be not too
severe. Nevertheless, with you providing a remedy for the evil, I
proceed more happily and more entertainingly; so much so that it
will be exceedingly pleasant for me to be frequently terrified, provided that it be permitted me to be revived and refreshed as many
times by you. But oh, in the meanwhile, the remarkable power in

8 Another reference, apparently, to the controversy between the scholastics
and the Baconians at Cambridge. Cf. the First Prolusion (extract 17).

you and the extraordinary virtue, which like that famous spear of Achilles, gift of Vulcan, wounds and heals!

Besides, let no one wonder if I, stationed as it were among the stars, rejoice exceedingly that so many men renowned for scholarship and that almost the whole flower of the academic world have flocked hither. Indeed, I can hardly believe that in olden times greater numbers came to Athens to hear the two most distinguished orators, Demosthenes and Aeschines, contending for oratorical supremacy; nor that ever this felicity happened to Hortensius when pleading; nor that so many men so remarkably versed in letters graced with their presence a Ciceronian display of oratory. Accordingly, although I may bring this task to a finish with little grace, nevertheless I shall regard it as an honour, not to be despised, even to have uttered words in so great a gathering and assemblage of most eminent men.

Moreover, by Hercules, I cannot but applaud myself at this moment with a little more unction because I am luckier by far in my body of judges than either Orpheus or Amphion; for they merely applied their fingers cunningly and skilfully to little strings attuned with pleasing harmony; and an equal portion of the charm of both lay in the strings themselves and in the proper and correct movement of the hands; whereas, if I shall win any praise here today, it will certainly be wholly and truly mine by as much as a superior work of genius conquers and excels the craft of the hands. Further, they drew to themselves rocks, beasts, and trees, and, if there were any men, those who were rude and rustic: but I behold ears, most learned, loaned to me and hanging upon my lips. Lastly, those rustics and many wild beasts followed a harmony of strings already sufficiently known and clearly heard; but you, expectation alone has drawn hither and now detains.

But, however it be, fellow students, I wish you to bear in mind especially at this time that I have not made these remarks boastingly, for would that just at this moment that honey-sweet, or, more truly, nectarian, flood of eloquence were granted to me, such as once in former times saturated and bedewed as though from heaven

the Attic and Roman genius! Would that it were permitted me to
suck out from the innermost recesses all the marrow of persuasion,
and to filch from the chests of Mercury himself, and to empty to
the bottom all the coffers of elegant sayings, so that I might be able
to deliver something worthy of such great expectation, of such a renowned assembly, and finally of ears so pure and fastidious.

Behold, my auditors, whither a most violent desire and inclination for pleasing you carries me off and drives me, since unexpectedly I feel that I have been swept into a certain excessive desire to
please, a sacrilege, but a pure and virtuous one, if such a thing can
be. And undoubtedly, I am of the opinion that there is hardly any
need for me to beseech and implore aid of the Muses, because I believe I am surrounded by those who are full of all the Muses and
Graces; and I imagine that all Helicon, and whatsoever shrines of
the Muses there are in addition, have poured forth all their foster
children for the purpose of taking part in the exercises of this day;
so that it is credible, on account of their absence at this very moment, that the laurels of Parnassus weep and drop their flowers;
whence indeed it will be vain to seek anywhere on earth for the
Muses and Graces and Goddesses of delight, except in this place.
If this is so, it necessarily follows at once that Barbarism itself,
Error, Ignorance, and all that sort, detested by the Muses, will flee
as speedily as possible at the sight of you and hide themselves far
away under a different sky; and then indeed what opposes the removal at once from my oration of any barbarous, inelegant, and
obsolete expression; and, by your inspiration and secret instigation,
my suddenly becoming fluent and polished.

At any rate, however, I conjure you, my hearers, not to repent
that any of you have had just a little leisure for my foolish remarks;
for all of the gods themselves, laying aside for a time the adminis-
tration of heavenly affairs, are said to have been present frequently
at the spectacle of little human beings violently contending; also at
different times, not despising humble circumstances and housed
in poor quarters, they are said to have partaken of beans and greens.
Accordingly I hope and pray you, most excellent listeners, that

this little so-so feast of mine may please your dainty and acute palates.

But even though I have known very many smatterers with whom it is quite the custom to contemn arrogantly and ignorantly in others that of which they know nothing, just as if it were a disgrace for anyone to spend his energies upon it: for instance, one fellow rails foolishly at Dialectic, which he never will be able to comprehend; another regards Philosophy as of no value, because, forsooth, Nature, most beautifully formed of the goddesses, has never deemed him worthy of such an honour that she would permit him to gaze upon her naked: nevertheless I shall not consider it a burden to praise, according to my ability, pleasantries and witty sallies, in which I acknowledge my capabilities are quite limited; if I shall have added first this one thing, which may seem rather difficult and not at all easy: that I am about to speak seriously today in praise of jocularity. And this is done not without cause indeed, for what is it that more quickly conciliates and retains friendships longer than a cheerful and agreeable disposition? And truly you will hardly find one is pleasing and welcome who lacks sportive remarks and pleasantries and elegant little witticisms.

19. Familiar Letter 3, to Alexander Gill. 1628.

From the Latin.
    Alexander Gill was Milton's teacher at St. Paul's, where the elder Gill was headmaster.

In my former letter [9] I did not so much reply to you as stave off my turn of replying. I silently promised with myself, therefore, that another letter should soon follow, in which I should answer somewhat more at large to your most friendly challenge; but even if I had not promised this, it must be confessed on the highest grounds of right to be your due, inasmuch as I consider that each single letter of yours cannot be balanced by less than two of mine—nay, if the account were more strict, not by even a hundred of mine. The

9 Familiar Letter 2, a note of acknowledgement for some verses sent by Gill, and of fulsome praise of the verses.—Columbia *Milton*, Vol. XII, pp.7–9.

matter respecting which I wrote to you rather obscurely you will find contained and expanded in the accompanying sheets.[10] I was labouring upon it with all my might when your letter came, being straitened by the shortness of the time allowed me: for a certain Fellow of our College who had to act as Respondent in the philosophical disputation in this Commencement chanced to entrust to my puerility the composition of the verses which annual custom requires to be written on the questions in dispute,[11] being himself already long past the age for trifles of that sort, and more intent on serious things. The result, committed to type, I have sent to you, as to one whom I know to be a very severe judge in poetical matters and a very candid critic of my productions. If you shall deign to let me have a sight of your verses in return, there will assuredly be no one who will more delight in them, though there may be, I admit, who will more rightly judge of them according to their worth. Indeed, every time I recollect your almost constant conversations with me (which even in this Athens, the University itself, I long after and miss), I think immediately, and not without grief, what a quantity of benefit my absence from you has cheated me of—me, who never left your company without a manifest increase and growth of literary knowledge, just as if I had been to some emporium of learning. Truly, amongst us here, as far as I know, there are hardly one or two that do not fly off unfeathered to Theology while all but rude and uninitiated in either Philology or Philosophy—content also with the slightest possible touch of Theology itself, just as much as may suffice for sticking together a little sermon anyhow, and stitching it over with worn patches obtained promiscuously: a fact giving reason for the dread that by degrees there may break in among our clergy the priestly ignorance of a former age.[12] For myself, finding almost no real companions in study here, I should certainly be looking straight back to London, were I not meditating a retirement during

10 The Fifth Prolusion.
11 Here is another evidence that Milton had become an important person at Cambridge, at least that his gifts were recognized.
12 Milton's disappointment in his fellow students is thus early translated into distrust of the clergy.

this summer vacation into a deeply literary leisure, and a period of hiding, so to speak, in the bowers of the Muses. But as this is your own daily practice, I think it almost a crime to interrupt you longer with my din at present. Farewell.

Cambridge: July 2, 1628.

20. Familiar Letter 4, to Thomas Young. 1628.

From the Latin.

On looking at your letter, most excellent preceptor, this alone struck me as superfluous, that you excused your slowness in writing; for, though nothing could be more welcome to me than your letters, how could I or ought I to hope that you should have so much leisure from serious and more sacred affairs as to have time always to answer me, especially as that is a matter entirely of kindness and not at all of duty? That I should suspect that you had forgotten me, however, your so many recent kindnesses to me by no means allow. I do not see, either, how you could dismiss into oblivion one laden with so great benefits by you. Having been invited to your part of the country, as soon as spring is a little advanced, I will gladly come, to enjoy the delights of the season, and not less of your conversation, and will withdraw myself from the din of town for a while to your Stoa of the Iceni,[13] as to that most celebrated Porch of Zeno or the Tusculan Villa of Cicero, where you, with moderate means but regal spirit, like some Serranus or Curius, placidly reign in your little farm, and, contemning fortune, hold as it were a triumph over riches, ambition, pomp, luxury, and whatever the herd of men admire and are amazed by. But, as you have deprecated the blame of slowness, you will also in turn, I hope, pardon me the fault of haste; for, having put off this letter to the last, I have preferred writing little, and that in a rather slovenly manner, to not writing at all. Farewell, much to be respected sir.

Cambridge: July 21, 1628.

13 Cf. Familiar Letter 3 (extract 19), where Milton is 'meditating a retirement during this summer vacation into a deeply literary leisure.' *Stoa* is a word-play; Young had become vicar of Stowmarket upon his return from Hamburg.

21. From Elegy VI, to Charles Diodati. 1629.

From the Latin.

> The foreword and the beginning of the poem. The elegy is
> more important for its light on Milton's literary ambition (ex-
> tract 51).

When Diodati had written, on the Ides of December, asking that, if
his verses should be less good than usual, their shortcomings should
be forgiven, because, so he affirmed, amid the splendid entertain-
ments wherewith he had been greeted by his friends he had not
been able to give to the Muses auspicious services, he had this
answer.

> With a stomach anything but full, I send you a prayer for sound
> health, of which, perhaps, you, with your stomach stretched to its
> uttermost, may be in sore need. But why does *your* Muse seek to
> lure forth *mine*? Why does your Muse not suffer mine to court the
> obscurity she craves? Should you wish to know through verses of
> mine how warmly I love you, how dearly I cherish you, *that*, be-
> lieve me, you could scarce learn through this present song, for my
> love is not hemmed within close-gripping measures, nor does it
> come whole and sound to feet that are lame [the elegiac distich].

22. Familiar Letter 5, to Alexander Gill. 1634.

From the Latin.

If you had presented to me a gift of gold, or of preciously embossed
vases, or whatever of that sort mortals admire, it were certainly to
my shame not to have some time or other made you a remuneration
in return, as far as my faculties might serve. Your gift of the day
before yesterday, however, having been such a sprightly and elegant
set of hendecasyllabics, you have, just in proportion to the superiority of that gift to anything in the form of gold, made us the more
anxious to find some dainty means by which to repay the kindness of so pleasant a favour. We had, indeed, at hand some things
of our own of this same kind, but such as I could nowise deem fit

to be sent in contest of equality of gift with yours. I send, therefore, what is not exactly mine, but belongs also to the truly divine
poet, this ode of whom, only last week, with no deliberate intention
certainly, but from I know not what sudden impulse before day-
break, I adapted, almost in bed, to the rule of Greek heroic verse:[14]
with the effect, it seems, that, relying on this coadjutor who sur-
passes you no less in his subject than you surpass me in art, I should
have something that might have a resemblance of approach to a
balancing of accounts. Should anything meet you in it not coming
up to your usual opinion of our productions, understand that since
I left your school this is the first and only thing I have composed in
Greek—employing myself, as you know, more willingly in Latin
and English matters, inasmuch as whoever spends study and pains
in this age on Greek composition runs a risk of singing mostly to the
deaf. Farewell, and expect me on Monday (if God will) in London
among the booksellers. Meanwhile, if with such influence of friendship as you have with that Doctor, the annual President of the College, you can anything promote our business, take the trouble, I
pray, to go to him as soon as possible in my behalf.[15] Again, farewell.

From our suburban residence: December 4, 1634.

23. Familiar Letter 6, to Charles Diodati. 1637.

From the Latin.
    Diodati is in the north of England, among the 'hyperboreans,'
    where he has begun his medical practice.

Now at length I see plainly that what you are driving at is to vanquish me sometimes in the art of obstinate silence; and, if it is so,
bravo! have that little glory over us, for behold! we write first. All
the same, if ever the question should come into contention why
neither has written to the other for so long, do not think but that I
shall stand by many degrees the more excused of the two—manifestly so indeed, as being one by nature slow and lazy to write, as
you well know; while you, on the other hand, whether by nature or

14 The 114th Psalm.
15 What the errand is to which this refers, I do not know.

by habit, are wont without difficulty to be drawn into epistolary correspondence of this sort. It makes also for my favour that I know your method of studying to be so arranged that you frequently take breath in the middle, visit your friends, write much, sometimes make a journey, whereas my genius is such that no delay, no rest, no care or thought almost of anything, holds me aside until I reach the end I am making for, and round off, as it were, some great period of my studies.[16] Wholly hence, and not from any other cause, believe me, has it happened that I am slower in approaching the voluntary discharge of good offices; but in replying to such, O our Theodotus, I am not so very dilatory; nor have I ever been guilty of not meeting any letter of yours by one of mine in due turn. How happens it that, as I hear, you have sent letters to the bookseller, to your brother too not unfrequently, either of whom could conveniently enough, on account of their nearness, have caused letters to have been delivered to me, if there had been any? What I complain of, however, is that, whereas you promised that you would take up your quarters with us for a passing visit on your departure from the city, you did not keep your promise, and that, if you had but once thought of this neglect of your promise, there would not have been wanting necessary occasion enough for writing. All this matter of deserved lecture, as I imagine, I have been keeping against you. What you will prepare in answer see for yourself. But, meanwhile, how is it with you, pray? Are you all right in health? Are there in those parts any smallish learned folks with whom you can willingly associate and chat, as we were wont together? When do you return? How long do you intend to remain among those hyperboreans? Please to answer me these questions one by one: not that you are to make the mistake of supposing that only now have I your affairs at heart—for understand that in the beginning of the autumn I turned

16 Professor Hanford concludes from his study of the Commonplace Book that Milton set for himself during his retirement at Horton, 'a clearly conceived program of historical study, to be continued with characteristic fidelity and thoroughness well into the period of his middle life.'—'The Chronology of Milton's Private Studies,' *Publications of the Modern Language Association*, XXXVI (1921), pp.288-289.

out of my way on a journey to see your brother for the purpose of knowing what you were doing. Lately also, when it had been fallaciously reported to me in London by some one that you were in town, straightway and as if by storm I dashed to your crib; but 'twas the vision of a shadow! for nowhere did you appear. Wherefore, if you can without inconvenience, fly hither all the sooner, and fix yourself in some place so situated that I may have a more pleasant hope that somehow or other we may be able at least sometimes to exchange visits—though I would you were as much our neighbour in the country as you are when in town. But this as it pleases God! I would say more about myself and my studies, but would rather do so when we meet; and now tomorrow we are to return to that country-residence of ours, and the journey so presses that I have hardly had time to put all this on the paper. Farewell.

London: September 2, 1637.

24. From *Scazons to Salsilli, a Roman Poet, as He Lay Ill*. 1638 or 1639.

From the Latin.

> Salsilli was one of Milton's Florentine friends. Among the *testimonia* before the Latin poems in the 1645 edition is one by Salsilli: 'on John Milton, Englishman, who deserves a coronal fashioned of the triple laurel of poesy—Greek, Latin, and Italian.
>
> 'Yield, Meles, yield; let Mincius, too, lowering his urn, yield; let Sebetus cease to have Tasso forever on his tongue. But let the Thames, victor now, sweep on with billows o'ertopping those of every other stream, for, thanks to you, Milton, he will be, in his single self, full match for the other three.'[17]

O Muse, who of choice dost trail a limping foot, and, slow of progress, dost take joy in the gait of Vulcan, and dost think such gait no less charming in its due season than when golden-tressed Deïope moves her comely ankles, now one, now other, before the golden couch of Juno, stand by me, I pray, and bear, if you will, these few words to Salsilli, who takes my Muse so warmly to his heart, preferring her—undeservedly—to the truly mighty poets. These verses

17 Columbia *Milton*, Vol. I, pt. 1, p.157.

that fosterling [of yours] at London, Milton, sends to him, Milton, who, in these latter days, quitting his proper nest and his own expanse of heaven, where the worst of winds all powerless to control its mad lungs swiftly plies panting blasts 'neath the skies, came to the fruitful glebe of Italy's soil, to see its cities, known by proud report, its lordly men, and the fine natures of its learned youth; he prays for you full many a blessing, Salsilli, and a state, a habit wholly sound for your exhausted body. At this present, overflowing bile assails your reins and firmly lodged within your frame breathes ruin. Nor did the impious bile spare you for all that you, a man of culture true, mould Lesbian song with your Roman lips.

25. From the Foreword of *To Manso*. 1639.

From the Latin.
> There are selections from the poem in extract 58.

When the author was tarrying in Naples, Manso attended him with unbounded good will, and bestowed upon him many kindly services, born of his true humanity. To him, therefore, the sojourner, before he left the city, sent this poem, that he might show himself not ungrateful.

26. Familiar Letter 9, to Lucas Holstenius. 1639.

From the Latin.
> Milton's respect for Holstenius, the Vatican Librarian, and for
> Cardinal Barberini, and his friendship with Holstenius as revealed
> in this letter, make the account in the *Second Defence* (extract 2) of
> his militant Protestantism while he was in Italy a little more palat-
> able. He was not fanatic enough to be blind to the worth of learn-
> ing and manners wherever he found them.

Although I both can and often do remember many courteous and most friendly acts done me by many in this my passage through Italy, yet, for so brief an acquaintance, I do not know whether I can justly say that from anyone I have had greater proofs of good will than those which have come to me from you. For, when I went up to the Vatican for the purpose of meeting you, though a total

stranger to you—unless perchance anything had been previously
said about me to you by Alexander Cherubini—[18] you received me
with the utmost courtesy. Admitted at once with politeness into the
Museum, I was allowed to behold the superb collection of books,
and also very many manuscript Greek authors set forth with your
explanations—some of whom, not yet seen in our age, seemed now,
in their array, like Virgil's

> souls enclosed deep within a green valley and
> ready to approach the threshold of the world above

to demand the active hands of the printer and a delivery into the
world, while others, already edited by your care, are eagerly received everywhere by scholars:—dismissed, too, richer than I came,
with two copies of one of these last presented to me by yourself.
Then I could not but believe that it was in consequence of the mention you made of me to the most excellent Cardinal Francesco
Barberini[19] that, when he a few days after gave that public musical
entertainment with truly Roman magnificence,[20] he himself, waiting at the doors, and seeking me out in so great a crowd, almost
seizing me by the hand indeed, admitted me within in a truly most
honourable manner. Further, when on this account I went to pay
my respects to him next day, you again were the person that both
made access for me and obtained me an opportunity of leisurely conversation with him—an opportunity such as, with so great a man—
than whom, on the topmost summit of dignity, nothing more kind,
nothing more courteous—was truly, place and time considered, too
ample rather than too sparing. I am quite ignorant, most learned
Holstenius, whether I am exceptional in having found you so
friendly and hospitable, or whether, in respect of your having spent
three years in study at Oxford, it is your express habit to confer

18 A young scholar in Rome.
19 Prime Minister of Rome.
20 It is commonly assumed that it was on this occasion that Milton heard
    Leonora Baroni sing. It was to her that he addressed his three Latin epi-
    grams *Ad Leonoram*.

such obligations on all Englishmen. If the latter, truly you are pay-
ing back finely to our England the expenses of your schooling there,
and you eminently deserve equal thanks on private grounds from
each of us and on public grounds for our country. If the former is
the case, then that I should have been held distinguishable by you
above the rest, and should have seemed worthy so far of a wish on
your part to form a bond of friendship with me, while I congratulate myself on this opinion of yours, I would at the same time attribute it to *your* frankness rather than to *my* merit. The commission
which you seemed to give me, relating to the inspection of a Medi-
cean codex, I have already carefully reported to my friends, who,
however, hold forth for the present very small hope of effecting that
matter. In that library, I am told, nothing can be copied unless by
leave first obtained; it is not permitted even to bring a pen to the
tables. But they tell me that Giovanni Battista Doni [21] is now in
Rome; having been called to Florence to undertake the public
lectureship in Greek, he is daily expected; and through him, they
say, it will be easy for you to compass what you want. Still it would
have been truly a most gratifying accident for me if a matter of a
kind so eminently desirable had advanced somewhat farther by my
little endeavour, the disgrace being that, engaged as you are in
work so honourable and illustrious, all men, methods, and circumstances, are not everywhere at your bidding.—For the rest, you will
have bound me by a new obligation if you salute His Eminence the
Cardinal with all possible respect in my name, whose great virtues
and regard for what is right, singularly evident in his readiness to
forward all the liberal arts, are always present before my eyes, as
well as that meek, and, if I may so say, submissive loftiness of
mind which alone has taught him to raise himself by self-depression,
concerning which it may truly be said, as is said of Ceres in Callimachus, though with a turn of the sense: 'Feet to the earth still
cling, while the head is touching Olympus.' This may be a proof to

---

21 A Florentine scholar and musician. Dr. MacKellar cites Doni's statement
   that Leonora and her mother would not suffer by comparison with
   Sappho.—*Latin Poems*, p.39.

most other princes how far asunder and alien from true magnanimity is the sour superciliousness and courtly haughtiness too common. Nor do I think that, while he is alive, men will miss any more
the Este, the Farnese, or the Medici, formerly the favourers of
learned men.—Farewell, most learned Holstenius; and, if there is
any more than average lover of you and your studies, I should wish
you to reckon me along with him, should you think that of such
consequence, wheresoever in the world my future may be.

Florence: March 30, 1639.

27. From *Damon's Epitaph*. 1640.

From the Latin.
   The present extract consists of Milton's foreword to the poem
   and a passage at the beginning of the poem concerned with his
   affection for Diodati. Extract 59 is also from *Damon's Epitaph*.

Thyrsis and Damon, shepherds of the same neighbourhood, devoted to the same pursuits, were friends from boyhood up, friends
as close as e'er men were. Thyrsis, while on a journey for pleasure's
sake, received, in foreign lands, a message telling of his friend's
death. Later, after his return home, when he found that the message
was true, he bemoaned himself and his loneliness.

   In this poem, by 'Damon' is meant Charles Diodati, descended on
his father's side from the Etruscan city of Lucca. In all things else
he was an Englishman, a youth, the while he lived, pre-eminent in
intellect, in learning, and in all the other brightest and fairest virtues.

   Nymphs of Himera—ye keep in mind Daphnis and Hylas both,
and the fate of Bion, long, long lamented—sing a strain truly Sici-
lian through the cities by the Thames, the cries that, in his woe,
Thyrsis poured forth, the ceaseless plainings wherewith he harried
the grots, and the wide-ranging rivers, and the retreats within the
woods, while he made lament that Damon had been wrested from
him before his time. Nor did he exempt from his griefs the deeps of
the night, as he wandered o'er lonely places. Twice already the

stalk was rising high with the green ears of grain, and the granaries were counting as many golden harvests, since his last day had borne Damon away within the shades, and Thyrsis was not yet by his side! for that shepherd the sweet love of the Muse was keeping in a Tuscan city. But when Thyrsis' mind, filled full, and concern for the flock he had left behind, called him home, then, verily, soon as he had set him down 'neath the accustomed elm, he was conscious that his friend was lost, and he began thus to disburden his limitless pain.

> *Go home, unpastured, my lambs:*
> *Your master has no leisure now.*

Woe is me! What powers divine shall I name on earth, what in heaven, since they have swept you off, Damon, by a merciless death? Is it thus, thus, that you leave me? Is merit such as yours to pass thus, nameless, and to be joined with a host of obscure shades? But he that with his golden wand parts the souls would not wish *that*; no, he would guide you to a host worthy of yourself, and would fend far off from you all the worthless herd of the voiceless [dead].

> *Go home, unpastured, my lambs:*
> *Your master has no leisure now.*

Whate'er shall come, one thing is sure: unless a wolf shall see me first, you, Damon, will not be crushed in an unlamented tomb, but your honours will be firmly fixed, firm set for you, and will long have vigorous life among the shepherds. To you, as second only to Daphnis, the shepherds will joy to pay their vows, they will joy to sing of you, as second only to Daphnis, as long as Pales, as long as Faunus shall love the countryside, if it counts for aught to have cherished faith like the faith of olden days, to have cherished righteousness, and the arts of Pallas, and to have had as comrade a man of song.

> *Go home, unpastured, my lambs:*
> *Your master has no leisure now.*

These sure rewards await you, Damon, they will be yours for aye. But what of me? What loyal comrade will cling to my side, as you were wont oft to do, in the days of unrelenting cold, in places pregnant with frosts, or under the devouring sun, when the plants were dying of thirst, or when there was need to face in hand to hand encounter the monstrous lions or to frighten the hungry wolves away from the high folds? Who will make it his habit with talking and with song to lay the day to rest?

> *Go home, unpastured, my lambs:*
> *Your master has no leisure now.*

To whom shall I entrust my soul? Who will teach me to lighten consuming cares, who to beguile the long nights with sweet converse, when the mellow pears shall be set hissing by the cheery fire, and the hearth shall crackle with the nuts, the while the evil South Wind confounds all the world outdoors and thunders down through the elm?

> *Go home, unpastured, my lambs:*
> *Your master has no leisure now.*

Or in the summer-time, when the day is revolving in mid heaven, when Pan, hidden away in the shade of the oak, courts slumber, and the nymphs seek again their familiar seats 'neath the waters, and the shepherds hide, the farmer snores under the hedge, who will renew for me your blandishments, your laughter, your sallies of Cecropian wit, and your cultured graces?

28. Familiar Letter 10, to Charles Dati. 1647.

From the Latin.

Dati is in the list of Florentine friends mentioned in the *Second Defence* (extract 2) as ever to be remembered. Only eighteen years old when Milton was in Florence, Dati was nevertheless dearest to Milton of his Florentine friends.

With how great and what new pleasure I was filled, my Charles, on the unexpected arrival of your letter, since it is impossible for me to describe it adequately, I wish you may in some degree understand from the very pain with which it was dashed, such pain as is almost the invariable accompaniment of any great delight yielded to men. For, on running over that first portion of your letter, in which elegance contends so finely with friendship, I should have called my feeling one of unmixed joy, and the rather because I see your labour to make friendship the winner. Immediately, however, when I came upon that passage where you write that you had sent me three letters before, which I now know to have been lost, then, in the first place, that sincere gladness of mine at the receipt of this one began to be infected and troubled with a sad regret, and presently a something heavier creeps in upon me, to which I am accustomed in very frequent grievings over my own lot: the sense, namely, that those whom the mere necessity of neighbourhood, or something else of a useless kind, has closely conjoined with me, whether by accident or by the tie of law, *they* are the persons, though in no other respect commendable, who sit daily in my company, weary me, nay, by heaven, all but plague me to death whenever they are jointly in the humour for it, whereas those whom habits, disposition, studies, had so handsomely made my friends, are now almost all denied me, either by death or by most unjust separation of place, and are so for the most part snatched from my sight that I have to live well-nigh in a perpetual solitude.[22] As to what you say, that from the time of my departure from Florence you have been anxious about my health and always mindful of me, I truly congratulate myself that a feeling has been equal and mutual in both of us, the existence of

22 Milton's wife's family took refuge in his house in the summer of 1646, when the Powells were ruined in the failure of the Royalists, and remained for almost a year. It is to them he is joined by 'mere necessity of neighbourhood . . . by accident or by the tie of law' and it is they who weary him and all but plague him to death. Of those whose absence he laments Miss Darbishire says, 'he is thinking not only of his Italian friends in Florence . . . but of Charles Diodati. . . . And more deeply still he is lamenting the loss of his father, who died only a month before.'—*Early Lives*, p.xlvii.

which on my side only I was perhaps claiming to my credit. Very sad to me also, I will not conceal from you, was that departure, and it planted stings in my heart which now rankle there deeper as often as I think with myself of my reluctant parting, my separation as by a wrench, from so many companions at once, such good friends as they were, and living so pleasantly with each other in one city, far off indeed, but to me most dear. I call to witness that tomb of Damon, ever to be sacred and solemn to me, whose adornment with every tribute of grief was my weary task, till I betook myself at length to what comforts I could, and desired again to breathe a little—I call that sacred grave to witness that I have had no greater delight all this while than in recalling to my mind the most pleasant memory of all of you, and of yourself especially. This you must have read for yourself long ere now, if that poem reached you,[23] as now first I hear from you it did. I had carefully caused it to be sent, in order that, however small a proof of talent, it might, even in those few lines introduced into it emblem-wise, be no obscure proof of my love towards you.[24] My idea was that by this means I should lure either yourself or some of the others to write to me; for, if I wrote first, either I had to write to all, or I feared that, if I gave the preference to any one, I should incur the reproach of such others as came to know it, hoping as I do that very many are yet there alive who might certainly have a claim to this attention from me. Now, however, you first of all, both by this most friendly call of your letter, and by your thrice-repeated attention of writing before, have freed the reply for which I have been some while since in your debt from any expostulation from the others. There was, I confess, an additional cause for my silence in that most turbulent state of our Britain, subsequent to my return home, which obliged me to divert my mind shortly afterwards from the prosecution of my studies to the defence anyhow of life and fortune. What safe retirement for literary leisure could you suppose given one among so many battles

---

23 The *Epitaphium Damonis*.
24 Lines 125 to 138 of the *Epitaph* are concerned with Milton's Italian friendships. Dati and Francini are specifically mentioned (extract 59).

of a civil war, slaughters, flights, seizures of goods? Yet, even in the midst of these evils, since you desire to be informed about my studies, know that we have published not a few things in our native tongue, which, were they not written in English,[25] I would willingly send to you, my friends in Florence, to whose opinions I attach very much value. The part of the poems which is in Latin I will send shortly, since you wish it; and I would have done so spontaneously long ago, but that, on account of the rather harsh sayings against the Pope of Rome in some of the pages,[26] I had a suspicion they would not be quite agreeable to your ears. Now I beg of you that the indulgence you were wont to give, I say not to your own Dante and Petrarch in the same case, but with singular politeness to my own former freedom of speech, as you know, among you, the same you, Dati, will obtain (for of yourself I am sure) from my other friends whenever I may be speaking of your religion in our peculiar way. I am reading with pleasure your description of the funeral ceremony to King Louis, in which I recognize your style—not that one of street bazaars and mercantile concerns which you say jestingly you have been lately practising, but the right eloquent one which the Muses like, and which befits the president of a club of wits. It remains that we agree on some method and plan by which henceforth our letters may go between us by a sure route. This does not seem very difficult when so many of our merchants have frequent and large transactions with you, and their messengers run backwards and forwards every week, and their vessels sail from port to port not much seldomer. The charge of this I shall commit, rightly I hope, to Bookseller James, or to his master, my very familiar acquaintance. Meanwhile farewell, my Charles; and give best salutations in my name to Coltellini, Francini, Frescobaldi, Malatesti, Clementillo the younger,[27] anyone else you know that remembers

25 The early anti-prelaty tracts, the divorce pamphlets, and the *Poems* of 1645.
26 In *In Quintum Novembris*, on the Gunpowder Plot. Milton has apparently learned a little reticence since his experience with Manso recorded in the *Second Defence* (extract 2). He is at any rate very eager indeed to retain the good will of his Italian friends.
27 More of Milton's Florentine friends. Coltellini, Francini, Frescobaldi,

me with some affection, and, in fine, to the whole Gaddian Academy. Again farewell!

London: April 21, 1647.

29. From a copy of *Eikonoklastes* presented to the Earl of Carbery. 1650.

For my very good friend Mr. William Thomas[28] at Laherne, to be presented to the Earl of Carbery.[29]

30. From the Album of Christopher Arnold. 1651.

From the Greek and Latin.

Christopher Arnold, a German scholar later to become Professor of History at Nuremberg, writes of Milton to George Richter, Vice-chancellor of the University of Altorf, August 7, 1651: 'The strenuous Defender of the same [i.e. the Republic], Milton, enters readily into talk: his style is pure and his writing most terse. Of the old English Theologians and their commentaries on the Books of Holy Scripture . . . he seemed to me altogether to entertain a too harsh, if not an unjust, opinion.'[30]

'My strength is made perfect in weakness.'[31] To the most learned man, and my most cultured champion, Mr. Christopher Arnold, I have given this, in memory of his virtue and my zeal towards him.

London: November 19, 1651.

John Milton.

Clementillo, and Dati himself, with Bonmattei instead of Malatesti, make the list in the *Second Defence* (extract 2).

28 A leader of the Independents in Wales.

29 Richard Vaughan, second Earl of Carbery, who married about 1653 the Lady Alix Egerton who had played the part of 'The Lady' in *Comus* sixteen years before (Masson, *Life*, Vol. VI, p.300). After the Restoration the Earl of Carbery was made President of Wales by Charles. The earlier accession to this office of the Earl of Bridgewater was the occasion which *Comus* celebrated.

30 Masson, *Life*, Vol. IV, p.350.

31 2 Cor. xii, 9. The scriptural text is from the Greek testament. Milton uses the same text as a complete entry in another album in 1656.—Columbia *Milton*, Vol. XVIII, p.271.

31. Familiar Letter 13, to Richard Heath. 1652.

From the Latin.
  Beyond what this letter tells, I know nothing of Richard Heath.

If I have ever been able, my much respected friend, to give aid, whether in promoting your studies or in procuring furtherance in them—and such aid has assuredly been either nothing or very slight—I am glad on more than one account that it should have been bestowed so well and fortunately on a nature of such promise, though known rather late, and that it has been so fruitful as to have produced an upright pastor of the church, a good citizen of his country, and at the same time an agreeable friend for myself. All this I am easily sure of, both from the rest of your life and your excellent state of sentiment about religion and state, and also, and especially, from that singular affectionateness of your mind which can be extinguished or lessened by no amount of absence, no lapse of time. Nor is it possible, unless you had made more than ordinary progress in virtue and piety and in study of the best things, that you should be so grateful to those who have conferred even the least assistance towards those acquisitions. Wherefore, my pupil (for I willingly call you by that name, if you allow it), I would have you believe that you have a high place in my regards, and that nothing would be more desirable for me than that, if your convenience and your plans permitted (and this I see to be also in your own wishes), you should be able to live somewhere near me, so that there might be more frequent and pleasant intercourse of life and studies be-tween us. But of that as God pleases and you find expedient! Further, as to what you say about writing in English, do so if you please (though you have really made no small advance in Latin), lest at any time the trouble of writing should make either of us slow to write, and in order that our ideas, not being bound by any fetters of an alien speech, may the more freely express themselves. You will, I believe, with the greatest propriety entrust your letters to any one of the servants of the family I have mentioned to you. Farewell.
  Westminster: December 13, 1652.

32. Sonnet XX. 1655.

The sonnet is addressed to Edward Lawrence, elder son of the President of the Council, Henry Lawrence. Edward Lawrence was one of Milton's pupils. He was a friend as well, drawing from Milton this sonnet, one of the most familiar and charming of his poems—an invitation to dinner, perhaps.[32]

> Lawrence, of virtuous father virtuous son,
>> Now that the fields are dank, and ways are mire,
>> Where shall we sometimes meet, and by the fire
>> Help waste a sullen day; what may be won
> From the hard season gaining? Time will run
>> On smoother, till Favonius re-inspire
>> The frozen earth, and clothe in fresh attire
>> The lily and rose, that neither sowed nor spun.
> What neat repast shall feast us, light and choice,
>> Of Attic taste, with wine, whence we may rise
>> To hear the lute well touched, or artful voice
> Warble immortal notes and Tuscan air?
>> He who of those delights can judge, and spare
>> To interpose them oft, is not unwise.

33. Sonnet XXI, to Cyriack Skinner. 1655.

Cyriack Skinner was another of Milton's pupils. They remained friends until Milton's death. Perhaps this sonnet is an invitation to the same dinner to which 'young Lawrence' is bid.

> Cyriack, whose grandsire on the Royal Bench
>> Of British Themis with no mean applause
>> Pronounced and in his volumes taught our laws,
>> Which others at their bar so often wrench,
> Today deep thoughts resolve with me to drench
>> In mirth that after no repenting draws;
>> Let Euclid rest and Archimedes pause,
>> And what the Swede intend, and what the French.

---

32 The identification of Edward Lawrence is Smart's (*Sonnets*, pp.111–115). Most of the biographers, including Masson, think the younger son,

To measure life learn thou betimes, and know
Toward solid good what leads the nearest way;
For other things mild Heaven a time ordains,
And disapproves that care, though wise in show,
That with superfluous burden loads the day,
And when God sends a cheerful hour, refrains.

34. From a copy of the *Poems* of 1645 presented to Peter Heim-bach.[33] 1655 or 1656.

From the Latin.

John Milton, the author, to his friend the truly outstanding gentle-man, elegant poet, flowery orator, keen philosopher, Peter von Heimbach, counsellor-at-law.

35. Familiar Letter 18, to Henry Oldenburg. 1656.

From the Latin.

Oldenburg came to London as agent to the Commonwealth for the city of Bremen, but settled in England to undertake a scholarly career culminating in a Fellowship in the Royal Society. He was the son-in-law of Milton's friend John Durie, and at the time of this letter tutor to Richard Jones, 'young Ranelagh.' They are in Oxford.

Your letter, brought by young Ranelagh, has found me rather busy, and so I am forced to be briefer than I should wish. You have certainly kept *your* departing promise of writing to me, and that with a punctuality surpassed, I believe, by no one hitherto in the payment of a debt. I congratulate you on your present retirement, to my loss though it be, since it gives pleasure to you; I congratulate you also on that happy state of mind which enables you so easily to set aside at once the ambition and the ease of city life, and to lift your thoughts to higher matters of contemplation. What advantage that retirement affords, however, besides plenty of books, I know

Henry, was Milton's friend. Edward Phillips speaks only of 'young Lawrence,' which may refer to either of the sons.
33 See headnote, extract 146.

not; and those persons you have found there as fit associates in your studies I should suppose to be such rather from their own natural constitution than from the discipline of the place—unless perchance, from missing you here, I do less justice to the place for keeping you away. Meanwhile you yourself rightly remark that there are too many there whose occupation it is to spoil divine and human things alike by their frivolous quibblings, that they may not seem to be doing absolutely nothing for those many endowments by which they are supported so much to the public detriment. All this you will understand better for yourself. Those ancient annals of the Chinese from the Flood downwards which you say are promised by the Jesuit Martini are doubtless very eagerly expected on account of the novelty of the thing; but I do not see what authority or confirmation they can add to the Mosaic books. Our Cyriack,[34] whom you bade me salute, returns the salutation. Farewell.

Westminster: June 25, 1656.

36. Familiar Letter 20, to Peter Heimbach. 1656.

From the Latin.

Most amply, my Heimbach, have you fulfilled your promises and all the other expectations one would have of your goodness, with the exception that I have still to long for your return. You promised that it would be within two months at farthest; and now, unless my desire to have you back makes me misreckon the time, you have been absent nearly three. In the matter of the Atlas you have abundantly performed all I requested of you, which was not that you should procure me one, but only that you should find out the lowest price of the book. You write that they ask 130 florins: it must be the Mauritanian mountain *Atlas*, I think, and not a book, that you tell me is to be bought at so huge a price. Such is now the luxury of typographers in printing books that the furnishing of a library seems to have become as costly as the furnishing of a villa. Since to me at least, on account of my blindness, painted maps can hardly be

34 Cyriack Skinner. See headnote, extract 33.

of use, vainly surveying as I do with blind eyes the actual globe of the earth, I am afraid that the bigger the price at which I should buy that book the greater would seem to me my grief over my deprivation. Be good enough, pray, to take so much farther trouble for me as to be able to inform me, when you return, how many volumes there are in the complete work, and which of the two issues, that of Blaeu or that of Jansen, is the larger and more correct. This I hope to hear from yourself personally, on your speedy return, rather than by another letter. Meanwhile, farewell, and come back to us as soon as you can.

Westminster: November 8, 1656.

37. From a copy of *Paradise Lost* given to Francis Rea. 1667.

For my loving friend Mr. Francis Rea, bookbinder in Worcestershire.

Milton speaks further of his friends or of friendship in extracts 1, 2, 38, 41, 45, 48, 51–54, 56–59, 63, 65, 81, 105, 130, 132, 133, 136–149, *and* 153–157.

VI. MORALITY

To scorn delights and live laborious days.

38. From the Sixth Prolusion. 1628.

From the Latin.

As later he was to excuse himself for similar offences by blaming them upon his opponents in pamphlet warfare, here, after apologizing for the length of the oration he is finishing, Milton explains the 'looseness' and 'licentiousness' of the oratorical buffoonery that is to follow in terms of the taste of his audience and the genius of the place—Cambridge. Milton is providing 'comic entertainment' in celebration of the end of the summer term in 1628. 'That Milton was chosen to give it [the oration]—before almost the entire University, as he tells us—[extract 18, also from the Sixth Prolusion] proves that he was by this time a popular and respected person.'—Tillyard, *Correspondence and Academic Exercises*, p.xxx.

But I fear, fellow students, that I have spun out the thread of my discourse longer than is proper. I shall not present excuses, as I might, lest, by apologizing, the fault should be accentuated. Now, freed from oratorical laws, we will break forth into comic licence; in which, if by chance I should swerve from my habit, if from the rigid laws of modesty, as they say, a finger's breadth, be it known, fellow students, that I have stripped off and laid aside for a short time my former custom out of good feeling for you; or, if anything shall be said loosely, if anything licentiously, you may consider that not my mind and disposition, but the procedure of the occasion and the genius of the place has indeed suggested it to me. Accordingly, like that which the comic actors used to beg at their exit, I at the very beginning entreat: Clap your hands and laugh.

39. From the Sixth Prolusion. 1628.

From the Latin.

The famous 'Lady of Christ's' passage.

From some I have lately heard the epithet 'Lady.' But why do I seem to those fellows insufficiently masculine? Was it any disgrace to Priscian? Really, the silly grammaticasters attribute to the feminine gender signs which belong to the masculine! Doubtless it was because I was never able to gulp down huge bumpers in pancratic fashion; or because my hand has not become calloused by holding the plough-handle; or because I never lay down on my back under the sun at midday, like a seven-year ox-driver; perhaps, in fine, because I never proved myself a man in the same manner as those gluttons. But would that they could as easily lay aside their asshood as I whatever belongs to womanhood.[1]

But notice how stupidly, how thoughtlessly they have taunted me about that which I, on the best authority, shall turn to my honour. For truly, even Demosthenes was called by his rivals and opponents a little man. Likewise Quintus Hortensius, most renowned of all the orators, after Marcus Tullius, was called by Lucius Torquatus 'Dionysia the citharess.' To him he replied: 'I would prefer indeed to be Dionysia than what you are, Torquatus—unrefined, boorish, ill-bred.' But I put far away and repel from me whatsoever pertains to Lord and Lady; I do not desire to be a 'Lord,' fellow students, except on your rostrum and in your tribunal. Who now will stop me from enjoying an omen so auspicious and happy, and from exulting with joy that I have been united in company with such great men under the same reproach! Meanwhile, as I think that all good and excellent men are placed above envy, so I believe these malicious fellows are so far the lowest down of all that they are not worth reviling.

40. From the Album of Count Camillus Cardouin. 1639.

> . . . if Virtue feeble were,
> Heaven itself would stoop to her.[2]
> 'I change my sky but not my spirit when I cross the sea.'[3]
>   John Milton, Englishman.
> June 10, 1639.

[1] Milton's explanation of the epithet is probably better than Aubrey's: 'He was so fair that they called him the Lady of Christ's College.'—Darbishire, *Early Lives*, p.3.   [2] *Comus*, ll.1022–1023.

[3] Horace, Epistle I, xi, 27. Milton quotes the original, of course.

41. From *An Apology for Smectymnuus*. 1642.

After recalling his opponent's confessed ignorance of his habits, and
after apology for writing of himself, Milton undertakes to answer
specific charges brought against him in *A Modest Confutation* to
the effect that he had been 'vomited forth' from the University and
was a haunter of playhouses and brothels. He responds with an
account of his position at Cambridge and an account of the actual
disposition of the hours he has been supposed to spend in de-
bauchery. He then replies to general charges of unchastity by tracing the growth in himself of the conviction that chastity is the most
important of virtues to a prospective poet. This involves a full
treatment of the intellectual and artistic forces that have shaped
his mind, a statement of his own high literary ambitions, and a
statement of his resolution to be true to them. This passage is
second in importance for its biographical significance only to the
long autobiographical passage in the *Second Defence* (extract 2),
if second to that. It is of first importance as an account of Milton's
development as a poet, his conception of the poetic function relating it very closely to the virtuous life, for 'he who would . . .
write well hereafter . . . ought himself to be a true poem.'

Thus having spent his first onset not in confuting, but in a reason-
less defaming of the book, the method of his malice hurries him to
attempt the like against the author:[4] not by proofs and testimonies,
but 'having no certain notice of me,' as he professes, 'further than
what he gathers from the *Animadversions*,' blunders at me for the
rest, and flings out stray crimes at a venture, which he could never,
though he be a serpent, suck from anything that I have written; but
from his own stuffed magazine and hoard of slanderous inventions,
over and above that which he converted to venom in the drawing.
To me readers, it happens as a singular contentment, and let it be
to good men no slight satisfaction, that the slanderer here confesses
he has 'no further notice of me than his own conjecture.' Although
it had been honest to have inquired before he uttered such infamous words; and I am credibly informed he did inquire; but

4 Milton is replying as if to Bishop Hall alone. Actually, *A Modest Confutation*, to which this is a response, was a collaboration of Bishop Hall and his
son.

finding small comfort from the intelligence which he received
whereon to ground the falsities which he had provided, thought it
his likeliest course under a pretended ignorance to let drive at random, lest he should lose his odd ends which from some penurious
book of characters he had been culling out and would fain apply.
Not caring to burden me with those vices whereof, among whom
my conversation hath been, I have been ever least suspected,
perhaps not without some subtlety to cast me into envy by bringing
on me a necessity to enter into mine own praises, in which argument I know every wise man is more unwillingly drawn to speak
than the most repining ear can be averse to hear. Nevertheless,
since I dare not wish to pass this life unpersecuted of slanderous
tongues, for God hath told us that to be generally praised is woeful,
I shall rely on His promise to free the innocent from causeless
aspersions: whereof nothing sooner can assure me than if I shall
feel Him now assisting me in the just vindication of myself, which
yet I could defer, it being more meet that to those other matters of
public debatement in this book I should give attendance first, but
that I fear it would but harm the truth for me to reason in her behalf so long as I should suffer my honest estimation to lie unpurged
from these insolent suspicions. And if I shall be large, or unwonted
in justifying myself to those who know me not, for else it would be
needless, let them consider that a short slander will oft-times reach
farther than a long apology, and that he who will do justly to all
men must begin from knowing how, if it so happen, to be not unjust
to himself. I must be thought, if this libeller (for now he shows
himself to be so) can find belief, after an inordinate and riotous
youth spent at 'the University,' to have been at length 'vomited out
thence.' For which commodious lie, that he may be encouraged in
the trade another time, I thank him; for it hath given me an apt
occasion to acknowledge publicly with all grateful mind that more
than ordinary favour and respect which I found above any of my
equals at the hands of those courteous and learned men, the Fellows
of that college wherein I spent some years, who at my parting, after
I had taken two degrees, as the manner is, signified many ways how

much better it would content them that I would stay, as by many
letters full of kindness and loving respect both before that time, and
long after, I was assured of their singular good affection towards
me.[5] Which being likewise propense to all such as were for their
studious and civil life worthy of esteem, I could not wrong their
judgements and upright intentions so much as to think I had that
regard from them for other cause than that I might be still encouraged to proceed in the honest and laudable courses of which they
apprehended I had given good proof. And to those ingenuous and
friendly men who were ever the countenancers of virtuous and
hopeful wits, I wish the best and happiest things that friends in absence wish one to another. As for the common approbation or
dislike of that place, as now it is, that I should esteem or disesteem
myself or any other the more for that, too simple and too credulous
is the confuter, if he think to obtain with me or any right discerner.
Of small practice were that physician who could not judge by what
both she or her sister hath of long time vomited that the worser
stuff she strongly keeps in her stomach, but the better she is ever
kecking at, and is queasy. She vomits now out of sickness, but ere
it be well with her, she must vomit by strong physic. In the meanwhile that 'suburb sink,'[6] as this rude scavenger calls it, and more
than scurrilously taunts it with the 'plague,' having a worse plague
in his middle entrail, that suburb wherein I dwell shall be in my
account a more honourable place than his university.[7] Which as in
the time of her better health and mine own younger judgement I
never greatly admired, so now much less. But he follows me to the
city, still usurping and forging beyond his book notice, which only
he affirms to have had; 'and where my morning haunts are he wisses

---

5 See Introduction, pp.xxix–xxx, and the *Second Defence* (extract 2).

6 Edward Phillips: 'A pretty garden-house he took in Aldersgate Street.'
  —Darbishire, *Early Lives*, p.62.

7 Cambridge. Milton is seldom kind in his judgements of his alma mater.
  His disappointment was twofold: first in his fellow students, finding among
  them, as he writes to Alexander Gill, 'almost no real companions in study'
  (extract 19), and second in the curriculum, in the scholastic subjects by
  which 'the mind is neither delighted nor instructed, nor indeed is any
  common good promoted' as he argues in the Third Prolusion (extract 148).

not.' 'Tis wonder, that being so rare an alchemist of slander, he
could not extract that as well as the university vomit and the suburb
sink which his art could distil so cunningly, but because his limbec
fails him, to give him and envy the more vexation, I'll tell him.
Those morning haunts are where they should be, at home, not
sleeping or concocting the surfeits of an irregular feast, but up and
stirring, in winter often ere the sound of any bell awake men to
labour or to devotion, in summer as oft with the bird that first
rouses, or not much tardier, to read good authors, or cause them to
be read,[8] till the attention be weary or memory have his full fraught.
Then with useful and generous labours preserving the body's
health and hardiness, to render lightsome, clear, and not lumpish,
obedience to the mind, to the cause of religion, and our country's
liberty, when it shall require firm hearts in sound bodies to stand
and cover their stations, rather than to see the ruin of our protestation and the enforcement of a slavish life. These are the morning
practices;[9] proceed now to the afternoon; 'in playhouses,' he says,
'and the bordellos.' Your intelligence, unfaithful spy of Canaan?
He gives in his evidence, that 'there he hath traced me.' Take him
at his word, reader, but let him bring good sureties, ere ye dismiss
him, that while he pretended to dog others he did not turn in for
his own pleasure; for so much in effect he concludes against himself,
not contented to be caught in every other gin, but he must be such
a novice as to be still hampered in his own hemp. 'In the *Animadversions*,' saith he, 'I find the mention of old cloaks, false beards,
night-walkers, and salt lotion; therefore the animadverter haunts

8 'Or cause them to be read.' This is Milton's schoolmastering period; the
reference is to his students, not to a reader. Milton's blindness is nearly ten
years away.
9 Aubrey gives Milton's schedule in his later life: 'He was an early riser (at
4 o'clock manè). Yea, after he lost his sight. He had a man to read to him:
the first thing he read was the Hebrew Bible, and that was at 4 manè to
$4\frac{1}{2}$+. Then he contemplated. At 7 his man came to him again and then
read to him and wrote till dinner; the writing was as much as the reading.
His daughter Deborah could read to him Latin, Italian, and French and
Greek. The other sister is Mary, more like her mother. After dinner he
used to walk 3 or 4 hours at a time. He always had a garden where he lived.
Went to bed about 9.'—Darbishire, *Early Lives*, p.6.

playhouses and bordellos; for if he did not, how could he speak of such gear?' Now that he may know what it is to be a child and yet to meddle with edged tools, I turn his antistrophon upon his own head: the confuter knows that these things are the furniture of playhouses and bordellos; therefore by the same reason the confuter himself hath been traced in those places. Was it such a dissolute speech, telling of some politicians who were wont to eavesdrop in disguises, to say they were often liable to a night-walking cudgeller, or the emptying of a urinal? What if I had writ as your friend the author of the aforesaid mime, *Mundus Alter et Idem*,[10] to have been ravished, like some young Cephalus or Hylas, by a troop of camping huswives in Viraginia, and that he was there forced to swear himself an uxorious varlet, then after a long servitude to have come into Aphrodisia, that pleasant country, that gave such a sweet smell to his nostrils among the shameless courtesans of Desvergonia? Surely he would have then concluded me as constant at the bordello as the galley-slave at his oar. But since there is such necessity to the hearsay of a tire, a periwig, or a visard, that plays must have been seen, what difficulty was there in that, when in the colleges so many of the young divines, and those in next aptitude to divinity, have been seen so oft upon the stage, writhing and unboning their clergy limbs to all the antic and dishonest gestures of Trinculos, buffoons, and bawds, prostituting the shame of that ministry which either they had, or were nigh having, to the eyes of courtiers and court-ladies, with their grooms and mesdemoiselles? There while they acted, and overacted, among other young scholars, I was a spectator; they thought themselves gallant men, and I thought them fools; they made sport, and I laughed; they mispronounced, and I misliked; and to make up the atticism, they were out, and I hissed. Judge now whether so many good text-men were not sufficient to instruct me of false beards and visards without more expositors. And how can this confuter take the face to object to me the seeing of that which his reverent prelates allow, and incite their young disciples to act? For if it be unlawful to sit and

10 Bishop Hall is himself the author of *Mundus Alter et Idem*.

behold a mercenary comedian personating that which is least unseemly for a hireling to do, how much more blameful is it to endure the sight of as vile things acted by persons either entered or presently to enter into the ministry, and how much more foul and ignominious for them to be the actors.[11]

But because as well by this upbraiding to me the bordellos as by other suspicious glancings in his book he would seem privily to point me out to his readers as one whose custom of life were not honest, but licentious, I shall entreat to be borne with though I digress and in a way not often trod acquaint ye with the sum of my thoughts in this matter through the course of my years and studies. Although I am not ignorant how hazardous it will be to do this under the nose of the envious, as it were in skirmish to change the compact order, and instead of outward actions to bring inmost thoughts into front. And I must tell ye, readers, that by this sort of men I have been already bitten at; yet shall they not for me know how slightly they are esteemed, unless they have so much learning as to read what in Greek Ἀπειροχαλία is, which together with envy is the common disease of those who censure books that are not for their reading. With me it fares now, as with him whose outward garment hath been injured and ill bedighted; for having no other shift, what help but to turn the inside outwards, especially if the lining be of the same, or, as it is sometimes, much better. So if my name and outward demeanour be not evident enough to defend me, I must make trial if the discovery of my inmost thoughts can. Wherein of two purposes, both honest, and both sincere, the one perhaps I shall not miss; although I fail to gain belief with others of being such as my perpetual thoughts shall here disclose me, I may yet not fail of success in persuading some to be such really themselves as they cannot believe me to be more than what I feign. I had my time, readers, as others have who have good learning bestowed upon them, to be sent to those places where the opinion was it might be soonest attained, and as the manner is was not unstudied

11 See Introduction, pp.xxxii–xxxv, for a discussion of Milton's probable attendance at the theatres.

in those authors which are most commended: whereof some were grave orators and historians, whose matter methought I loved indeed, but as my age then was, so I understood them; others were the smooth elegiac poets, whereof the schools are not scarce, whom both for the pleasing sound of their numerous writing, which in imitation I found most easy and most agreeable to nature's part in me, and for their matter, which, what it is there be few who know not, I was so allured to read that no recreation came to me better welcome. For that it was then those years with me which are excused though they be least severe, I may be saved the labour to remember ye. Whence, having observed them to account it the chief glory of their wit, in that they were ablest to judge, to praise, and by that could esteem themselves worthiest to love, those high perfections which under one or other name they took to celebrate, I thought with myself by every instinct and presage of nature, which is not wont to be false, that what emboldened them to this task might with such diligence as they used embolden me, and that what judgement, wit, or elegance was my share, would herein best appear and best value itself, by how much more wisely and with more love of virtue I should choose (let rude ears be absent) the object of not unlike praises. For albeit these thoughts to some will seem virtuous and commendable, to others only pardonable, to a third sort perhaps idle, yet the mentioning of them now will end in serious. Nor blame it, readers, in those years to propose to themselves such a reward as the noblest dispositions above other things in this life have sometimes preferred, whereof not to be sensible, when good and fair in one person meet, argues both a gross and shallow judgement, and withal an ungentle and swainish breast. For by the firm settling of these persuasions I became, to my best memory, so much a proficient that if I found those authors anywhere speaking unworthy things of themselves, or unchaste of those names which before they had extolled, this effect it wrought with me: from that time forward their art I still applauded, but the men I deplored, and above them all preferred the two famous renowners of Beatrice and Laura, who never write but honour of

them to whom they devote their verse, displaying sublime and pure
thoughts without transgression. And long it was not after when I
was confirmed in this opinion, that he who would not be frustrate
of his hope to write well hereafter in laudable things, ought himself
to be a true poem, that is, a composition and pattern of the best
and honourablest things, not presuming to sing high praises of
heroic men or famous cities unless he have in himself the experience
and the practice of all that which is praiseworthy.[12] These reasonings, together with a certain niceness of nature, an honest haughtiness, and self-esteem either of what I was, or what I might be
(which let envy call pride), and lastly that modesty, whereof though
not in the title-page[13] yet here I may be excused to make some be-
seeming profession, all these uniting the supply of their natural
aid together, kept me still above those low descents of mind beneath

12 Cf. Familiar Letter 23, to Henry DeBrass: 'This, then, is my view: that he
who would write of worthy deeds worthily must write with mental endowments and experience of affairs not less than were in the doer of them,
so as to be able with equal mind to comprehend and measure even the
greatest of them, and, when he has comprehended them, to relate them
distinctly and gravely in pure and chaste speech.'—Columbia *Milton*,
Vol. XII, p.93.
   An extended description of the proper discipline for an epic poet, akin
to an historian, is included in Elegy VI, to Diodati: 'But if a poet sings of
wars, of Heaven controlled by a Jove full grown, of duty-doing heroes, of
captains that are half gods, if he sings now the holy counsels of the gods
above, now the realms deep below wherein howls a savage hound, let him
live a simple, frugal life, after the fashion of the teacher who came from
Samos, let herbs offer him food that works no harm, let pellucid water
stand near him, in a tiny cup of beechen wood, and let him drink only
sober draughts from a pure spring. On such a poet are imposed, too, a
youth free from crime, pure and chaste, and a character unyielding, and a
name without taint; such an one must he be as *you* are, augur, as resplendent with holy vestments and with lustral waters, you rise, minded
to go forth to face the angry gods. . . . For the bard is sacred to the gods;
the secret deeps of his soul, and his very lips alike breathe forth Jove.'
—Columbia *Milton*, Vol. I, pt. 1, pp.211–213.
   See also section X, note 18, and extract 105, also from the *Apology*:
'So that how he should be truly eloquent who is not withal a good man, I
see not.'
13 Milton gave himself the full opportunity to rail against Hall's claim of
modesty by including Hall's title in his own, which is in full, *An Apology
against a Pamphlet called 'A Modest Confutation of the Animadversions of
the Remonstrant against Smectymnuus.'*

which he must deject and plunge himself that can agree to salable
and unlawful prostitutions. Next (for hear me out now, readers,
that I may tell ye whither my younger feet wandered) I betook me
among those lofty fables and romances which recount in solemn
cantos the deeds of knighthood founded by our victorious kings,
and from hence had in renown over all Christendom. There I read
it in the oath of every knight that he should defend to the expense
of his best blood, or of his life if it so befell him, the honour and
chastity of virgin or matron. From whence even then I learned
what a noble virtue chastity sure must be, to the defence of which
so many worthies by such a dear adventure of themselves had
sworn. And if I found in the story afterward any of them by word
or deed breaking that oath, I judged it the same fault of the poet as
that which is attributed to Homer, to have written undecent things
of the gods. Only this my mind gave me, that every free and gentle
spirit without that oath ought to be born a knight, nor needed to
expect the gilt spur or the laying of a sword upon his shoulder to
stir him up both by his counsel and his arm to secure and protect
the weakness of any attempted chastity. So that even those books
which to many others have been the fuel of wantonness and loose
living, I cannot think how, unless by divine indulgence, proved to
me so many incitements, as you have heard, to the love and steadfast observation of that virtue which abhors the society of bordellos.
Thus from the laureate fraternity of poets, riper years and the
ceaseless round of study and reading led me to the shady spaces of
philosophy, but chiefly to the divine volumes of Plato and his equal,
Xenophon. Where if I should tell ye what I learned of chastity and
love (I mean that which is truly so, whose charming cup is only
virtue which she bears in her hand to those who are worthy—the
rest are cheated with a thick intoxicating potion which a certain
sorceress, the abuser of love's name, carries about—and how the
first and chiefest office of love begins and ends in the soul, produc-
ing those happy twins of her divine generation, knowledge and
virtue, with such abstracted sublimities as these), it might be worth
your listening, readers, as I may one day hope to have ye in a still

time, when there shall be no chiding; not in these noises, the adversary as ye know, barking at the door, or searching for me at the
bordellos where it may be he has lost himself, and raps up without
pity the sage and rheumatic old prelatess with all her young Corin-
thian laity to inquire for such a one. Last of all, not in time, but as
perfection is last, that care was ever had of me, with my earliest
capacity not to be negligently trained in the precepts of Christian
religion. This that I have hitherto related hath been to show that
though Christianity had been but slightly taught me, yet a certain
reservedness of natural disposition and moral discipline learned
out of the noblest philosophy was enough to keep me in disdain of
far less incontinences than this of the bordello. But having had the
doctrine of Holy Scripture unfolding those chaste and high mysteries with timeliest care infused, that 'the body is for the Lord and
the Lord for the body,' thus also I argued to myself, that if unchastity in a woman, whom Saint Paul terms the glory of man, be
such a scandal and dishonour, then certainly in a man, who is both
the image and glory of God, it must, though commonly not so
thought, be much more deflowering and dishonourable, in that he
sins both against his own body which is the perfecter sex, and his
own glory which is in the woman, and that which is worst, against
the image and glory of God which is in himself.[14] Nor did I slumber
over that place expressing such high rewards of ever accompanying
the Lamb, with those celestial songs to others inapprehensible, but
not to those who were not defiled with women, which doubtless
means fornication: for marriage must not be called a defilement.
Thus large I have purposely been, that if I have been justly taxed
with this crime, it may come upon me after all this my confession
with a tenfold shame. But if I have hitherto deserved no such opprobrious word or suspicion, I may hereby engage myself now
openly to the faithful observation of what I have professed. I go on
to show you the unbridled impudence of this loose railer, who

14 If we remember that *An Apology for Smectymnuus* was published only
   two or three months before the probable date of Milton's first marriage,
   this passage gives us a more significant understanding of the extent of his
   disillusionment in the marriage and the pain it gave him.

having once begun his race regards not how far he flies out beyond all truth and shame, who from the single notice of the *Animadversions*, as he protests, will undertake to tell ye the very clothes I wear, though he be much mistaken in my wardrobe. And like a son of Belial without the hire of Jezebel charges me 'of blaspheming God and the King,' as ordinarily as he imagines me 'to drink sack and swear,' merely because this was a shred in his commonplace-book, and seemed to come off roundly, as if he were some empiric of false accusations to try his poisons upon me whether they would work or no. Whom what should I endeavour to refute more, whenas that book which is his only testimony returns the lie upon him, not giving him the least hint of the author to be either a swearer or a sack drinker. And for the readers, if they can believe me, principally for those reasons which I have alleged, to be of life and purpose neither dishonest nor unchaste, they will be easily induced to think me sober both of wine and of word; but if I have been already successless in persuading them, all that I can further say will be but vain; and it will be better thrift to save two tedious labours, mine of excusing, and theirs of needless hearing.

42. From *An Apology for Smectymnuus*. 1642.

Milton is again writing in response to the calumnies of the Halls.

But he proceeds; and the familiar belike informs him that 'a rich widow, or a lecture, or both, would content me'; whereby I perceive him to be more ignorant in his art of divining than any gipsy. For this I cannot omit without ingratitude to that Providence above, who hath ever bred me up in plenty, although my life hath not been unexpensive in learning and voyaging about: so long as it shall please Him to lend me what He hath hitherto thought good, which is enough to serve me in all honest and liberal occasions, and something over besides, I were unthankful to that highest bounty if I should make myself so poor as to solicit needily any such kind of 'rich hopes' as this fortune-teller dreams of. And that he may further learn how his astrology is wide all the houses of heaven in spelling marriages, I care not if I tell him thus much professedly, though it be to the losing of my 'rich hopes,' as he calls them, that I think with them who both in prudence and elegance of spirit would choose a virgin of mean fortunes honestly bred before the wealthiest widow.[15] The fiend therefore that told our Chaldean the contrary was a lying fiend.

43. From the *Defence of Himself*. 1655.

From the Latin.

> This long and not very pleasant extract shows Milton almost at his controversial worst. He is replying, one by one, to accusations brought against him by Alexander More in the *Public Faith of Alexander More*. We must not excuse the violence of the attacks upon More which are mixed with Milton's remarks about himself on the ground that he has been given great provocation without remembering that More had been similarly, indeed even more strongly, provoked. See Introduction, pp.xxii–xxvii.

You even threaten me with a lying fame—namely, that it is famed, 'I judge of other men's dispositions by my own manners, and that there is not a vice inveighed against by me to which I am not myself prone.' Therefore I am a fornicator, therefore I am an adulterer, as that lying fame reports: for these vices I inveigh against as yours. Make trial now of fame; come, bring your charge; if you have anything to say, speak out distinctly and boldly; make known the time and place, not forgetting names—the plan I adopt in respect of yourself. Say with what Claudia Pelletta, with what Pontia; tell us in what garden, in what house, whether by night or by day; whether I was ever called to account, whether I ever refused to appear: all these things may be affirmed of you, all these things I have proved against you! [16] You will find, in fact, that to the investigation of my own injuries and of your crimes I have brought along with me this liberty of speech as the clearest discovery and fruit of my past and

15 Mr. Tillyard suggests the possibility that Milton is here making specific reference to Mary Powell.—*Milton*, p.139.
16 In the *Second Defence*. Milton repeats the charges made there in the present extract, below, in the form of an invitation to More to deny them.

as the least questionable aim of my future life. You will never hear
me repent of this liberty, as it is said Lucius Crassus formerly re-
pented that he had ever impeached Caius Carbo when he found
that by this his severity he was considered by everyone to have
narrowed and circumscribed the licence of his subsequent mode of
life. Lucius Crassus called to the bar of the senate and of the people
of Rome, Caius Carbo as a profligate citizen: I, More, deliver you
over to the bar of posterity, in my own name, and in the name of the
people of England, to whom, by publishing that infamous *Cry*, you
gave the first provocation, as one blacker far than that Carbo, and as
shifting off the sentence of your country. In the meantime I feel
perfectly secure, whatever your hungry emigrants may mutter or
prate about me. You will find that I have within me that pleasing
testimony of my life, that I have that esteem among good men,
that confidence from the past, that hope so fair of the future, that
nothing can hinder, nothing can deter me, should you persist in
provocation, from tracing your crimes with still greater freedom
and diligence, and from easily seeing through and exposing to
derision your meditated corruptions of fame.

Meanwhile, that no doubt may remain of your having found,
after the keenest search, absolutely nothing that will bear the name
of crime, or if you had, of your instantly proclaiming it, of your
magnifying it in every possible way with the utmost eagerness of
malice, let us see how you treat as crimes things which are not
criminal—nay, how hatefully you slander things correctly done.
In the first place, you ask—'Why I should return an answer to the
Cry of an anonymous author, and not to so many others who have
published their names?' Why should I give the reason to an adversary who asks questions so foolish, and so foreign to the subject?
However, that you may see with what temper I deal with you, I
will tell you the reason. You ask why I should answer the author of
the *Cry*? I reply, because I was publicly ordered so to do by those
whose authority ought to have weight with me; else I had hardly
laid a hand upon you. Again, because I was expressly injured: for,
however little you may like that I also should pay some regard to

my own character, you yourself will think allowable in this particular, though against your inclination, what I am sure is most freely
allowed by all good men. Yet why 'not answer others?' say you.
'They also raise a cry, and with no less noise.' I again reply as before, because I go not uncalled to public business. Secondly, because I did not feel myself injured—no trivial reason, though it is
your supreme wish, after injuring another, to escape with impunity.
Thirdly, because, agreeably to your own opinion, we have shown
so much consideration for Salmasius as not to suppose that any
other person after him should have anything to say worth notice:
for you yourselves are accustomed to style him the royal defender,
as if he were the only one, and himself equal to all the rest. Would
you have more reasons? Because it was at my own option; because I
had not leisure; in fine, because I am a man, because my composition is human, not of iron, though you may be an Alexander of
brass. It appears to me that something else is necessary to stop
effectually the mouths of so many outrageous criers. How many
things have been cried by that anonymous Stentor of yours which
had been before cried and proclaimed by Salmasius! and to which
things, so often repeated, though I have wearied myself even to
pain in replying still more often; yet, because it was not at my
choice to contend always with that wordy vociferator, 'my language
grows feeble, whenever I plead for the people': that is as you think,
who are of opinion, that not to be tautologous is to be 'more frigid
than Gallican snow.' And if I have pleaded with a more earnest
diligence for myself, it is not that I am more concerned for myself
than for the people, but because your *Cry*, by supplying something
new, allowed me an occasional respite from your nauseous cabbage!
Your facetious remark, therefore, that 'it is not improperly said
to be a second defence of the people,' as it is a happy one, I take
for my omen; and the rather, as it is from the mouth of an enemy.
You may utter a new cry every year, but you will be left to burst
yourself with crying before it is said you have uttered a second
cry.

My other crime is that I went out of my way to introduce an

eulogium on the most serene the Queen of Sweden,[17] though the occasion was furnished me by my adversary himself. That I might assume no merit to myself on the ground of my having the Queen so favourable to me, in opposition, as it appeared, to the royal cause, I had declared, among other things (and in my judgement, with abundant modesty), that I really knew not by what chance it had happened. I chose rather to seem to refer the thing to chance, to the stars, to the consent or guidance of spirits or of things, if there be any such invisible agency, than to any supposed manifestations of my genius, my acuteness, or of my fertility. But you, laying hold of this as matter for slander and parasitism, begin to bluster away about it as of pernicious example; when the mud collected in your inward parts begins also, as is most commonly the case, to work upward towards your mouth. Come then, vomit it out; and what is it? 'the reason' (you say) 'of your bepraising her so zealously, is, that you may reconcile her to your mud.' Are you Morus, or Momus? Or are both one and the same person? I am in doubt by which name I should call you: for who but Morus or Momus could ever have interpreted this matter in so absurd, so left-handed a manner? What language is there, though of unexampled modesty, which malice like this might not deprave and pervert? Then you draw also from your own slave's hoard the servile and parasitical remark—'Christina was not aware that she was upon terms of such familiarity with you.' And do you, the mere footstool of a man! take it upon you to suggest to Christina, out of your commonplaces and your pollutions, what she was not aware of, or what she might say? And yet, from her unparalleled favour towards literary men, she was aware of being upon terms of familiarity with Salmasius; and of her own accord, from her own uninfluenced opinion, has been said to have more than once expressed a preference of me to him.[18]

17 In the *Second Defence* (extract 126).
18 Salmasius was an honoured recipient of Christina's bounty as a patroness of learning when the *First Defence* arrived in Stockholm and was admired by the Queen. Six months later Salmasius had left Sweden, with his reputation greatly weakened. He was never again the figure in European letters that he had been, and the response to Milton announced as forthcoming

But, say you, 'This single consideration—the Queen had not merited praises from you.' What—she has merited praises then from you, the least of all men praiseworthy? Granted without dispute: for if you choose to contaminate by your touch the praises of anyone, however much against his will, who can help it? Come then, try your skill. Only put the finishing stroke to what you foist in here as a choice specimen of your praises: 'whom an extraordinary energy of nature, an astonishing effulgence of genius, has raised above the sphere of mortality.' Go on, I say, and prosper in this strain; from such a beginning, you have my permission to take your flight to any elevation you please: for, if you proceed at this rate, we shall behold you, from a groundwork thus deeply laid, erecting a fabric of that stupendous loftiness as to go near to prop the clouds! It does not suit me, I confess, to mount so high: for in the instant, I should unavoidably tumble thence in ridiculous plight, or, among the clouds, should be frozen to death. You proceed, however—'you are eminent for those endowments, which, when relaxing their minds, can give solace to heroes.' Beyond a doubt; there are likewise endowments, and especially writings of your own, which might give solace to heroes, when relaxing in another way. And first of all, that short but most sapient address of yours to printers, which follows next in order, and is worthy of a paltry minister like you; I therefore pass it by.

For I am come now to my third crime; namely, that I said I went abroad with one servant.[19] This is a weighty crime: for under this appellation I receive a rub for it in more places than one. The very mention of this was no doubt ominous, since your versifiers might

---

from his pen never came. When Salmasius died, Milton modestly refrained from saying that he himself was responsible: 'And how he died I shall not undertake to say: for I will not impute to him his death as a crime, as he did to me my blindness. There are not wanting, however, those who lay the guilt of his death upon me, and upon those stings of mine which were but too sharp—and which by resisting he caused to sink the deeper. . . . He is said, after three years of chagrin, to have died, worn away by sickness of mind more than from any bodily disease.'— In the *Second Defence* (extract 124).

19 See section II, note 7.

be found out to have sung falsely: for they had versified that, in consequence of this revolution of things among us, I rose from I know not what beggarliness of origin! You jest, however, in this place; as it is so rare a bird, I am unable to pass by: 'I certainly could never have meant to quarrel' with you, 'printers, any more than with the servant whom Milton took with him abroad.' How miserably far-fetched! What would you be at with this head of yours, which so resembles a pumpkin? from which, with all your sweating, you cannot hammer out a single grain of wit. Yet you are a quiet man and a hater of quarrels; and therefore intend none with my servant, nor even with your own, though a fugitive from your domestic shame, and the divulger of your more secret vices—your abominable lusts.

The fourth is, since what is your lie must be called my crime, that I 'had the impudence to censure, and gravely to speechify about the commonwealth and the duty of citizens in the very book,' surely, 'which,' as you will have it, 'is full of the gaieties of loose wassailers.' Who would not think you now a true follower of Epicurus, who has neither polish in his manners nor elegance in his writings? From this character, it is not to be wondered at that you should be an enemy to all the forms of wit, both because they are denied to you, and because you are galled by them: it is not to be wondered at, I say, that you who are so full of sores should have an antipathy to salt. It is this which is rather to be wondered at, that you, who are a professor, should be so angry with me for being so anxious to preserve your salary for you. And as to those 'jests' which you falsely affirm 'to have been taken from the brothel and the tavern' (unless you understand by the expression 'taken from the brothel,' that they took you thence who were lurking there), if those jests are allowed by the rest of mankind to be such as are not unbecoming a man of honour and liberality, but at once polite and honourable, and to be given you as salt with which to rub over your mass of corruption—then, that professor's ignorance of yours, which is not seasoned with one particle of salt, as it is sufficiently manifest on other occasions, so is it in your declaring that to be out

of place which Marcus Tullius, when speaking with the highest admiration of an oration of Lucius Crassus against Cn. Domitius,
pronounced to be the sovereign excellence of an orator. His words
are: 'Never was there a more masterly harangue, never was there
an oration which had a greater effect upon the people, and which
was more seasoned with wit and gaiety, than the oration of this
man against his late colleague in the censorship.' And a little after
he says, that 'of all orators, it was the fortune of Crassus alone not
only to be, but also to appear, at once the most charming and witty,
the most impressive and severe.' And it was the opinion of Plato
and the Socratic philosophers, that there was nothing more appro-
priate, more suitable to decorum, than the intermixture, the sprink-
lings of wit on the gravest subjects. That I have before made these
things plain,[20] and now once again, to men of learning and intelligence, I cannot doubt: nevertheless, I blame not you for observing
that 'the transition from the nose to the brow ought to have been
more gentle': for you have not yet forgotten, I ween, the fingers of
Pontia, and how little gentleness there was in her transition from
your nose to your brows: indeed you would have been a happy
man, could you then have persuaded that frail woman of the truth
of this observation of yours; but a very different sort of judgement,
More, is necessary with respect to the transition of orators!

Again, 'I prescribe rules' (and this is my fifth crime) 'not only
for the people, but for those who have no need of me for a preceptor.' Most trifling and arrogant man! And do you presume to inform me, of whom anyone may stand in need? Do the United
States[21] stand in need of you for a speechifier, 'from a higher place,'
and shall not our own people stand in need of me so much as for a
voluntary adviser, from a lower place—an office which belongs of
right to every citizen?[22] When I observe you to assume so much

20 In *An Apology for Smectymnuus* (extract 105), notably. But the theme is
   recurrent in Milton, appearing, we have seen, even in the Sixth Prolusion
   (extract 38). There are many returns to it in the *Defence of Himself*. See
   also section X.B entire.
21 Of Holland. More's professorship was in Amsterdam.
22 Milton's consciousness of superiority because he owes no paid allegiance,
   but speaks as a 'voluntary adviser,' is recurrent. Thus in the *Second*

in a foreign country, is it possible I should think myself of no utility in my own? Is there any reason why you, a preacher for hire, should be able to advise better than I, who deliver gratuitous, and as I trust, sounder admonitions? These are my five deadly sins: for to make seven of them I think was not in your power. From charges so trifling, we may collect how perfectly frivolous those offences must have been which you say you have 'pardoned' in me.

But perhaps you will have it to be criminal that I called God to witness; and certainly, there wanted little of your reckoning even that also in the number of my crimes: for 'hence (you remark) that really too anxious protestation.' And what protestation was that, More? You shall hear, though you desire nothing less: nor shall it now be a mere recitation, but, as I feel no shame for what I have done, and as you here calumniate even my travelling, I again call God to witness, in the very words I first used,[23] that in all those places where so much licence is given I lived free and untouched of all defilement and profligate behaviour, having it ever in my thought, that if I could escape the eyes of men, I certainly could not escape the eyes of God. This is your 'too anxious protestation,' More, who have as little anxiety about calling God to witness as when called upon to forswear Him. You are not ignorant by what numbers you are accused, and of offences how various! If you have any honesty, if you have any purity in you, dare only to defend yourself in those same words in which I have now set you an example. Pronounce according to these words—I call God to witness that I have always lived innocent and untouched of all those flagitious crimes with which I have been charged; that I have neither committed whoredom nor adultery with Claudia, nor Pontia, nor with any other woman whatsoever. Though you are said to pay little regard to an oath, you will not have the courage, I think, to

Defence (extract 2) Milton tells of his determination to write *Of Reformation* confident that he 'should not write worse than those who contended for their own lucre and most iniquitous domination.' Ultimately, of course, he devoted a pamphlet to the hired clergy, *Considerations touching the Likeliest Means to Remove Hirelings out of the Church*, 1659.

23 In the *Second Defence* (extract 2).

follow me in these words. But if you dare not implore the faith of God, at least implore the faith of men. Return, I say, to Geneva; there surrender yourself to the magistrates and to the people; say to them, as becomes a chaste and innocent man falsely accused: People of Geneva, I am accused by you of many and weighty crimes: if it shall be made appear by proper witnesses and proofs that I have thus lived, that I have thus demeaned myself among you, here I am, prepared to undergo that just sentence which I have before evaded! That you will never have courage enough to do this, I know well. You had rather, as I have said before, have recourse to subterfuge; like an old fornicator as you are, you had rather skulk, and shift, and seek refuge from other quarters. However, you allow it to have been an 'honest declaration' of mine, though 'little in unison with the preceding one.' With what preceding one, I beseech you? I could wish you to be more particular; for I am very sure that a few pages back not the slightest trace of obscenity is to be found, since in that short interval no mention is made of you. And if you mean any other place, where there are some pungent animadversions upon your vices, I would have you to know, in spite of your distorted quotation from 'Plato,' that to reprobate with severity and with wit what is scandalous, and at the same time 'to think of God,' even in the same book (for you will never find there the expressions of 'profligate modesty'), is neither immodest nor foreign to the purpose. If, indeed, this maxim of the orator be just and commendable, that modesty and severity are compatible in the same countenance, why, in like manner, should they not be compatible in the same mouth? The modesty of no modest person is impaired by a vehement and galling reprobation, or even by the derision of turpitude; but there is nothing which seems so effectually to crush the growth of all modesty in one who had it not before as impudence in a culprit. I would have you take care, preacher adulterate! that your eternal lying be compatible with modesty, and 'with thinking of God,' when you could affirm me to have written that 'at Rome I was a candidate for martyrdom; that the Jesuits laid a plot for my life!' To dissipate both of which lies, it is only necessary to examine the passage itself in the book;[24] and the reason why I wrote anything at all on that subject may be easily conjectured by anyone, provided only he does not think it credible that the man who so often incurred danger in Italy by the confession of his faith 'was obliged to fly thither by reason of his debaucheries.'[25]

After this, you have a good deal of trash on a variety of topics: though flogged as a slave by Pontia, you yet presume to prate about 'swords and legions.' But these things have already afforded us sufficient merriment. Attend now, I entreat, to a brave and notable slander, that ye may learn what sort of faith he has even in sacred learning, which, to the heavy disgrace of the church, he professes; that ye may learn how little scruple has this falsifying preacher to corrupt, should he think it for his advantage, even the sanctity of God's word itself. With a view to undeceive those who are in the habit of bestowing, however absurdly, the title and surname of great upon a grammarian or critic, I had written thus: 'He alone deserves the appellation of great, who either achieves great things himself or teaches how they may be achieved, or who describes with suitable dignity the great achievements of others.'[26] Who, but a grammarian, could be offended with a sentiment thus founded in truth? What says our professor to this? That is, he remarks, who teaches great things 'like Milton on the subject of divorce'; or who describes them with suitable dignity, 'like the same Milton, in his defence of the people; and he is here doubly great.' A shrewd interpretation, More, no doubt, and evidently of a piece with your interpretation of that passage of the Gospel concerning divorce, which was given, however, not in words but in deeds. It is lawful to dismiss either a wife or a betrothed mistress for fornication; More fornicated with Pontia, who was betrothed to him; therefore, it is lawful for More to dismiss a betrothed mistress for fornication! Come, now, 'O ye number of princely personages, ye many nobles,

24 The *Second Defence*.
25 See extract 2, and Introduction, pp.xxx–xxxii.
26 See section X, note 18.

churches, colleges, which either honour this man by espousing his cause, or caress him by your good wishes!' manifest an eager contention in your invitations of one who is so faithful, so religious an interpreter, whether of sacred or of profane learning—who would be able to make even sacred learning profane among you, by his actions as well as by his glosses. Or, if ye have no sort of inclination for this, as ye seem to have long since caught the scent of this glozing doctor from all quarters, give and grant at least this gentle fomentation to the puffed-up tumour of a man—invite, I beseech you, this chaired actor by your very honourable letters; but, if ye would be safe, with the secret caution, with the most polite proviso, that he should at no rate accept the invitation. Amidst so many professorial chairs, in his dreamy expectations of professorships, and prelections, and murmurs, and applauses, and new Pontias, he will make his plays truly admirable!

Milton also discusses his standards of personal morality in extracts 1, 2, 4, 7, 14, 30, 32, 33, 40, 44–46, 48, 56, 58, 105, *and* 124.

VII. BLINDNESS

O dark, dark, dark, amid the blaze of noon.

44. Sonnet XIX. 1652?

Milton never comes nearer to despair of success in the fulfilment of his ambitions because of his blindness than in this favourite among his sonnets. Since Milton could hardly have given up hope of a useful literary life after writing the *Second Defence*, we date it early with Tillyard and Smart. Dr. Eleanor Brown dates it 1655 because she does not believe that Milton could have achieved early in his blindness the calm of mind expressed in the last lines.

> WHEN I consider how my light is spent
>   Ere half my days in this dark world and wide,
>   And that one talent which is death to hide
>   Lodged with me useless, though my soul more bent
> To serve therewith my Maker, and present
>   My true account, lest He returning chide;
>   'Doth God exact day-labour, light denied?'
>   I fondly ask. But Patience to prevent
> That murmur, soon replies, 'God doth not need
>   Either man's work or His own gifts. Who best
>   Bear His mild yoke, they serve Him best. His state
> Is Kingly. Thousands at His bidding speed,
>   And post o'er land and ocean without rest:
>   They also serve who only stand and wait.'

45. Familiar Letter 15, to Leonard Philaras, Athenian. 1654.

From the Latin.

   After a paragraph of compliment to Philaras and to Athens, Milton gives the account of the 'causes and symptoms' of his blindness which has been the basis of many (and various) at-

94

tempts at medical diagnosis since that of Thevenot, for whom the account is supplied.[1]

As I have been from boyhood an especial worshipper of all bearing the Greek name, and of your Athens in chief, so I have always had a firm private persuasion that that city would some time or other requite me splendidly for my affection towards her. Nor, in truth, has the ancient genius of your noble country failed my augury, since in you, an Athenian born, I have had bestowed upon me one of the most loving of friends. When I was known to you by writings only, and you were yourself separated from me by place, you opened a communication with me most courteously by letter;[2] and, coming afterwards unexpectedly to London, and visiting a man incapable any more of seeing his visitors, even in that calamity by which I am rendered an object of more regard to none, and perhaps of less regard to many, you continue now to show me the same kind attention. As you have, therefore, suggested to me that I should not give up all hope of recovering my sight, and told me that you have a friend and close companion in the Paris physician, Thevenot, especially distinguished as an oculist, and that you will consult him about my eyes if I furnish you with means for his diagnosis of the causes and symptoms, I will do what you advise, that I may not haply seem to refuse any chance of help offered me providentially.

It is ten years, I think, more or less, since I felt my sight getting weak and dull, and at the same time my viscera generally out of sorts. In the morning, if I began, as usual, to read anything, I felt my eyes at once thoroughly pained and shrinking from the act of reading, but refreshed after moderate bodily exercise. If I looked at a lit candle, a kind of iris seemed to snatch it from me. Not very long after, a darkness coming over the left part of my left eye (for that eye became clouded some years before the other) removed from my vision all objects situated on that side. Objects in front also, if I chanced to close the right eye, seemed smaller. The other

1 For a full study see *Milton's Blindness*, by Eleanor Gertrude Brown, New York, 1934.
2 See Milton's first letter to Philaras (extract 153).

eye also failing perceptibly and gradually through a period of three years, I observed, some months before my sight was wholly gone, that objects I looked at without myself moving seemed all to swim, now to the right, now to the left. Inveterate mists now seem to have settled in my forehead and temples, which weigh me down and depress me with a kind of sleepy heaviness, especially from meal-time to evening; so that not seldom there comes into my mind the description of the Salmydessian seer, Phineus, in the *Argonautics*:

> All round him then there grew
> A purple thickness; and he thought the earth
> Whirling beneath his feet, and so he sank,
> Speechless at length, into a feeble sleep.

But I should not forget to mention that, while yet a little sight remained, when first I lay down in bed, and turned myself to either side, there used to shine out a copious glittering light from my shut eyes; then that, as my sight grew less from day to day, colours proportionally duller would burst from them, as with a kind of force and audible shot from within; but that now, as if the sense of lucency were extinct, it is a mere blackness, or a blackness dashed, and as it were inwoven, with an ashy grey, that is wont to pour itself forth. Yet the darkness which is perpetually before me, by night as well as by day, seems always nearer to a whitish than to a blackish, and such that, when the eye rolls itself, there is admitted, as through a small chink, a certain little trifle of light.

And so, whatever ray of hope also there may be for me from your famous physician, all the same, as in a case quite incurable, I prepare and compose myself accordingly; and my frequent thought is that, since many days of darkness, as the wise man warns us, are destined for everyone, my darkness hitherto, by the singular kindness of God, amid rest and studies, and the voices and greetings of friends, has been much easier to bear than that deathly one. But if, as is written, 'Man shall not live by bread alone, but by every word that proceedeth out of the mouth of God,' what should prevent one from resting likewise in the belief that his eyesight lies not in his eyes alone, but enough for all purposes in God's leading and providence? Verily, while only He looks out for me and provides for me, as He doth, leading me and leading me forth as with His hand through my whole life, I shall willingly, since it has seemed good to Him, have given my eyes their long holiday. And to you, dear Philaras, whatever may befall, I now bid farewell, with a mind not less brave and steadfast than if I were Lynceus himself for keenness of sight.

Westminster: September 28, 1654.

46. From the *Second Defence*. 1654.

From the Latin.

Would it were equally in my power to confute this inhuman adversary on the subject of my blindness![3] But it is not. Then let us bear it. To be blind is not miserable; not to be able to bear blindness, that is miserable. But why should I be unable to bear that which it behoves everyone to be prepared to bear, should the accident happen to himself, without repining? Why should I be unable to bear what I know may happen to any mortal being—what I know has actually happened to some of the most eminent and the best of men on the records of memory? Or shall I mention those old poets, ancientest and wisest, whose calamity the gods are said to have recompensed with far more excelling gifts, and men to have honoured with that high honour as to choose rather to blame the gods themselves than to impute their blindness to them as a crime. What is handed down of the augur Tiresias is well known. Of Phineus thus sang Apollonius in his *Argonautics*:

> Not Jove himself he feared; his daring ken
> With truth disclosed the will of fate to men;
> With length of years did Jove him hence requite,
> But his eyes bereft of the day's sweet light.

3 As on the subject of his personal appearance (extract 4).

But God himself is truth; and the more closely anyone adheres to truth, in teaching it to mankind, the more nearly must he resemble God, the more acceptable must he be to Him. It is impious to believe God to be jealous of truth, or to be an enemy to the utmost freedom of its communication to men. It does not appear, therefore, that it was for any crime that this ancient sage, who was so zealous to enlighten humankind, and that many among the philosophers, were deprived of light. Or, should I mention those men of old, so deserving of admiration for their civil wisdom, as also for their great actions? And first, Timoleon of Corinth, the deliverer of his own city and of all Sicily, than whom a better man or more revered in the commonwealth no age has produced. Next, Appius Claudius, who, by nobly declaring his sentiments in the senate, delivered Italy from Pyrrhus, a formidable enemy; but himself delivered not from blindness. Then Cæcilius Metellus the high-priest, who lost his eyes in saving from the flames not the city only, but the palladium, on which hung the destiny of the city, as also the most sacred of the religious mysteries; though on other occasions it is certain that God has declared that His favour attends a devotedness so extraordinary, even among the Gentiles. What therefore has happened to such a man, I can hardly think should be considered as an evil. Why should I add others of later times—as Dandolo, Prince of Venice, the first man by far of all his compatriots; or Ziska, the gallant Duke of Bohemia, champion of the orthodox faith? Why divines of highest name, Hieronymus Zanchius, with some others? when it is well known that the patriarch Isaac himself, than whom no mortal was ever more dear to God, lived blind no small number of years; and for some time, perhaps Jacob also, his son, of God no less beloved; when, in fine, it is beyond all doubt, from the divine testimony of Christ our Saviour, that the man whom He healed had been blind even from the womb, for no sin either of himself or of his parents. As for myself, I call Thee, O God, to witness, the searcher of the inmost spirit, and of every thought, that I am not conscious of any offence (though to the utmost of my power I have often seriously examined myself on this point, though I have visited all the recesses of my heart) recently committed, or long ago, the heinousness of which could have justly caused, could have called down this calamity upon me above others. Whatever I have written, yea, at any time (since the Royalists in their exultation imagine I am now suffering for it, by way of atonement, as they will have it) I call the same God to witness, that I have written nothing which I was not persuaded at the time, and am still persuaded, was right, and true, and pleasing to God; and this without being moved by ambition, by lucre, or by glory, but solely by a sense of duty, of grace, and of devotion to my country; that, above all, I have done this with a view not only to the deliverance of the commonwealth, but likewise of the church. Hence, when that office against the royal defence was publicly assigned me, and at a time when not only my health was unfavourable, but when I had nearly lost the sight of my other eye, and my physicians expressly foretold that if I undertook the task I should in a short time lose both—in no wise dismayed at this warning, methought it was no physician's voice I heard—not the voice even of Æsculapius from the shrine of Epidaurus—but of some diviner monitor within; methought, that, by a certain fatality in my birth, two destinies were set before me, on the one hand, blindness, on the other, duty—that I must necessarily incur the loss of my eyes, or desert a sovereign duty.[4] Nor did I fail to recollect the twofold destiny which the son of Thetis reports that his mother brought back concerning himself when she went to consult the oracle at Delphi:

4 The anonymous *Life* has this account: 'While he was thus employed' in prose controversy 'his eyesight totally failed him; not through any immediate or sudden judgement, as his adversaries insultingly affirmed, but from a weakness which his hard nightly study in his youth had first occasioned, and which by degrees had for some time before deprived him of the use of one eye: and the issues and seatons made use of to save or retrieve that, were thought by drawing away the spirits which should have supplied the optic vessels to have hastened the loss of the other. He was indeed advised by his physicians of the danger, in his condition, attending so great intentness as that work required. But he who was resolute in going through with what upon good consideration he at any time designed, and to whom the love of truth and his country was dearer than all things, would not for any danger decline their defence.'—Darbishire, *Early Lives*, p.28.

Two fates conduct me to the realms of night:
If staying here around Troy-town I fight,
I return no more; but my glory fair
Shall shine immortal, and my deeds declare:
If to my dear and native land I'm led,
Long is my life; but my glory is fled.

Iliad 9.

Hence I thought with myself, that there were many who purchased a less good with a greater evil; for example—glory, with death. On the contrary, I proposed to purchase a greater good with a less evil; namely, at the price of blindness only, to perform one of the noblest acts of duty; and duty, being a thing in its own nature more substantial even than glory, ought on that account to be more desired and venerated. I decided, therefore, that as the use of light would be allowed me for so short a time, it ought to be enjoyed with the greatest possible utility to the public. These are the reasons of my choice; these the causes of my loss. Let the slanderers, then, of the judgements of God cease their revilings; let them desist from their dreamy forgeries concerning me; in fine, let them know that I neither repine at nor repent me of my lot; that I remain fixed, immovable in my opinion; that I neither believe nor have found that God is angry; nay, that in things of the greatest moment I have experienced, and that I acknowledge His mercy, and His paternal goodness towards me; that above all, in regard of this calamity, I acquiesce in His divine will, for it is He Himself who comforts and upholds my spirit—being ever more mindful of what He shall bestow upon me than of what He shall deny me; last of all, that I would not exchange my own consciousness of what I have done for any act of theirs however well performed, or lose the recollection of it, which is always so calm and delightful to me. As to blindness, I would rather at last have mine, if it must be so, than either theirs, More, or yours. Yours, immersed in the lowest sense, so blinds your minds that you can see nothing sound or solid; mine, with which you reproach me, deprives things merely of their colour and surface, but takes not from the mind's contemplation whatever is real and permanent in them. Besides, how many things are there which I should choose not to see, how many which I might be unwilling to see, and how few remaining things are there which I could desire to see! Neither am I concerned at being classed, though you think this a miserable thing, with the blind, with the afflicted, with the sorrowful, with the weak; since there is a hope, that on this account I have a nearer claim to the mercy and protection of the Sovereign Father. There is a way, and the Apostle is my authority, through weakness to the greatest strength. May I be one of the weakest, provided only in my weakness that immortal and better vigour be put forth with greater effect; provided only in my darkness the light of the divine countenance does but the more brightly shine: for then I shall at once be the weakest and the most mighty, shall be at once blind, and of the most piercing sight.[5] Thus, through this infirmity should I be consummated, perfected; thus, through this darkness should I be enrobed in light. And in truth we who are blind are not the last regarded by the providence of God, who as we are the less able to discern anything but Himself beholds us with the greater clemency and benignity. Woe be to him who makes a mock of us; woe be to him who injures us; he deserves to be devoted to the public curse. The divine law, the divine favour, has made us not merely secure, but as it were sacred, from the injuries of men, nor would seem to have brought this darkness upon us so much by inducing a dimness of the eyes as by the overshadowing of heavenly wings, and not unfrequently is wont to illumine it again, when produced, by an inward and far surpassing light. To this I attribute the more than ordinary civilities, attentions, and visits of friends, of whom there are some with whom, as with true friends, I may hold the dialogue of Pylades and Orestes:

5 Cf. *Paradise Lost*, Bk. III, ll.51–53 (extract 47):
    So much the rather thou celestial Light
    Shine inward, and the mind through all her powers
    Irradiate. . . .

Orest. Go slowly on, and be the rudder of my feet.
Py. Precious is my charge.

Eurip. in Orest.

And in another place:

Give your hand to your friend and helper.
Throw your arm about my neck, and I will be your guide.

Id. in Her. furent.

For they do not suppose that by this misfortune I am rendered altogether a nullity; they do not suppose that all which belongs to a man of sense and integrity is situated in his eyes. Besides, as I am not grown torpid by indolence since my eyes have deserted me, but am still active, still ready to advance among the foremost to the most arduous struggles for liberty, I am not therefore deserted even by men of the first rank in the state. On the contrary, such men, considering the condition of humanity, show me favour and indulgence, as to one who has completed his services, and readily grant me exemption and retirement. They despoil me of no dignity, they deprive me not of any public office I before held; they disparage not the benefit which may have accrued from that particular service; and though they are aware that they are now to confer their favours upon one who is become less useful, they think it ought to be done with no less benignity—indeed, with the same honour, as if like the Athenians in ancient times they had decreed a maintenance for me in the Prytaneum.[6] Thus, while I can derive consolation in my

6 In March 1652 the Council appointed Weckherlin to serve as Milton's assistant. In November 1652 Thurloe took over Weckherlin's duties and some of Milton's. In 1653 Meadows became Milton's assistant. In January 1654 Meadows became Latin Secretary, Milton being retained in the service of the Council, but his title not specified. In May 1654 he published the *Second Defence.* Presumably he had been relieved of his duties to write it, for Meadows apparently was doing all his official work. In April 1655 Milton's annual salary was reduced from £288 to £150 to be paid to him 'during his life out of his Highness's Exchequer.' He did not discontinue his services, even returning to routine duties of the office, until he was discharged in 1660.—The Council Order Books, Masson, *Life, passim.*

blindness both from God and man, let no one be troubled that I have lost my eyes in an honourable cause; and far be it from me to be troubled at it; far be it from me to possess so little spirit as not to be able without difficulty to despise the revilers of my blindness, or so little placability as not to be able with still less difficulty to forgive them.

I return to you, whoever you are,[7] who, with no little inconsistency, will one while have me to be a dwarf, another while, an Antæus. But, at last, you express a wish: 'Nothing better could befall the United Provinces of Holland than that they may make an end of this war as easily and as successfully as Salmasius will make an end of Milton.' In which wish I shall readily acquiesce, and am of opinion that I am neither presaging ill nor praying ill for our success, and for the cause of England.

47. From *Paradise Lost*. 1655–1665.[8]

The Invocation of Book III.

> Hail holy Light, offspring of Heav'n first-born,
> Or of th'Eternal co-eternal beam
> May I express thee unblamed? since God is Light,
> And never but in unapproached light
> Dwelt from eternity, dwelt then in thee,
> Bright effluence of bright essence increate.
> Or hear'st thou rather pure ethereal stream,
> Whose fountain who shall tell? Before the sun,
> Before the heavens thou wert, and at the voice
> Of God, as with a mantle didst invest
> The rising world of waters dark and deep,
> Won from the void and formless infinite.
> Thee I revisit now with bolder wing,
> Escaped the Stygian pool, though long detained
> In that obscure sojourn, while in my flight

7 This seems to be a confession, even in the *Second Defence*, of some doubt at least of More's authorship of the *Cry*.
8 Mr. Tillyard finds reason to assign this passage to 1655.—*Milton*, p.195.

Through utter and through middle darkness borne,
With other notes than to the Orphean lyre
I sung of chaos and eternal night,
Taught by the heavenly Muse to venture down
The dark descent, and up to re-ascend,
Though hard and rare. Thee I revisit safe,
And feel thy sovran vital lamp; but thou
Revisit'st not these eyes, that roll in vain
To find thy piercing ray, and find no dawn;
So thick a drop serene hath quenched their orbs,
Or dim suffusion veiled. Yet not the more
Cease I to wander where the Muses haunt
Clear spring, or shady grove, or sunny hill,
Smit with the love of sacred song; but chief
Thee, Sion, and the flowry brooks beneath,
That wash thy hallowed feet, and warbling flow,
Nightly I visit: nor sometimes forget
Those other two equalled with me in fate,
So were I equalled with them in renown,
Blind Thamyris and blind Mæonides,
And Tiresias and Phineus, prophets old.
Then feed on thoughts that voluntary move
Harmonious numbers; as the wakeful bird
Sings darkling, and in shadiest covert hid
Tunes her nocturnal note. Thus with the year
Seasons return, but not to me returns
Day, or the sweet approach of ev'n or morn,
Or sight of vernal bloom, or summer's rose,
Or flocks, or herds, or human face divine;
But cloud instead, and ever-during dark
Surrounds me, from the cheerful ways of men
Cut off, and for the book of knowledge fair
Presented with a universal blanc
Of Nature's works to me expunged and rased,
And wisdom at one entrance quite shut out.

So much the rather thou celestial Light
Shine inward, and the mind through all her powers
Irradiate; there plant eyes; all mist from thence
Purge and disperse, that I may see and tell
Of things invisible to mortal sight.

48. Sonnet XXII. 1655.

To Mr. Cyriack Skinner upon his blindness.

Cyriack, this three years' day these eyes, though clear
    To outward view of blemish or of spot,
    Bereft of light, their seeing have forgot;
    Nor to their idle orbs doth sight appear
Of sun or moon or star throughout the year,
    Or man or woman. Yet I argue not
    Against Heaven's hand or will, nor bate a jot
    Of heart or hope; but still bear up and steer
Right onward. What supports me, dost thou ask?
    The conscience, friend, to have lost them overplied
    In liberty's defence, my noble task,
Of which all Europe talks from side to side.
    This thought might lead me through the world's vain mask
    Content though blind, had I no better guide.

49. Sonnet XXIII. 1658?

This is the last of Milton's sonnets. It was written after the death of
    Katharine Woodcock, his second wife, with whom we may judge
    from this poem Milton found his greatest domestic happiness.

Methought I saw my late espoused saint
    Brought to me like Alcestis from the grave,
    Whom Jove's great son to her glad husband gave,
    Rescued from death by force, though pale and faint.
Mine, as whom washed from spot of child-bed taint
    Purification in the old law did save,
    And such as yet once more I trust to have
    Full sight of her in Heaven without restraint,

Came vested all in white, pure as her mind.
  Her face was veiled; yet to my fancied sight
  Love, sweetness, goodness, in her person shined
So clear, as in no face with more delight.
  But O as to embrace me she inclined
  I waked, she fled, and day brought back my night.

Milton's blindness is mentioned also in extracts 2, 4, 5, 36, 65, 74, 124, 131, 144, 155, and 157.

VIII. POETIC ASPIRATIONS AND ACHIEVEMENTS

And sing thee an elaborate song to generations.

50. From the Sixth Prolusion. 1628.

This is the end of Milton's part in the revelries beginning the summer vacation in 1628. As published among Milton's poems, without the prose speech to which it is an appendage, *At a Vacation Exercise* is preceded by the following heading: '*Anno Aetatis* 19. At a Vacation Exercise in the college, part Latin, part English. The Latin speeches ended, the English thus began.' The verses were followed by further prose entertainment of other authorship. It is characteristic of Milton that he should feel obliged to acknowledge his high poetic ambitions even upon so unsuitable an occasion. The prose sentences introducing the verses here are from the Latin.

Now, leaping over the academic laws, as over the walls of Romulus, I pass from Latin to English. You to whom such things are pleasing give now to me attentive ears and minds.

> Hail native language, that by sinews weak
> Didst move my first endeavouring tongue to speak,
> And mad'st imperfect words with childish trips,
> Half unpronounced, slide through my infant lips,
> Driving dumb Silence from the portal door,
> Where he had mutely sat two years before:
> Here I salute thee, and thy pardon ask
> That now I use thee in my latter task.
> Small loss it is that thence can come unto thee;
> I know my tongue but little grace can do thee.
> Thou need'st not be ambitious to be first,
> Believe me I have thither packed the worst:

And, if it happen as I did forecast,
The daintiest dishes shall be served up last.
I pray thee then deny me not thy aid
For this same small neglect that I have made,
But haste thee straight to do me once a pleasure,
And from thy wardrope bring thy chiefest treasure:
Not those new-fangled toys and trimming slight
Which takes our late fantastics with delight,
But cull those richest robes and gay'st attire,
Which deepest spirits and choicest wits desire:
I have some naked thoughts that rove about
And loudly knock to have their passage out,
And weary of their place do only stay
Till thou hast decked them in thy best array,
That so they may without suspect or fears
Fly swiftly to this fair assembly's ears.
Yet I had rather, if I were to choose,
Thy service in some graver subject use,[1]
Such as may make thee search thy coffers round
Before thou clothe my fancy in fit sound:
Such where the deep transported mind may soar
Above the wheeling poles, and at Heaven's door
Look in and see each blissful deity,
How he before the thunderous throne doth lie,
Listening to what unshorn Apollo sings
To th' touch of golden wires, while Hebe brings
Immortal nectar to her kingly sire:

1 In the Seventh Prolusion, too, Milton tells his fellow students of his literary ambitions (extract 28), as later he was to make similar public promises
of future work in the *Reason of Church Government* (extract 1). That he had
chosen English so early does not contradict the account he gives in the
Reason of Church Government of the resolution to write English made during or after the Italian journey. The example of Ariosto was a genuine
example and the authority of the Pleiade a real authority; but Milton must
have experienced some new doubts about forsaking Latin when he saw
how little known Spenser was on the continent and how widely known
Buchanan. See Tillyard, *Milton*, pp.91ff.

Then passing through the spheres of watchful fire,
And misty regions of wide air next under,
And hills of snow and lofts of piled thunder,
May tell at length how green-eyed Neptune raves,
In Heaven's defiance mustering all his waves;
Then sing of secret things that came to pass
When beldam Nature in her cradle was;
And last of kings and queens and heroes old,
Such as the wise Demodocus once told
In solemn songs at King Alcinous' feast,
While sad Ulysses' soul and all the rest
Are held with his melodious harmony
In willing chains and sweet captivity.
But fie my wandring Muse how thou dost stray!
Expectance calls thee now another way;
Thou know'st it must be now thy only bent
To keep in compass of thy predicament:
Then quick about thy purposed business come,
That to the next I may resign my room.

51. From Elegy VI. 1629.

From the Latin.

Addressed to Charles Diodati.

Except that the 'infant cry of God' and the 'stabling under a poor roof' do not receive in the poem the fulness of treatment the account here leads us to expect, we can hardly ask better commentary than this upon the *Nativity Ode*.

If you shall seek to learn what *I* am doing (if only you think it worth your while to seek to know what I am doing), I am hymning the King of Heavenly Seed, Bringer of Peace, and the blessed generations covenanted by the holy books, and the infant cry of God, and the stabling under a poor roof of Him who with His Father cherishes the realms on high, and of the star-begetting skies, of the companies attuning their strains in the high heavens, and of the [heathen] gods, of a sudden crushed, at their own fanes. This song

I offered as gift on the birthday of Christ; the first light, as the dawn drew near, gave me this song.[2]

For you other strains too are waiting, strains oft practised, strains struck out from my native country's reeds: you shall serve as the critic to whom I shall recite them.

52. From the Seventh Prolusion. 1632?

From the Latin.

> The Seventh Prolusion, of which the present extract is the introduction, Mr. Tillyard has called one of Milton's major works. It is an important document in the controversy between the 'humanists' and the 'scholastics.' Mr. Tillyard also calls attention to the great rhetorical skill of this introduction.[3]

Although, my hearers, nothing is more delightful and pleasing to me than your presence, and than an attentive throng of gowned gentlemen, also than this honour-bearing oratorical exhibition, in which at one time and another I have taken part among you, the task being not disagreeable; nevertheless, if it be allowable to mention what is a fact, it always so happens that, although neither my natural bent nor course of studies are very much at variance with this oratorical activity, I hardly ever undertake speaking of my own free will and accord. If it had been in my power, I would gladly indeed have avoided the exertion of this evening especially, because I have learned from books and from the opinions of the most learned men this, that in the orator as in the poet nothing common-

---

2 Professor Hanford points out that the *Nativity Ode* and Elegy VI together begin a new period in Milton's literary activity, that although 'the materials of Milton's future poetry are as yet but vaguely defined, . . . his mind is plainly set toward the mysteries of Heaven and Hell and the deeds of "pious heroes and leaders part divine." ' He is bidding farewell to the elegiac mood and to 'all amatory trifling.' This farewell he makes specific in the epilogue to Elegy VII (extract 7).

For the epic, Hanford goes on, Milton did not yet feel ready, and by way of preparation for it proposes to himself a series of poems on religious subjects, of which the *Nativity Ode* was finished, *The Passion* begun, and of which *Upon the Circumcision* may be a third.—*Youth of Milton*, pp.126–127.

3 *Correspondence and Academic Exercises*, pp.xxxiii–xxxix.

place or mediocre can be allowed, and that he who wishes deservedly to be and to be considered an orator ought to be equipped and perfected with a certain encompassing support of all the arts and of all science. Since my age does not permit this, I have preferred up to the present, while providing myself with these supports, to strive earnestly after that true reputation by long and severe toil, rather than to snatch a false reputation by a hurried and premature mode of expression.

While I am wholly afire and ablaze every day with this plan and purpose of mind, I have never felt any hindrance and delay more pressing than this frequent annoyance of interruption; indeed nothing has more nourished my ability and conserved its good health, contrary to what takes place in the body, than learned and abundant leisure. This I have believed to be the prophetic sleep of Hesiod, those nocturnal trysts of Endymion with the moon, that retreat of Prometheus under the leadership of Mercury into the deepest solitudes of Mount Caucasus, where he became the wisest of gods and men, insomuch that Jupiter himself is said to have asked his advice about the nuptials of Thetis.

I myself invoke the glades and streams and beloved elms of the farms, under which during the summer just gone by (if it be permitted to mention the secrets of the goddesses) I recall to mind with pleasant memories that I enjoyed the highest favour of the Muses, where amid fields and remote woodlands I have even seemed to myself to have been able to grow up as it were in seclusion. In this place likewise I might have hoped for myself the same opportunity also of hiding, had not this inconvenient annoyance of speaking interposed itself quite unseasonably, which so hindered in a disagreeable way my sacred slumbers, so distracted a mind fixed on other things, and so impeded and burdened amid the rugged difficulties of the arts, that having lost all hope of obtaining quiet, I began to think sorrowfully how far I was removed from that tranquillity which letters at first promised me, that life would be painful among these surgings and tossings, that it would be better to forget the arts completely. Accordingly, hardly master of myself, I

undertook the rash design of praising Ignorance, which would
certainly involve none of these commotions, and I advanced the
proposition for debate: which of the two, Knowledge or Ignorance,
would render its devotees the happier?

I do not know what happened: either my fate or my genius did
not wish me to depart from my early love of the Muses. Nay, even
blind Chance herself, become suddenly as it were prudent and fore-
sighted, seemed likewise not to wish this. More speedily than I had
supposed, Ignorance has found her champion; to me is left the defence of Knowledge. I truly rejoice that I was thus mocked, nor do
I feel ashamed that Fortune, though blind, has restored my sight.
For this boon I give thanks to her. Now at least I may praise the
illustrious one from whose embrace I had been torn away, and by
a speech I may almost console the grief of absence. Now this is
clearly not an interruption; for who may call it an interruption when
he praises and defends what he loves, what he cherishes, what he
wishes with all his heart to pursue?

53. Letter to a Friend. 1633?[4]

The inclusion of this letter, and even of the sonnet which it contains,
in a section devoted to Milton's statements of his literary aspirations requires explanation and is based upon reading between the
lines. Professor Hanford comments on the letter:

'It is odd but characteristic that Milton should, in this statement, say nothing whatever regarding his literary purposes and
ambitions. No reader previously unacquainted with his thoughts
on this subject could possibly infer them from the letter, the plain
implication of the language being that he intends, when he is
ready, to labour in the vineyard as a minister. It is possible, of
course, that in the suggestion about a congregation and preaching
Milton was maintaining a mental reservation, having already determined to interpret his ministry in terms of the poetic enuncia-
tion of divine truth. More probably he had not yet altogether
abandoned the plan of entering the church. In any case there is a

4 The assignment of the letter to 1633, and the sonnet it contains therefore
to December 1632, is Mr. W. R. Parker's.—'Some Problems in the Chronology of Milton's Early Poems,' *Review of English Studies*, XI (1935).

misleading suppression of a part of his full mind, which we may regard as a characteristic manifestation of Miltonic strategy. The friend is representative of the normal judgment of the world. He is not, therefore, an intimate of the inner shrine of Milton's purposes and, since he presumably holds the common inadequate view of art, would misunderstand and condemn a confession of the important place which poetry occupied in his thought. In his undergraduate days Milton had freely enough proclaimed his interest to the circle of his academic contemporaries. Since he had come to take a more serious view of himself he had reserved his confidences, communicating them privately to the entirely sympathetic Diodati, and now, with an apologia based on the true and elevated conception of poetry, to his father.'[5]

Sir, besides that in sundry respects I must acknowledge me to profit by you whenever we meet, you are often to me, and were yesterday especially, as a good watchman to admonish that the hours of the night pass on (for so I call my life as yet obscure and unserviceable to mankind) and that the day is at hand wherein Christ commands all to labour while there is light. Which, because I am persuaded you do to no other purpose than out of a true desire that God should be honoured in everyone, I am ever ready, you know, when occasion is, to give you account, as I ought though unasked, of my tardy moving according to the precept of my conscience, which I firmly trust is not without God. Yet now I will not strain for any set apology, but only refer myself to what my mind shall have at any time to declare herself at her best ease. Yet if you think, as you said, that too much love of learning is in fault, and that I have given up myself to dream away my years in the arms of studious retirement, like Endymion with the Moon on Latmus Hill, yet consider that if it were no more but this, to overcome this, there is on the other side both ill more bewitchful to entice away, and natural cares more swaying, and good more available, to withdraw to that which you wish me: as first all the fond hopes which forward youth and vanity are fledge with, none of which can sort with this Pluto's helmet, as

5 *Youth of Milton*, p.130. Mr. Hanford assigns *To My Father* to 1632 rather than with us to 1637.

Homer calls it, of obscurity and would soon cause me to throw it off if there were nothing else in't but an affected and fruitless curiosity of knowing; and then a natural desire of honour and repute, which I think possesses the breast of every scholar—as well of him that shall, as of him that never shall, obtain it (if this be altogether bad), which would quickly oversway this phlegm and melancholy of bashfulness, or that other humour, and prevail with me to prefer a life that had at least some credit in it, some place given it before a manner of living much disregarded and discountenanced. There is besides this, as all well know, about this time of a man's life, a strong inclination, be it good or no, to build up a house and family of his own in the best manner he may, to which nothing is more helpful than the early entering into some credible employment, and nothing more cross than my way, which my wasting youth would presently bethink her of and kill one love with another, if that were all. But what delight or what peculiar conceit, may you in charity think, could hold out against the long knowledge of a contrary command from above, and the terrible seizure of him that hid his talent? Therefore commit grace to grace or nature to nature, there will be found on the other way more obvious temptations to bad—as gain, preferment, ambition; more winning presentments of good, and more prone affections of nature to encline and dispose (not counting outward causes, as expectations and murmurs of friends, scandals taken, and such like) than the bare love of notions could resist; so that if it be that which you suppose, it had by this been round about begirt and overmastered, whether it had proceeded from virtue, vice, or nature in me. Yet that you may see that I am sometime suspicious of myself, and do take notice of a certain belatedness in me, I am the bolder to send you some of my nightward thoughts some while since, since they come in fitly, made up in a Petrarchian stanza:

> How soon hath Time, the subtle thief of youth,
>> Stol'n on his wing my three-and-twentieth year!
>> My hasting days fly on with full career,
>> But my late spring no bud or blossom shew'th.

Perhaps my semblance might deceive the truth
   That I to manhood am arrived so near,
   And inward ripeness doth much less appear,
   That some more timely-happy spirits indu'th.
Yet be it less or more, or soon or slow,
   It shall be still in strictest measure even
   To that same lot however mean or high
Toward which Time leads me, and the will of Heaven:
   All is, if I have grace to use it so,
   As ever in my great Taskmaster's eye.

54. Letter to a Friend, revised. 1633?

A revised and expanded second draft of the 'Letter to a Friend' in which the sonnet on the twenty-third birthday is included. The letter finally sent was probably based on this draft.

Sir, besides that in sundry other respects I must acknowledge me to profit by you whenever we meet, you are often to me, and were yesterday especially, as a good watchman to admonish that the hours of the night pass on (for so I call my life, as yet obscure and unserviceable to mankind) and that the day with me is at hand wherein Christ commands all to labour while there is light. Which, because I am persuaded you do to no other purpose than out of a true desire that God should be honoured in everyone, I therefore think myself bound, though unasked, to give you account, as oft as occasion is, of this my tardy moving, according to the precept of my conscience, which I firmly trust is not without God. Yet now I will not strain for any set apology, but only refer myself to what my mind shall have at any time to declare herself at her best ease. But if you think, as you said, that too much love of learning is in fault, and that I have given up myself to dream away my years in the arms of studious retirement, like Endymion with the Moon, as the tale of Latmus goes, yet consider that if it were no more but the mere love of learning, whether it proceed from a principle bad, good, or natural, it could not have held out thus long against so strong opposition on the other side of every kind. For if it be bad, why should

not all the fond hopes that forward youth and vanity are fledge with,
together with gain, pride, and ambition, call me forward more powerfully than a poor, regardless, and unprofitable sin of curiosity
should be able to withhold me, whereby a man cuts himself off
from all action and becomes the most helpless, pusillanimous, and
unweaponed creature in the world, the most unfit and unable to do
that which all mortals most aspire to—either to defend and be useful to his friends, or to offend his enemies. Or, if it be to be thought
an natural proneness, there is against that a much more potent inclination, and inbred, which about this time of a man's life solicits
most—the desire of house and family of his own, to which nothing
is esteemed more helpful than the early entering into credible employment, and nothing more hindering than this affected solitariness. And though this were enough, yet there is to this another act,
if not of pure, yet of refined nature, no less available to dissuade prolonged obscurity—a desire of honour and repute and immortal fame
seated in the breast of every true scholar, which all make haste to
by the readiest ways of publishing and divulging conceived merits
—as well those that shall, as those that never shall, obtain it. Nature
therefore would presently work the more prevalent way if there
were nothing but this inferior bent of herself to restrain her. Lastly,
if the love of learning as it is, be the pursuit of something good, it
would sooner follow the more excellent and supreme good known
and presented, and so be quickly diverted from the empty and fan-
tastic chase of shadows and notions, to the solid good flowing from
due and timely obedience to that command in the Gospel set out
by the terrible seizing of him that hid the talent. It is more probable therefore that not the endless delight of speculation, but this
very consideration of that great commandment, does not press forward as soon as may be to undergo, but keeps off with a sacred
reverence and religious advisement how best to undergo—not taking thought of being late so it give advantage to be more fit; for
those that were latest lost nothing when the master of the vineyard
came to give each one his hire. And here I am come to a stream-
head copious enough to disburden itself, like Nilus, at seven mouths

into an ocean. But then I should also run into a reciprocal contradiction of ebbing and flowing at once, and do that which I excuse myself for not doing—preach and not preach. Yet that you may see that I am something suspicious of myself, and do take notice of a certain belatedness in me, I am the bolder to send you some of my nightward thoughts some while since, because they come in not altogether unfitly, made up in a Petrarchian stanza, which I told you of:

after the stanza

By this I believe you may well repent of having made mention at all of this matter; for if I have not all this while won you to this, I have certainly wearied you to it. This therefore alone may be a sufficient reason for me to keep me as I am, lest having thus tired you singly, I should deal worse with a whole congregation, and spoil all the patience of a parish. For I myself do not only see my own tediousness, but now grow offended with it, that has hindered me thus long from coming to the last and best period of my letter, and that which must now chiefly work my pardon—that I am

Your true and unfeigned friend.

55. *To My Father*. 1637? [6]
From the Latin.

I would fain have the Pierian Springs divert, at this instant, their watercourses through my breast; I would fain have the stream loosed from the twin peaks and roll in all its fulness o'er my lips, to the end that forgetting all humble strains my Muse may rise on daring pinions to discharge her loving service to my father, a father worthy of all reverence. Be its welcome what it may, it is for you,

---

6 Mr. Tillyard's date (*Milton*, p.384). Professor Hanford and Mr. Visiak both assign the poem to 1632, connecting it in its content with the 'Letter to a Friend.' Certainly the biographical significance of the two documents is clarified if they are read together, but there is otherwise no reason for supposing them to have been written together. Professor Grierson puts *To My Father* after *Comus* in the Florence Edition.

worthy father, that my Muse is toiling o'er this slender achievement. I know not what gifts *from* me can make more fitting answer
to your gifts *to* me, though not even the greatest gifts can make
answer unto yours: far less can the gratitude that is rendered
through empty words, barren gratitude, be a match for gifts [sub-
stantial]. Yet after all this page sets forth my rating: all that I have
of wealth I have counted out on the sheet that is before you; and yet
that wealth is naught save what golden Clio has given me, what
slumbers have begotten for me within some grot sequestered, and
the laurel-thickets in the holy wood, shady dells on Parnassus.

Do not *you* look down on song divine, creation of the bard; for
naught graces more finely than does song his heavenly source, his
heavenly seed, his mind mortal in origin—for song still keeps holy
traces of Prometheus' fire. The gods above love song, and song has
power to rouse the quaking depths of Tartarus, to bind fast the
gods of the deeps below; song restrains with triple adamant the un-
feeling Manes. By song the secrets of the far-distant future are revealed by the daughters of Phœbus, and by quivering Sibyls, pale
of lips. The sacrificer composes [builds] songs at the holy altars,
whether he lays low the bull as it tosses its gilded horns, or, keen of
mind, consults the fates hidden away within the smoking entrails, or
in the *exta*, still warm, searches for [the will of] destiny. So I too,
when I shall revisit my native Olympus, and time shall stand immovable, endlessly delayed, I too shall go wearing a golden crown
through the realms of the skies, wedding sweet strains to the soft-
sounding *plectrum*: at those strains the stars and the vaults of the
twin poles will ring. At this instant too the fiery spirit that flies
round and round 'mid the swiftly whirling orbs is singing, himself,
amid the starry choirs, singing a never-dying melody, a song beyond all describing, while the ruddy Serpent checks his hot hiss-
ings, and savage Orion, with sword now lowered, turns gentle, and
Maurusian Atlas no longer feels his burden.

Songs were wont, in olden days, to adorn the rich feasts of kings,
when luxury and the limitless abyss of the bottomless gullet were
yet unknown, and the banquet tables foamed only with modest

wines. In those days, the bard, seated in accord with custom at the holiday feast, his unshorn locks bound with leaves from the oak tree, used to sing of the achievements of heroes, exploits worthy of imitation, and the foundations, laid broad and wide, of the world, and of gods creeping, and of acorns that formed food for gods, and of the lightning bolt not yet sought from Ætna's grot. In brief, what pleasure will there be in music well attuned if it is empty of voice, empty of words and of their meanings, and of numbers that talk? Such strains befit the woodland choirs, not Orpheus, who by his songs held fast the streams, and added ears to the oaks by his songs, not by his lyre, and by his singing compelled to tears the shades that were done with life: it is from his *song* that he has these praises.

Persist not, I pray you, to hold cheap the holy Muses, nor think them idle, poor; for through their bounty you yourself skilfully compose a thousand strains to measures fit, and since you have been trained to vary your tuneful voice by a thousand modulations, you would of right be heir of Arion's fame. Wherein is it strange if it has fallen to your lot to sire me, a poet, if we [you and I], knit so closely together by dear ties of blood, should pursue arts of one blood, and kindred studies? Phœbus, wishing to divide himself between us twain, gave one half of his gifts to me, the other half to my father, and so we, father and son, possess the god in shares.[7]

Though you pretend that you loathe the dainty Muses, none the less you loathe them not, methinks; for, Father, you did not bid me go where a highway lies open, wide and broad, where the ground slopes more straightly to gain, and the golden hope of storing away money shines with steady lustre. You are not now dragging me off to the laws, the ill-guarded statutes of our nation, nor are you condemning my ears to the tasteless clamours [of the laws]. But eager to enrich yet more my mind, you drew me away from the din and the uproar of the city into seclusions deep, and you suffered me to go amid the delightful leisure of the Aonian stream, a blessed comrade at Apollo's side.

7 Milton's father was a musician of some skill. Several of his compositions were included in seventeenth-century collections of songs.

I hold my peace about the service rendered by every father to dear son: on *me* larger demands are made. When, at your expense, best of fathers, the eloquence of Romulus' tongue was opened wide to me, and all its Latin graces, when there lay open to me the exalted words of the Greeks, masters of a noble tongue, words that become the great mouth of Jove himself, you urged me to add the flowers [of language] whereof Gaul boasts, and the talk that the newer Italian pours forth from his degenerate lips, bearing witness by his utterance to barbarian uprisings; you urged me to learn, too, the mysteries that the seers and the prophets of Palestine speak forth. In a word, whatever is contained within the sky, in Mother Earth, spread out beneath the skies, or in the air that streams 'twixt earth and sky, whatever the waters cover and the heaving marble of the sea, all this, thanks to you, it is my privilege to know, thanks to you, if it shall be my pleasure to know it. Nay, more, sweeping the clouds apart, Science comes to be viewed, and naked she inclines her bright face to my kisses, unless I should wish to flee, unless I should find it burdensome to taste her kisses.

Go to, now, match your wealth [with mine], whoso'er, unsound of mind, makes his first choice the age-old treasures of Austria, and of the kingdoms of Peru. What greater wealth could have been given by a father, even, if you will, by Jove himself, though he had given all the world, the sky alone excepted? No choicer gifts, e'en had they been safe, gave he who entrusted to his youthful son the light that is common property of all mankind, and Hyperion's chariot, and the reins of the day, and the tiara undulating with radiant light. Therefore, since I am already a part, albeit the lowliest, of the learned [poetic] throng, I shall sit amid the victors' crowns of ivy and of laurel; no more now shall I mingle, a figure obscure, with the witless populace, but my footsteps will avoid eyes profane. Keep yourselves far away, wakeful Cares, keep yourselves far away, Complaints, and the eye of Envy with its crooked leer. Stretch not wide, merciless Calumny, your snake-bearing jaws. Most loathsome crew, *you* possess naught of baneful power against me, nor am I in *your* control. Safe, with breast secure, I shall stride on, uplifted high from your viper blows.

But for you, Father dear, since the power is not vouchsafed me to make just return to your deserts, or to balance your gifts by my achievements, let it be enough that I have made mention of them, that with grateful heart I am telling the tale of your gifts, and am storing them away in a loyal mind.

And now, verses of mine, song of my youth, my sport and frolic, if only you shall venture to hope for never-ceasing years, and to outlive your master's funeral pyre, and then to gaze on the light, and if black forgetfulness shall not whirl you 'neath crowded Orcus, perhaps you will jealously guard these praises, and my father's name, thus lauded in song, guarding them, I mean, to serve as an example for a time far distant.

56. From *Lycidas*. 1637.

There are perhaps in the epic poems and in *Comus* and *Samson Ago-nistes* utterances as personal, almost, as these from *Lycidas*. While they are excluded from our text except when avowedly autobiographical, these lines are included because there is here no pretence of assignment of speeches to a fictitious character. Well within the pastoral tradition, Milton is here avowedly speaking in his own person, as in *Damon's Epitaph* he speaks in his own person.

In this monody the author bewails a learned friend,[8] unfortunately drowned in his passage from Chester on the Irish Seas, 1637. And by occasion foretells the ruin of our corrupted clergy then in their height.

> Yet once more, O ye laurels, and once more
> Ye myrtles brown, with ivy never sere,
> I come to pluck your berries harsh and crude,
> And with forced fingers rude
> Shatter your leaves before the mellowing year.

8 Edward King. But it has been often noted that *Lycidas* depends for much of its force and effectiveness upon the probability that throughout Milton is thinking as much of himself as of King.

Bitter constraint, and sad occasion dear,
Compels me to disturb your season due:
For Lycidas is dead, dead ere his prime,
Young Lycidas, and hath not left his peer.
Who would not sing for Lycidas? he knew
Himself to sing, and build the lofty rhyme.
He must not float upon his watry bier
Unwept, and welter to the parching wind,
Without the meed of some melodious tear.
　　Begin then, Sisters of the sacred well
That from beneath the seat of Jove doth spring,
Begin, and somewhat loudly sweep the string.
Hence with denial vain, and coy excuse:
So may some gentle Muse
With lucky words favour my destined urn,
And as he passes turn
And bid fair peace be to my sable shroud.
For we were nursed upon the self-same hill,
Fed the same flock, by fountain, shade, and rill.[9]
　　Together both, ere the high lawns appeared
Under the opening eyelids of the morn,
We drove afield, and both together heard
What time the grey-fly winds her sultry horn,
Batt'ning our flocks with the fresh dews of night,
Oft till the star that rose, at ev'ning, bright,
Toward Heaven's descent had sloped his westering wheel.
Meanwhile the rural ditties were not mute,
Tempered to th' oaten flute;
Rough Satyrs danced, and Fauns with cloven heel
From the glad sound would not be absent long;
And old *Damœtas*[10] loved to hear our song.

· · ·

9 Milton and King were both at Christ's College.
10 Damœtas has been variously identified. Masson observes that 'personal
　identification is, of course, now as futile as it is unnecessary; but, while

Alas! What boots it with uncessant care
To tend the homely slighted shepherd's trade,
And strictly meditate the thankless Muse?
Were it not better done as others use,
To sport with Amaryllis in the shade,
Or with the tangles of Neæra's hair?
Fame is the spur that the clear spirit doth raise
(That last infirmity of noble mind)
To scorn delights and live laborious days;
But the fair guerdon when we hope to find,
And think to burst out into sudden blaze,
Comes the blind Fury with th'abhorred shears,
And slits the thin-spun life. 'But not the praise,'
Phœbus replied, and touched my trembling ears;
'Fame is no plant that grows on mortal soil,
Nor in the glistering foil
Set off to th' world, nor in broad rumour lies,
But lives and spreads aloft by those pure eyes,
And perfet witness of all-judging Jove;
As he pronounces lastly on each deed,
Of so much fame in Heaven expect thy meed.'

. . .

Thus sang the uncouth swain to th' oaks and rills,
While the still morn went out with sandals grey:
He touched the tender stops of various quills,
With eager thought warbling his Dorick lay;
And now the sun had stretched out all the hills,
And now was dropt into the western bay.
At last he rose, and twitched his mantle blue:
Tomorrow to fresh woods, and pastures new.[11]

Milton wrote, a vision of some particular person at Cambridge did certainly pass across his mind.'—*Works*, Vol. III, p.257.
11 To Italy, or into new poetic endeavours, or both?

57. Familiar Letter 7, to Charles Diodati. 1637.

From the Latin.
    After a long response to a letter from Diodati, and a rebuke to
Diodati for not having been a more satisfactory correspondent,
Milton affirms the depth of his friendship for Diodati perhaps
even more strongly than in *Damon's Epitaph*, outlining the Platonic basis of it in his deep-rooted love of the good and the beautiful, of which Diodati is a manifestation, and then tells his friend
once more of his high literary aspirations, of his hope for literary
immortality.

While other friends generally in their letters think it enough to
express a single wish for one's health, I see now how it is
that you convey the same salutation so many times; for to those
mere wishes on the subject which were all that you yourself could
in former times offer, and which are all that others have to offer
yet, you would now have me understand, I suppose, that there is
the gigantic addition of your art and all the force of your medical
practitionership. You bid me be well six hundred times, well as I
wish to be, well as I can be, and so forth even more superlatively.
Verily you must have lately been made the very steward of the
larder, the clerk of the kitchen, to Health, such havoc you make of
the whole store of salubrity; or, doubtless, Health ought now to be
your parasite, you so act the king over her and command her to be
obedient. I therefore congratulate you, and find it consequently
necessary to return you thanks on a double account—your friendship for one thing, and your excellence in your profession for
another. I did indeed, since it had been so agreed, long expect letters from you; but, having never received any, I did not, believe me,
on that account suffer my old good will to you to cool in the least;
nay, that very excuse for your delay which you have employed in
the beginning of your letter I had anticipated in my own mind you
would offer, and that rightly and in accordance with our relations
to each other. For I would not have true friendship turn on bal-
ances of letters and salutations, all which may be false, but that it
should rest on both sides in the deep roots of the mind and sustain

itself there, and that, once begun on sincere and sacred grounds, it should, though mutual good offices should cease, yet be free from suspicion and blame all life long. For fostering such a friendship as this, what is wanted is not so much written correspondence as a loving recollection of virtues on both sides. Nor even should you have persisted in not writing would there be lack of means with me for supplying that good office. Your probity writes for me in your stead, and inscribes true letters on my inmost consciousness; your frank innocence of character writes to me, and your love of the good; your genius also, by no means an everyday one, writes to me and commends you to me more and more. Don't, therefore, now that you have possessed yourself of that tyrannic citadel of Medicine, wave those terrors before me, as if you meant to draw in bit by bit and to demand back from me your six hundred healths till only one was left, if by chance (which God forbid) I should become a traitor to friendship. Remove that terrible battery which you seem to have planted right at me in your resolution that it shall not be lawful for me to get ill without your good leave. For, lest you should threaten too much, know that it is impossible for me not to love men like you. What besides God has resolved concerning me I know not, but this at least: He has instilled into me, if into anyone, a vehement love of the beautiful. Not with so much labour, as the fables have it, is Ceres said to have sought her daughter Proserpina as it is my habit day and night to seek for this Idea of the beautiful, as for a certain image of supreme beauty, through all the forms and faces of things (for many are the shapes of things divine) and to follow it as it leads me on by some sure traces which I seem to recognize. Hence it is that, when anyone scorns what the vulgar opine in their depraved estimation of things, and dares to feel and speak and be that which the highest wisdom throughout all ages has taught to be best, to that man I attach myself forthwith by a kind of real necessity, wherever I find him. If, whether by nature or by my fate, I am so circumstanced that by no effort and labour of mine can I myself rise to such an honour and elevation, yet that I should always worship and look up to those who have attained that glory, or happily aspire to it, neither gods nor men, I reckon, have bidden nay.

But now I know you wish to have your curiosity satisfied. You make many anxious inquiries, even as to what I am at present thinking of. Hearken, Theodotus, but let it be in your private ear, lest I blush; and allow me for a little to use big language with you. You ask what I am thinking of? So may the good Deity help me, of immortality! And what am I doing? Growing my wings and meditating flight; but as yet our Pegasus raises himself on very tender pinions. Let us be lowly wise!

I will now tell you seriously what I am thinking of. I am thinking of migrating into some Inn of the Lawyers where I can find a pleasant and shady walking-ground, because there I shall have both a more convenient habitation among a number of companions if I wish to remain at home, and more suitable headquarters if I choose to make excursions in any direction. Where I am now, as you know, I live obscurely and in a cramped manner. You shall also have information respecting my studies. I have by continuous reading brought down the affairs of the Greeks as far as to the time when they ceased to be Greeks. I have been long engaged in the obscure business of the state of Italians under the Longobards, the Franks, and the Germans, down to the time when liberty was granted them by Rudolf, King of Germany: from that period it will be better to read separately what each city did by its own wars. But what are *you* doing? How long will you hang over domestic matters as a son of the family, forgetting your town companionships? Unless this stepmotherly war be very bad indeed,[12] worse than the Dacian or the Sarmatian, you will certainly have to make haste, so as to come to us at least for winter quarters. Meanwhile, if it can be done without trouble to you, I beg you to send me Justiniani, the historian of the Venetians. I will, on my word, see that he is well kept against your arrival, or, if you prefer it, that he is sent back to you not very long after receipt. Farewell.

London: September 23, 1637.

12 Diodati's father had recently married a second time.

58. From *To Manso*. 1639.

From the Latin.

Milton repays the kindness shown him by Manso, generous host when he was a visitor to Naples, by addressing to him the poem from which the following lines are extracts. Few passages better attest the confidence which Milton had in his own powers in his youth, especially after the Italian journey.

Therefore, in the names of Clio and of mighty Phœbus, I dispatch to you, father Manso, my best wishes for your health through the long, long years, I, a youth from a foreign land, sent from the hyperborean quarter of the world. Since you are so gracious, you will not spurn a Muse that comes from afar, a Muse that, though nurtured but hardly 'neath the cold Bear, unthinkingly dared recently a flight through the cities of Italy.[13] I too, I am persuaded, have heard through the dark shadows of the night the swans as they attuned their strains in my own river, where the silvery Thames, bright-urned, wide-spreading stream, drenches his grey tresses with the swirling waters of ocean. Nay, nay, once on a time there came to these shores [of Italy] Tityrus [Chaucer].

. . .

Elder beloved of the gods! It must be that Jupiter and Phœbus and the kindly grandson of Atlas all alike with kindly eyes surveyed you at your birth, for, unless he shall be from his first hours dear to the gods above, a man will ne'er have power to befriend a mighty poet. This is why *your* old age keeps green amid clinging flowers,[14] and by its vigorous life gains for itself the spindles of Æson, preserving for you the graces of your brow, graces not yet fallen, the vigour of your intellect, and the full-grown keenness of your wit. O may my lot vouchsafe to me a friend so fine, one who knows so well how to honour the men of Phœbus, true men, if ever I shall bring back to my songs the kings of my native land, and Arthur, who set wars in train even 'neath the earth [i.e. in Fairyland], or

13 See section IX, note 8.
14 Manso was seventy-nine.

shall tell of the high-hearted heroes bound together as comrades at that peerless table, and—O may the spirit come to my aid—I shall break to pieces Saxon phalanxes under the might of Britons' warring. At last when, having measured to the full the span of a life not voiceless, a man full of years, I shall leave to the ashes their rights, that friend would stand with streaming eyes beside my bier: it will be enough if I shall say to him as he stands there, 'Let me be your concern.' My limbs, relaxed by black death, he would take pains to have bestowed softly, gently, in a tiny urn; mayhap he will carve my features out of marble, wreathing my locks with leafage of Parnassus' laurel; and so I shall rest in undisturbed peace. Then, too, if there is aught of good faith, of loyalty, anywhere, if there are sure rewards for good men, I myself, withdrawn to the ether of the gods that dwell in the skies, in some place to which toil and a clean heart and their own flaming manhood bear good men, from some corner of a world apart I shall see, so far as the Fates permit, all that happens here [i.e. in this world below], and with all my soul smiling calmly I shall have a crimson flush upon my face, and at the same time, full of joy, I shall applaud myself in skyey Olympus.

59. From *Damon's Epitaph*. 1640.

From the Latin.

Milton has been planning his future as an epic poet, even choosing Arthur for his subject, and has looked forward to confiding his hopes to Diodati. Now, since Diodati is dead, he tells of them in the poem to his memory.

Alas! what vagrant wandering drove me to go to stranger shores, across the skyey ridges and the snow-laden Alps? Was there anything worth its cost in the sight of buried Rome?—[would there have been] even if she were as splendid as in the days when Tityrus[15] went to see her, leaving the while his sheep and his country-

---

15 There is a similar reference to Chaucer's visit to Italy in the preceding extract, from *To Manso*, with the comparison Milton is making between himself and Chaucer even more clearly implied.

side—, anything worth so much that for it I could be without *you*, my sweet, sweet comrade, could set between you and me so many deep seas, so many mountains, so many forests, so many crags, so many sounding streams? Ah! I might at least have been privileged to touch for the last time your hand, and your dear eyes, decently composed as you died in peace, and to say, 'Fare you well, fare you well! Remember me, as you shall take your way to the stars.'

> *Go home, unpastured, my lambs:*
> *Your master has no leisure now.*

And yet I shall never regret that I kept you in mind, shepherds of Tuscany, youths busied with the Muses, for there dwells Charis, there Lepos abides. You, too, Damon, were a Tuscan, from the ancient city of Lucumo: thence you derive your lineage.[16] O, how wondrous great was I, when, stretched at ease by the prattlings of the cool Arno, in its poplar grove, where the grass was softest, I could pluck now violets, now the tips of the myrtles, and could hear Menalcas vying with Lycidas! I too ventured [then] to contend, and, methinks, I did not much displease, for I have in my possession even now the gifts you, one and all, gave me—baskets of rush, baskets of wicker, and the waxen fastenings of hemlock. Nay more, Dati and Francini made my name known to the beeches: well known were they both for their songs, and for their studies, and both were of the blood of the Lydians [Tuscans].[17]

> *Go home, unpastured, my lambs:*
> *Your master has no leisure now.*

16 In the *Second Defence* (extract 2) Milton tells of an excursion to Lucca, the home of the Diodati family. We may assume, surely, that his friendship for Diodati sent him there.

17 This passage refers to the friends with whom Milton spent his time in Florence, Dati and Francini important among them. Milton mentions both as men he will never forget in the *Second Defence* (extract 2) in the list of those whom he met in one of the private academies of which he thought so highly. A Latin letter to Dati is extant from 1647 (extract 28), in which Milton sends his greetings to the same friends.

Such strains the dewy moon used to dictate to me—glad was I in those days—while by myself I was penning my dainty kids within the hurdles. Ah! How many times I said, even when the black ashes possessed you, 'Damon is singing now, or else he is setting nets 'gainst the hares; now he is intertwining osiers to serve his varied needs.' And what then I with complaisant mind hoped would come to pass, I lightly forestalled in my prayers, and I portrayed it as already present. 'What ho, good sir! [I said to you, Damon] you're doing naught? Unless, perchance, something holds you back, are we off, and are we reclining a while in the tuneful shade, at the waters of the Colnus [the River Colne], or where the acres of Cassivellaunus [lie]? You will run through for me your healing potions, your herbs, the hellebore, and the lowly crocus, and the leaf of the hyacinth, all the herbs that yonder marsh possesses, and the arts, too, of the healers.'[18] Alas! perish the herbs, perish, too, the arts of the healers, the plants, since they profited not at all him who was their master. I myself too—my pipe was sounding forth some lofty strain, I know not what—another day is come, the day following the eleventh night—I myself, as it chanced, had set my lips to pipes of hemlock, pipes that were new: none the less, bursting their joinings, they leaped asunder, and could brook no longer the weighty strains. I misdoubt that I am over-swollen with pride. Still I will tell the tale. Yield, ye woods.

> *Go home, unpastured, my lambs:*
> *Your master has no leisure now.*

I myself shall sing of Dardan ships [making their way] through Rutupian [Kentish] waters, and of the realm, in days of old, of Imogene, daughter of Pandrasus; I shall sing of Brennus and Arviragus, captains [both], and of ancient Belinus, too, and of the settlers from Armorica, subject at last to Britons' laws. Next I shall sing of Igraine, mother-to-be, through fateful trickery, of Arthur; I shall sing of lying features, of the taking of the arms of Gorloïs, guile, all,

18 Diodati was a physician. See Familiar Letter 7 (extract 57).

of Merlin. O if only life shall endure for me, you, my Pan's pipe, will hang far away [from me] on an aged pine, utterly forgot by me, or else, transmuted, you will with the aid of native Muses sound forth a truly British strain. Why, pray, [speak I thus]? One man may not, one man may not hope [to achieve] all things [i.e. to win fame by working in Latin and in English both]. It is recompence in plenty, and high glory too, for me (even though I be unknown to endless time, and utterly without glory from the world without) should the yellow-tressed Usa [the Ouse], and he that drinks the Alanus [the River Alan], and Abra [the Humber], crowded with whirling eddies, and every grove of Treanta [the Trent], and my beloved Thames, before all others, and the Tamara [the Tamar], swart with metals, and the Orcades in the furthermost billows learn my songs.

> Go home, unpastured, my lambs:
> Your master has no leisure now.

All these [plans and dreams] I was guarding jealously for you, Damon,[19] under the pliant bark of the laurel, these, and more as well, and the cups,[20] too, that were given to me by Manso, by Manso, not the least glory of the Chalcidian [Cumæan, Italian] strand, cups two in number, wondrous creations of skill, given to me by Manso, himself a marvel. He had graven them round with a double theme. In the midst are the billows of the Red Sea, and fragrance-bearing spring, the long shores of Araby, and forests dripping with balsam. Among the trees is Phœnix, bird divine, without its like on earth, gleaming darkly with parti-coloured wings, watching Aurora as she rises from the glassy billows. Elsewhere are the sky, spreading without end, and mighty Olympus. Here—who would think

---

19 Cf. extract 27, also from *Damon's Epitaph*, 'To whom shall I entrust my soul?' The letters to Diodati also are full of Milton's hopes of literary greatness; e.g. Familiar Letter 7 (extract 57).

20 Cups or books. See Michele De Filippis, 'Milton and Manso: Cups or Books?' *Publications of the Modern Language Association*, LI (1936), pp.745–756.

it?—is Love, too, with his quiver painted amidst a cloud, Love with
his gleaming armoury, his torches, and his darts touched with the
colour of bronze. Not trivial souls and the ignoble hearts of the rabble does he smite thence [from the cloud, or, perhaps, with these
weapons]: but, rolling his flaming eyes, he scatters his shafts, always
straight upward, through the heavenly spheres, and never looks
with glance askant to ply downward blows. Through such strokes
holy minds are set ablaze, and shapes of the gods themselves.

60. From *Animadversions upon the Remonstrant's Defence against
    Smectymnuus.* 1641.

And he that now for haste snatches up a plain ungarnished present
as a thank-offering to Thee, which could not be deferred in regard
of Thy so many late deliverances wrought for us one upon another,
may then [21] perhaps take up a harp and sing Thee an elaborate song
to generations. [22]

61. Sonnet VIII. 1642.

In the Trinity College Manuscript of the minor poems, this sonnet
    has the heading, 'When the assault was intended to the city,' and
    the cancelled heading, 'On his door when the city expected an
    assault.' We may be certain, perhaps, that the sonnet was written
    during the period of alarm, but we must agree with Smart that
    while Milton's ability here to make the danger the subject matter

---

21 When God has perfected His glorious acts, when He has 'settled peace in
   the church and righteous judgement in the kingdom.'
22 Cf. *Of Reformation,* earlier in 1641: 'Then, amidst the hymns and hallelujahs of saints, someone may perhaps be heard offering at high strains in
   new and lofty measures to sing and celebrate Thy divine mercies and
   marvellous judgements in this land throughout the ages, whereby this
   great and warlike nation, instructed and inured to the fervent and continual practice of truth and righteousness, and casting far from her the
   rags of her whole vices, may press on hard to that high and happy emulation to be found the soberest, wisest, and most Christian people at that
   day, when Thou, the eternal and shortly expected king, shall open the
   clouds to judge the several kingdoms of the world, and . . . shalt put
   an end to all earthly tyrannies, proclaiming Thy universal and mild
   monarchy through heaven and earth.'—Columbia *Milton,* Vol. III, pt. 1,
   pp.78–79.

of a somewhat playful sonnet is proof of his 'inflexible composure' and calm detachment, it is hardly likely that the poem was actually placed on his door to disarm some Royalist commander (*Sonnets*, pp. 56–57). Nevertheless, whimsical though the poem may be, it is still another expression of Milton's estimate of the importance of poetry and of the certainty of his position as a poet.

> Captain, or colonel, or knight in arms,
>> Whose chance on these defenceless doors may seize,
>> If deed of honour did thee ever please,
>> Guard them, and him within protect from harms:
> He can requite thee, for he knows the charms
>> That call fame on such gentle acts as these,
>> And he can spread thy name o'er lands and seas,
>> Whatever clime the sun's bright circle warms.
> Lift not thy spear against the Muse's bower:
>> The great Emathian conqueror bid spare
>> The house of Pindarus when Temple and Tower
> Went to the ground; and the repeated air
>> Of sad Electra's poet had the power
>> To save th'Athenian walls from ruin bare.

62. Epilogue to *The Passion*. 1645?[23]

This subject the author finding to be above the years he had when he wrote it, and nothing satisfied with what was begun, left it unfinished.

63. Foreword to *Testimonia*. 1645.

From the Latin.
>   Before the Latin section of the 1645 volume, *Poems of Mr. John Milton, Both English and Latin . . .*, is a group of eulogies of Milton in Latin and Italian to which Milton wrote a Latin foreword, the following extract.

23 The date 1645 is assigned to this note on *The Passion*, written in 1630, on the ground that the most probable occasion for an explanation of the poem's fragmentary state was the publication of the *Poems* of 1645.

Here follow *testimonia* with respect to the author. He was perfectly well aware, himself, that they were uttered not so much *about* him as *over* him, because men of pre-eminent ability who are one's friends as well have a habit of phrasing their eulogies in such a way that they conjure up, eagerly, what from beginning to end befits their own merits rather than the truth. Yet the author was unwilling that the kindly feeling entertained for him by the writers of these *testimonia* should not be known, especially since others were very earnestly urging him to make them generally known. For, while he is seeking with might and main to fend off from himself the odium that excessive praise begets, and prefers that he should not be credited with more than is his due, he cannot in the meantime deny that he sees a signal honour to himself in the favourable judgement of men of intellect reinforced by high distinction.

64. From the *Ode to Rouse*. 1647.

From the Latin.

> Milton is again rejoicing, although somewhat playfully, in the thought of literary immortality, this time based upon the preservation of his minor poems in the library at Oxford.

To John Rouse, Librarian of the University of Oxford.

About a book of poems that had been lost. The librarian was asking that the book should be sent to him anew, that he might place it with others of my books in the general library.

Twin books, rejoicing in a single robe [i.e. binding],[24] bright, it may be, with double leaves of laurel [i.e. with two title-pages], and with neatness [of contents] not overlaboured, neatness that a boyish hand bestowed on you, an earnest, zealous hand, but as yet no sure poet's hand, while that poet, wandering where he would, frolicked now in the green places, still untainted of the people [i.e. had not yet taken part in matters political], and, far from the beaten tracks, gave free course to his native lute, or, presently, in like manner with

24 The Latin poems were printed in a group separate from the English and Italian poems in 1645, but they were bound together.

a Daunian quill struck out for them that were about him a song brought from far-off lands, the while he scarce touched the ground with his foot.

. . .

Therefore you shall go to view the lovely groves of the Muses; you shall go again to the house divine wherein Phœbus dwells in the Vale of Oxford, holding less dear Delos and the twin-cleft peak of Parnassus. You shall go in honour, after you too, having won a peerless destiny, shall, prevailed on by the entreaties of an auspicious friend, quit my side. There you will be read among the lofty names of authors, age-old beacons and true glories alike of the Grecian and the Latin race.

You, it seems at last, were not empty, idle things, toils of mine, whatever my barren intellect poured forth. I am bidding you now, late though it be, to hope for a calm and quiet rest, a rest that shall be done with envy; I bid you hope for the blest abodes that kindly Hermes and the skilful guardianship of Rouse will vouchsafe you, abodes into which the wanton tongue of the rabble will not make its way, from which the throngs of worthless readers will speed afar. But our latest children's children, and an age of sounder minds, will mayhap from hearts untainted apply juster judgements to all things. Then, when envy and malice shall be buried, if we deserve aught, the sound minds of after days will know it, thanks to Rouse's favour.

65. Familiar Letter 14, to Henry Oldenburg, Agent for Bremen. 1654.

From the Latin.

Oldenburg has apparently expressed a wish that Milton would devote himself to worthier things than the reply to the *Cry of the Royal Blood*. He has also become doubtful of More's authorship of the *Cry*. Milton here affirms the nobility of his cause, but agrees that there are other literary tasks that he would find more congenial.

Your former letter, honoured sir, was given to me when your messenger, I was told, was on the point of return, whence it happened that there was no opportunity of reply at that time. While I was afterwards purposing an early reply, some unexpected business took me off; but for which I should certainly not have sent you my book, *Defence* though it is called, in such a naked condition, without accompanying excuse. And now I have your second letter, in which your thanks are quite disproportioned to the slenderness of the gift. It was in my mind too more than once to send you back English for your Latin, in order that, as you have learned to speak our language more accurately and happily than any other foreigner of my acquaintance, you should not lose any opportunity of writing the same, which I believe you could do with equal accuracy. But in this, just as henceforward the impulse may be, let your own choice regulate. As to the substance of your communication, you plainly think with me that a 'Cry' of that kind 'to Heaven' transcends all bounds of human sense; the more impudent, then, must be he who declares so boldly he has heard it. You throw in a scruple after all as to who he is: but formerly whenever we talked on this subject, just after you had come hither from Holland, you seemed to have no doubt whatever but Morus was the author, inasmuch as that was the common report in those parts and no one else was named. If then, you have now at last any more certain information on the point, be so good as to inform me. As to the treatment of the argument, I should wish (why should I dissemble?) not to differ from you, if only because I would fain know what there is to which one would more readily yield than the sincere judgement of friendly men like yourself, and praise free from all flattery. To prepare myself, as you suggest, for other labours—whether nobler or more useful I know not, for what can be nobler or more useful in human affairs than the vindication of liberty?—truly, if my health shall permit, and this blindness of mine, a sorer affliction than old age, and lastly the 'cries' of such brawlers as there have been about me, I shall be induced to *that* easily enough. An idle ease has never had charms for me, and this unexpected contest with the adversaries of liberty took me off against my will[25] when I was intent on far different and altogether pleasanter studies: not that in any way I repent of what I have done, since it was necessary; for I am far from thinking that I have spent my toil, as you seem to hint, on matters of inferior consequence. But of this at another time: meanwhile, learned sir, not to detain you too long, farewell, and reckon me among your friends.

Westminster: July 6, 1654.

66. From *Paradise Lost*. 1655–1665.

The Invocation to Book I.
> After the long interlude of controversy, Milton has finally come to his task of prophecy, of writing for the glory of God 'an elaborate song to generations.'

> Of Man's first disobedience, and the fruit
> Of that forbidden tree whose mortal taste
> Brought death into the world, and all our woe,
> With loss of Eden, till one greater Man
> Restore us, and regain the blissful seat,
> Sing Heavenly Muse, that on the secret top
> Of Oreb, or of Sinai, didst inspire
> That shepherd, who first taught the chosen seed
> In the beginning how the heavens and earth
> Rose out of Chaos: or if Sion Hill
> Delight thee more, and Siloa's brook that flow'd
> Fast by the oracle of God, I thence
> Invoke thy aid to my adventrous song,
> That with no middle flight intends to soar
> Above th'Aonian mount, while it pursues
> Things unattempted yet in prose or rhyme.

25 Milton refers here to the writing of the defences, in the first part of the letter specifically to the assignment in the *Second Defence* of the *Cry of the Royal Blood* to Alexander More. In the request for any further information that Oldenburg may have, Milton is not yet contemplating the *Defence of Himself*, for the *Public Faith of Alexander More* in response to which it was written did not appear until October 1654, three months after the date of this letter.

And chiefly Thou, O Spirit, that dost prefer
Before all temples th'upright heart and pure,
Instruct me, for Thou know'st; Thou from the first
Wast present, and with mighty wings outspread
Dove-like satst brooding on the vast abyss
And mad'st it pregnant: what in me is dark
Illumine, what is low raise and support;
That to the heighth of this great argument
I may assert Eternal Providence,
And justify the ways of God to men.

67. Note on the Versification of *Paradise Lost*. 1668.

This note, with the 'Argument' of the poem, added 'for the satisfaction of many that have desired it,' was inserted in 1668 in copies of
the first edition of *Paradise Lost* that still remained unsold in the
hands of the printer, Simmons. It is described by Simmons in a
note to the reader as 'a reason of that which stumbled many others,
why the poem rhymes not.'

The measure is English heroic verse without rhyme, as that of Homer in Greek and of Virgil in Latin, rhyme being no necessary ad-
junct or true ornament of poem or good verse, in longer works especially, but the invention of a barbarous age to set off wretched matter and lame metre, graced indeed since by the use of some famous
modern poets, carried away by custom, but much to their own vexation, hindrance, and constraint to express many things otherwise,
and for the most part worse, than else they would have expressed
them. Not without cause therefore some both Italian and Spanish
poets of prime note have rejected rhyme both in longer and shorter
works, as have also long since our best English tragedies, as a thing
of itself to all judicious ears, trivial and of no true musical delight
—which consists only in apt numbers, fit quantity of syllables, and
the sense variously drawn out from one verse into another, not in
the jingling sound of like endings, a fault avoided by the learned ancients both in poetry and all good oratory. This neglect then of
rhyme so little is to be taken for a defect, though it may seem so

perhaps to vulgar readers, that it rather is to be esteemed an example set, the first in English, of ancient liberty recovered to heroic poem from the troublesome and modern bondage of rhyming.

68. Foreword to *Samson Agonistes*. 1668–1671?

'Of that sort of dramatic poem which is called tragedy.'

Tragedy, as it was anciently composed, hath been ever held the gravest, moralest, and most profitable of all other poems: therefore said by Aristotle to be of power by raising pity and fear, or terror, to purge the mind of those and such like passions, that is to temper and reduce them to just measure with a kind of delight stirred up by reading or seeing those passions well imitated. Nor is Nature wanting in her own effects to make good his assertion: for so in physic things of melancholic hue and quality are used against melancholy, sour against sour, salt to remove salt humours. Hence philosophers and other gravest writers, as Cicero, Plutarch, and others, frequently cite out of tragic poets, both to adorn and illustrate their discourse. The apostle Paul himself thought it not unworthy to insert a verse of Euripides into the text of Holy Scripture, I Cor. xv, 33, and Pareus commenting on the Revelation, divides the whole book as a tragedy into acts distinguished each by a chorus of heavenly harpings and song between.[26] Heretofore men in highest dignity have laboured not a little to be thought able to compose a tragedy. Of that honour Dionysius the elder was no less ambitious than before of his attaining to the tyranny. Augustus Cæsar also had begun his *Ajax*, but unable to please his own judgement with what he had begun, left it unfinished. Seneca the philosopher is by some thought the author of those tragedies (at least the best of them) that go under that name. Gregory Nazianzen, a Father of the Church, thought it not unbeseeming the sanctity of his person to write a tragedy, which he entitled, *Christ Suffering*. This is mentioned to vindicate tragedy from the small esteem, or rather infamy, which in

26 In the *Reason of Church Government* (extract 1) Milton writing in 1642 used the same argument and cited the same authority.

the account of many it undergoes at this day with other common interludes, happening through the poet's error of intermixing comic stuff with tragic sadness and gravity or introducing trivial and vulgar persons, which by all judicious hath been counted absurd, and brought in without discretion, corruptly, to gratify the people. And though ancient tragedy use no prologue, yet using sometimes, in case of self-defence or explanation, that which Martial calls an epistle, in behalf of this tragedy coming forth after the ancient manner, much different from what among us passes for best, thus much beforehand may be epistled: that chorus is here introduced after the Greek manner, not ancient only but modern, and still in use among the Italians. In the modelling therefore of this poem, with good reason, the ancients and Italians are rather followed, as of much more authority and fame. The measure of verse used in the chorus is of all sorts, called by the Greeks monostrophic, or rather apolelymenon, without regard had to strophe, antistrophe or epode, which were a kind of stanzas framed only for the music, then used with the chorus that sung—not essential to the poem, and therefore not material—, or being divided into stanzas or pauses, they may be called allæostropha. Division into act and scene referring chiefly to the stage (to which this work never was intended) is here omitted.

It suffices if the whole drama be found not produced beyond the fifth act. Of the style and uniformity, and that commonly called the plot, whether intricate or explicit—which is nothing indeed but such economy or disposition of the fable as may stand best with verisimilitude and decorum—, they only will best judge who are not unacquainted with Æschylus, Sophocles, and Euripides, the three tragic poets unequalled yet by any, and the best rule to all who endeavour to write tragedy. The circumscription of time wherein the whole drama begins and ends, is, according to ancient rule and best example, within the space of twenty-four hours.

Further light upon Milton's aspirations and his judgement of his achievements as a poet will be found in extracts 1, 2, 7, 8, 11, 14, 18, 19, 21, 22, 24, 28, 41, 47, 74–76, 107, 120, 147, *and* 151.

IX. INSPIRATION

Of my celestial patroness, who deigns
Her nightly visitation unimplored,
And dictates to me slumbring.

69. From Elegy V, *On the Coming of Spring.* 1629.

From the Latin.

The 'inspiration' of which Milton speaks here, the gift of spring, is the conventional inspiration of the poet, not the prophetic inspiration of which he speaks elsewhere. The apparent contradiction here of the report that Milton's inspiration came only between the fall and the spring equinoxes is hardly real.[1]

TIME, that rolls back upon itself in never-ending circuit, is already, since the spring is gaining in warmth, calling back the new Zephyrs; Earth, made anew, is clothing herself with a short-lived youth; and at last the ground, set free from the frost and the ice, is growing charmingly green. Am I beguiling myself? or is strength coming back into my songs also, and have I, thanks to the bounty of spring, inspiration at my call? *Is* inspiration here, by the gift of spring, and is it winning vigour from the spring—who would think it?—, and demanding now for itself some achievement, some creation? Castalia's waters dance before mine eyes, and the twice-cleft peak, and at night dreams bring to me Pirene. My soul is deeply stirred, is all aglow with mysterious impulses; the madness of inspiration and holy sounds stir me to my deeps within. The god of Delos himself is coming—I see his locks twined with Peneus' laurel—yes, the god of Delos is coming himself. Now my mind is whirled up to the heavenly steeps, and, freed from my body, I move 'mid the roving clouds; through the shades I go, moving through grottoes, the penetralia of the bards; the fanes of the gods are open wide for me, wide to their innermost depths; my soul gazes intently on whatever

1 See section IX, note 8.

141

is done in all Olympus' length and breadth, nor do the blind deeps
of Tartarus escape mine eyes.

What lofty strains is my soul sounding forth through my parted
lips? What is being born of this madness, this holy frenzy? The
spring, the spring that gave me inspiration shall be the theme of that
inspiration's songs; thus the gifts of spring will be repaid to her and
will bring her profit.

At last, Philomela, enveloped in new-born leaves, you are beginning your tuneful strains, while the wood everywhere is soundless:
let us twain begin together, in the city I, you in the woodland; let
us two, each in his own part, chant the coming of the spring. The
springtime—sing ho!—is come again in its due turn: let us honour
the springtime, and sound forth her praises; let this be the task
essayed by the never-dying Muse!

70. From the *Reason of Church Government*. 1642.

In the same work (extract 1) Milton refers to himself as writing while
green years are upon his head. He was thirty-three.

And if any man incline to think I undertake a task too difficult for
my years, I trust through the supreme enlightening assistance far
otherwise; for my years, be they few or many, what imports it? so
they bring reason, let that be looked on.

71. From the *Doctrine and Discipline of Divorce*. 1643.

In the present brief extract Milton speaks at greater length of his aim
and his accomplishment in the divorce pamphlets than of the
divine guidance that was his. The reference to the 'illuminating
spirit' which has favoured him is certainly the most personal note
in the passage, however, and accounts for its position here among
extracts dealing mainly with his inspiration.

Which agrees with that of the same Apostle to the Ephes. lv, 14, 15,
where he tell us that the way to get a sure undoubted knowledge of
things is to hold that for truth which accords most with charity.
Whose unerring guidance and conduct having followed as a load-
star with all diligence and fidelity in this question, I trust, through

the help of that illuminating Spirit which hath favoured me, to have done no everyday's work: in asserting after many ages the words of Christ with other Scriptures of great concernment from burdensome and remorseless obscurity, tangled with manifold repugnances, to their native lustre and consent between each other: hereby also dissolving tedious and Gordian difficulties, which have hitherto molested the church of God, and are now decided, not with the sword of Alexander, but with the immaculate hands of Charity, to the unspeakable good of Christendom.

72. From the *Judgement of Martin Bucer,*[2] *concerning Divorce.* 1644.

In this and the next extract from the same work Milton attempts to prove as he does elsewhere only with regard to the divorce pamphlets, on some other basis than the mere assertion of his immediate consciousness of inspiration, that he does indeed write from divine prompting. Since in different ages he and Martin Bucer have arrived at the same conclusions quite independently, it must be that 'God doth now again create the same doctrine in another unwritten table, and raises it up immediately out of His pure oracle to the convincement of a perverse age.'

Certainly if it be in man's discerning to sever providence from chance, I could allege many instances wherein there would appear cause to esteem of me no other than a passive instrument under some power and counsel higher and better than can be human, working to a general good in the whole course of this matter. For that I owe no light or leading received from any man in the discovery of this truth, what time I first undertook it in the *Doctrine and Discipline of Divorce*, and had only the infallible grounds of Scripture to be my guide, He who tries the inmost heart and saw with what severe industry and examination of myself I set down every period, will be my witness. When I had almost finished the first edition, I chanced to read in the notes of Hugo Grotius upon the fifth of Matthew, whom I straight understood inclining to

2 Martin Bucer, Professor of Divinity at Cambridge in 1550–1551, was a Protestant champion of international fame. His body was exhumed and burned as that of an heretic in the reign of Mary.

reasonable terms in this controversy: and something he whispered rather than disputed about the law of charity, and the true end of wedlock. Glad therefore of such an able assistant, however at much distance, I resolved at length to put off into this wild and calumnious world. For God, it seems, intended to prove me, whether I durst alone take up a rightful cause against a world of disesteem, and found I durst. My name I did not publish, as not willing it should sway the reader either for me or against me.[3] But when I was told that the style, which what it ails to be so soon distinguishable, I cannot tell, was known by most men, and that some of the clergy began to inveigh and exclaim on what I was credibly informed they had not read, I took it then for my proper season both to show them a name that could easily contemn such an indiscreet kind of censure, and to reinforce the question with a more accurate diligence: that if any of them would be so good as to leave railing and to let us hear so much of his learning and Christian wisdom as will be strictly demanded of him in his answering to this problem, care was had he should not spend his preparations against a nameless pamphlet. By this time I had learned that Paulus Fagius,[4] one of the chief divines in Germany, sent for by Frederic the Palatine to reform his dominion, and after that invited hither in King Edward's days to be Professor of Divinity in Cambridge, was of the same opinion touching divorce which these men so lavishly traduced in me. What I found I inserted where fittest place was, thinking sure they would respect so grave an author, at least to the moderating of their odious inferences. And having now perfected a second edition, I referred the judging thereof to your high and impartial sentence, honoured Lords and Commons. For I was confident, if anything generous, anything noble and above the multitude, were left yet in the spirit of England, it could be nowhere sooner found and nowhere sooner understood than in that house of justice and true liberty where ye sit in council. Nor doth the event hitherto, for some reasons which

3 Milton is elsewhere frequently disdainful of anonymous publication; e.g. in *Colasterion* (extract 109).
4 See section X, note 4.

I shall not here deliver, fail me of what I conceived so highly. Nevertheless, being far otherwise dealt with by some of whose profession and supposed knowledge I had better hope, and esteemed the deviser of a new and pernicious paradox, I felt no difference within me from that peace and firmness of mind which is of nearest kin to patience and contentment: both for that I knew I had divulged a truth linked inseparably with the most fundamental rules of Christianity, to stand or fall together, and was not uninformed that divers learned and judicious men testified their daily approbation of the book. Yet at length it hath pleased God, who had already given me satisfaction in myself, to afford me now a means whereby I may be fully justified also in the eyes of men. When the book had been now the second time set forth well-nigh three months, as I best remember, I then first came to hear that Martin Bucer had written much concerning divorce: whom earnestly turning over, I soon perceived, but not without amazement, in the same opinion, confirmed with the same reasons which in that published book without the help or imitation of any precedent writer, I had laboured out and laid together. Not but that there is some difference in the handling, in the order, and the number of arguments, but still agreeing in the same conclusion. So as I may justly gratulate mine own mind, with due acknowledgement of assistance from above, which led me, not as a learner, but as a collateral teacher, to a sympathy of judgement with no less a man than Martin Bucer. And he, if our things here below arrive him where he is, does not repent him to see that point of knowledge which he first, and with an unchecked freedom, preached to those more knowing times of England, now found so necessary, though what he admonished were lost out of our memory, yet that God doth now again create the same doctrine in another unwritten table, and raises it up immediately out of His pure oracle to the convincement of a perverse age, eager in the reformation of names and ceremonies, but in realities as traditional and as ignorant as their forefathers. I would ask now the foremost of my profound accusers whether they dare affirm that to be licentious, new, and dangerous, which Martin Bucer so often and so urgently avouched to be most lawful, most necessary, and most Christian, without the least blemish to his good name among all the worthy men of that age and since, who testify so highly of him? If they dare, they must then set up an arrogance of their own against all those churches and saints who honoured him without this exception. If they dare not, how can they now make that licentious doctrine in another which was never blamed or confuted in Bucer or in Fagius? The truth is, there will be due to them for this their unadvised rashness the best donative that can be given them—I mean a round reproof, now that where they thought to be most magisterial, they have displayed their own want both of reading and of judgement. First, to be so unacquainted in the writings of Bucer, which are so obvious and so useful in their own faculty; next, to be so caught in a prejudicating weakness as to condemn that for lewd which (whether they knew or not) these elect servants of Christ commended for lawful; and for new, that which was taught by these almost the first and greatest authors of reformation, who were never taxed for so teaching, and dedicated without scruple to a royal pair of the first reforming kings in Christendom, and confessed in the public confession of a most orthodoxal church and state in Germany. This is also another fault which I must tell them: that they have stood now almost this whole year clamouring afar off, while the book hath been twice printed, twice bought up, and never once vouchsafed a friendly conference with the author, who would be glad and thankful to be shown an error, either by private dispute or public answer, and could retract as well as wise men before him —might also be worth the gaining, as one who heretofore hath done good service to the church by their own confession. Or if he be obstinate, their confutation would have rendered him without excuse, and reclaimed others of no mean parts who incline to his opinion.

73. From the *Judgement of Martin Bucer concerning Divorce.* 1644.

God, that I may ever magnify and record this His goodness, hath unexpectedly raised up as it were from the dead more than one famous light of the first reformation to bear witness with me and to do me honour in that very thing wherein these men thought to have blotted me, and hath given them the proof of a capacity which they despised, running equal and authentic with some of their chiefest masters unthought of, and in a point of sagest moment. However, if we know at all when to ascribe the occurrences of this life to the work of a special providence, as nothing is more usual in the talk of good men, what can be more like to a special providence of God, than, in the first reformation of England, that this question of divorce, as a main thing to be restored to just freedom, was written and seriously commended to Edward the Sixth, by a man called from another country to be the instructor of our nation, and now in this present renewing of the church and commonwealth, which we pray may be more lasting, that the same question should be again treated and presented to this parliament by one enabled to use the same reasons without the least sight or knowledge of what was done before. It were no trespass, Lords and Commons, though something of less note were attributed to the ordering of a heavenly power; this question therefore of such prime concernment both to Christian and civil welfare, in such an extraordinary manner, not recovered, but plainly twice born to these latter ages, as from a divine hand I tender to your acceptance and most considerate thoughts. Think not that God raised up in vain a man of greatest authority in the church to tell a trivial and licentious tale in the ears of that good prince, and to bequeath it as his last will and testament, nay rather as the testament and royal law of Christ to this nation, or that it should of itself after so many years, as it were in a new field where it was never sown, grow up again as a vicious plant in the mind of another, who had spoke honestest things to the nation, though he knew not that what his youth then reasoned without a pattern had been heard already, and well allowed, from the gravity and worth of Martin Bucer, till meeting with the envy of men ignorant in their own undertaken calling, God directed him to the forgotten writings of this faithful evangelist, to be his defence and warrant against the gross imputation of broaching licence.

74. From *Paradise Lost*. 1655–1665.

The Invocation of Book VII.

> Descend from Heaven, Urania, by that name
> If rightly thou art called, whose voice divine
> Following, above th'Olympian hill I soar,
> Above the flight of Pegasean wing.
> The meaning, not the name I call: for thou
> Nor of the Muses nine, nor on the top
> Of old Olympus dwell'st, but heavenly born,
> Before the hills appeared, or fountain flowed,
> Thou with eternal Wisdom didst converse,
> Wisdom thy sister, and with her didst play
> In presence of th'Almighty Father, pleased
> With thy celestial song. Up led by thee
> Into the Heaven of Heavens I have presumed,
> An earthly guest, and drawn empyreal air,
> Thy tempring; with like safety guided down,
> Return me to my native element,
> Lest from this flying steed unrein'd (as once
> Bellerophon, though from a lower clime)
> Dismounted, on th'Aleian field I fall,
> Erroneous there to wander and forlorn.
> Half yet remains unsung, but narrower bound
> Within the visible diurnal sphere:
> Standing on earth, not rapt above the pole,
> More safe I sing with mortal voice, unchanged
> To hoarse or mute, though fall'n on evil days,
> On evil days though fall'n, and evil tongues;
> In darkness, and with dangers compassed round,
> And solitude;[5] yet not alone, while thou

5 Milton's response to the Restoration might be thought another evidence of his identification of himself with his cause. But it is more than that. An ill fate for the Commonwealth is not merely figuratively an ill fate for him. For a time he was imprisoned. Even when he was not in prison, he had articulate enemies among the Royalists. Masson's note is that after the Restoration Milton found himself 'solitary, blind, and calumniated, while

Visit'st my slumbers nightly,[6] or when morn
Purples the east: still govern thou my song,

all that he thought worst was now in the ascendancy in England.'—*Works*,
Vol. III, p.487.

At times, if we may read personal feeling into a chorus of *Samson Agonistes* (ll.667–704), Milton seems to have felt his changed position to be an
instance of divine injustice:

> God of our Fathers, what is man!
> That Thou towards him with hand so various,
> Or might I say contrarious,
> Temperst Thy providence through his short course,
> Not evenly, as Thou rul'st
> The angelic orders and inferior creatures mute,
> Irrational and brute.
> Nor do I name of men the common rout,
> That wandring loose about,
> Grow up and perish, as the summer fly,
> Heads without name no more remembered,
> But such as Thou hast solemnly elected,
> With gifts and graces eminently adorned
> To some great work, Thy glory,
> And people's safety, which in part they effect:
> Yet toward these thus dignified, Thou oft
> Amidst their heighth of noon,
> Changest Thy countenance, and Thy hand with no regard
> Of highest favours past
> From Thee on them, or them to Thee of service.
> Nor only dost degrade them, or remit
> To life obscured, which were a fair dismission,
> But throw'st them lower than Thou didst exalt them high—
> Unseemly falls in human eye,
> Too grievous for the trespass or omission;
> Oft leav'st them to the hostile sword
> Of heathen and profane, their carcasses
> To dogs and fowls a prey, or else captived,
> Or to the unjust tribunals, under change of times,
> And condemnation of the ingrateful multitude.
> If these they 'scape, perhaps in poverty
> With sickness and disease Thou bow'st them down,
> Painful diseases and deformed,
> In crude old age;

(*Continued on p.150.*)

---

6 In *Paradise Lost*, Book IX (extract 75), Milton speaks

> Of my celestial patroness, who deigns
> Her nightly visitation unimplored,
> And dictates to me slumbring, or inspires
> Easy my unpremeditated verse.

Urania, and fit audience find, though few.[7]
But drive far off the barbarous dissonance
Of Bacchus and his revellers, the race
Of that wild rout that tore the Thracian bard
In Rhodope, where woods and rocks had ears
To rapture, till the savage clamour drowned
Both harp and voice; nor could the Muse defend
Her son. So fail not thou, who thee implores:
For thou art Heavenly, she an empty dream.

75. From *Paradise Lost*. 1655–1665.

Book IX ll.1–47.

No more of talk where God or angel guest
With man, as with his friend, familiar used
To sit indulgent, and with him partake
Rural repast, permitting him the while
Venial discourse unblamed: I now must change
Those notes to tragic: foul distrust and breach
Disloyal on the part of man, revolt,
And disobedience; on the part of Heaven
Now alienated, distance and distaste,
Anger and just rebuke, and judgement given,
That brought into this world a world of woe,
Sin and her shadow Death, and Misery,
Death's harbinger: Sad task! yet argument

Though not disordinate, yet causeless suffring
The punishment of dissolute days, in fine,
Just or unjust alike seem miserable,
For oft alike both come to evil end.

---

7 Although he is writing a poem 'doctrinal to the nations,' Milton speaks
frequently throughout his works of his disdain for a vulgar audience—most
particularly perhaps in the expression of doubt of his wisdom in writing
the divorce pamphlets in the vernacular (extracts 2 and 79) and in the foreword to the *Christian Doctrine* (extract 102), where he hopes for an audience of 'men of mature and manly understanding.' But the same disdain
for the unlearned mob and the same appeal to the learned few are to be
found in the books defending the Commonwealth to the world and to all
Englishmen—e.g. in *Eikonoklastes* (extract 88).

Not less but more heroic than the wrath
Of stern Achilles on his foe pursued
Thrice fugitive about Troy wall; or rage
Of Turnus for Lavinia disespoused,
Or Neptune's ire or Juno's, that so long
Perplexed the Greek and Cytherea's son;
If answerable style I can obtain
Of my celestial patroness, who deigns
Her nightly visitation unimplored,
And dictates to me slumbring, or inspires
Easy my unpremeditated verse:
Since first this subject for heroic song
Pleased me long choosing, and beginning late,
Not sedulous by nature to indite
Wars, hitherto the only argument
Heroic deemed, chief mast'ry to dissect
With long and tedious havoc fabled knights
In battles feigned (the better fortitude
Of patience and heroic martyrdom
Unsung), or to describe races and games,
Or tilting furniture, emblazoned shields,
Impresses quaint, caparisons and steeds,
Bases and tinsel trappings, gorgeous knights
At joust and tournament; then marshalled feast
Served up in hall with sewers, and seneshals;
The skill of artifice or office mean,
Not that which justly gives heroic name
To person or to poem. Me of these
Nor skilled nor studious, higher argument
Remains, sufficient of itself to raise
That name, unless an age too late, or cold
Climate,[8] or years damp my intended wing

8 Milton seems to have been really concerned lest the climate of England
prove unfriendly to poetry. In the *History of Britain*, Miss Darbishire
points out, Milton observes that the sun which England lacks 'ripens wits
as well as fruits' (*Early Lives*, pp.lvii–lviii). In the *Reason of Church Gov-*

> Depressed, and much they may, if all be mine,
> Not hers who brings it nightly to my ear.

76. From *Paradise Regained*. 1666–1670.

Book I, ll. 1–17.

> I who erewhile the happy garden sung,
> By one man's disobedience lost, now sing
> Recovered Paradise to all mankind,
> By one man's firm obedience fully tried
> Through all temptation, and the Tempter foiled
> In all his wiles, defeated and repulsed,
> And Eden raised in the waste wilderness.
>
>   Thou Spirit who ledst this glorious Eremite
> Into the desert, his victorious field
> Against the spiritual foe, and broughtst him thence
> By proof the undoubted Son of God, inspire,
> As thou art wont, my prompted song else mute,
> And bear through heighth or depth of nature's bounds
> With prosperous wing full summed to tell of deeds
> Above heroic, though in secret done,
> And unrecorded left through many an age,
> Worthy t'have not remained so long unsung.

Milton speaks further of his inspiration, of divine dictation, in ex-
tracts 1, 2, 46, 47, 52, 66, 102, 105, 108, 120, 123, *and* 124.

ernment (extract 1) Milton makes his promise of a great poem conditional
upon the provision 'that there be nothing adverse in our climate,' and in
To Manso he speaks of his Muse 'nurtured but hardly 'neath the cold Bear'
(extract 58), but reassures himself with the memory of Chaucer.

    This apparent fear of cold is curiously at variance with Aubrey's report
of Edward Phillips' statement that 'all the time of writing his *Paradise
Lost*, his vein began at the autumnal equinoctial and ceased at the vernal
or thereabouts (I believe about May)' (Darbishire, *Early Lives*, p.13).
But this report is itself at variance with Milton's enthusiastic welcome to
spring in Elegy V (extract 69). The point is, of course, that Milton's fears
for the climate were not based upon a distaste for cold weather which he
may or may not have felt, but upon the conviction shared with his age that
all the truly great literature of the world had come from the South, from
the Greeks, the Romans, and the Italians, that the sun 'ripens wits as well
as fruits.' Looking back from the seventeenth century, we shall need to
make very few exceptions to this judgement.

X. PROSE

Defence is a good cause, and Heaven be for us.

A. AIMS AND MOTIVES

Not to be all wanting to this noble cause.

77. From the *Doctrine and Discipline of Divorce*. 1643.

Milton speaks here specifically of his argument on divorce, but in
much of his prose he regarded himself as 'sole advocate of a discountenanced truth.' Many of the extracts in the present group
refer similarly to particular works, but many of those also similarly
express attitudes that Milton held toward much of his writing.

AND now the duty and the right of an instructed Christian calls me
through the chance of good or evil report to be the sole advocate of
a discountenanced truth: a high enterprise, Lords and Commons, a
high enterprise and a hard, and such as every seventh son of a seventh son does not venture on. Nor have I amidst the clamour of so
much envy and impertinence whither to appeal but to the concourse
of so much piety and wisdom here assembled.

78. From the *Doctrine and Discipline of Divorce*. 1643.

In the *Defence of Himself* (extract 43) in explanation of his answer to
the *Cry of the Royal Blood* by order of the Council and of his failure to answer other equally noisy pamphlets, Milton says he goes
not 'uncalled' to public business, but statements like the one in the
present extract of his feeling of obligation to take part in controversy on public matters solely at the call of conscience are frequent;
e.g. in the *Reason of Church Government* and *Of Civil Power in
Ecclesiastical Causes* (extracts 1 and 95).

Yet if the wisdom, the justice, the purity of God be to be cleared
from foulest imputations which are not yet avoided, if charity be not

to be degraded and trodden down under a civil ordinance, if matrimony be not to be advanced like that exalted perdition written of to the Thessalonians, 'above all that is called God,' or goodness, nay against them both, then I dare affirm there will be found in the contents of this book that which may concern us all. You it concerns chiefly, worthies in Parliament, on whom, as on our deliverers, all our grievances and cares by the merit of your eminence and fortitude are devolved: me it concerns next, having with much labour and faithful diligence first found out, or at least with a fearless and communicative candour first published to the manifest good of Christendom, that which, calling to witness everything mortal and immortal, I believe unfeignedly to be true. Let not other men think their conscience bound to search continually after truth, to pray for enlightening from above, to publish what they think they have so obtained, and debar me from conceiving myself tied by the same duties.

79. From the *Doctrine and Discipline of Divorce*. 1643.

For me, as far as my part leads me, I have already my greatest gain: assurance and inward satisfaction to have done in this[1] nothing unworthy of an honest life and studies well employed—with what event among the wise and right understanding handful of men, I am secure. But how among the drove of custom and prejudice this will be relished by such whose capacity, since their youth run ahead into the easy creek of a system or a medulla, sails there at will under the blown physiognomy of their unlaboured rudiments—for them, what their taste will be, I have also surety sufficient from the entire league that hath been ever between formal ignorance and grave obstinacy. Yet when I remember the little that our Saviour could prevail about this doctrine of charity against the crabbed textuists of His time, I make no wonder, but rest confident that who so prefers either matrimony or other ordinance before the good of man and the plain exigence of charity, let him profess Papist, or Protestant, or what he will, he is not better than a Pharisee, and understands

1 I.e. in writing of divorce.

not the Gospel: whom as a misinterpreter of Christ I openly protest against, and provoke him to the trial of this truth before all the world: and let him bethink him withal how he will solder up the shifting flaws of his ungirt permissions, his venial and unvenial dispences, wherewith the law of God pardoning and unpardoning hath been shamefully branded for want of heed in glossing, to have eluded and baffled out all faith and chastity from the marriage-bed of that holy seed, with politic and judicial adulteries. I seek not to seduce the simple and illiterate; my errand is to find out the choicest and the learnedest, who have this high gift of wisdom to answer solidly, or to be convinced.[2] I crave it from the piety, the learning, and the prudence which is housed in this place. It might perhaps more fitly have been written in another tongue: and I had done so, but that the esteem I have of my country's judgement, and the love I bear to my native language to serve it first with what I endeavour, made me speak it thus, ere I assay the verdict of outlandish readers.[3] And perhaps also here I might have ended nameless, but that the address of these lines chiefly to the Parliament of England might have seemed ingrateful not to acknowledge by whose religious care, unwearied watchfulness, courageous and heroic resolutions, I enjoy the peace and studious leisure to remain,

The honourer and attendant of their noble worth and virtues,

John Milton.

80. From the *Doctrine and Discipline of Divorce.* 1643.

But because he is but brief,[4] and these things of great consequence not to be kept obscure, I shall conceive it nothing above my duty either for the difficulty or the censure that may pass thereon, to communicate such thoughts as I also have had, and do offer them

2 See section IX, note 7 for comment upon Milton's frequent expression of a desire for 'fit audience though few.'

3 Milton came to regret that he had not written the divorce pamphlets in Latin. See the *Second Defence* and Familiar Letter 16, to Leo Van Aizema (extracts 2 and 130).

4 Paulus Fagius, in whose commentary on the Pentateuch there is a passage in which, Milton says, 'he doubted not to maintain that divorces might be

now in this general labour of reformation to the candid view both of church and magistrate, especially because I see it the hope of good men that those irregular and unspiritual courts have spun their utmost date in this land, and some better course must now be constituted.

81. From *Of Education*. 1644.

Of Education was apparently written at the request of Samuel Hartlib, to whom it is addressed as a letter.

Mr. Hartlib,

I am long since persuaded that to say or do aught worth memory and imitation, no purpose or respect should sooner move us than simply the love of God and of mankind. Nevertheless, to write now the reforming of education, though it be one of the greatest and noblest designs that can be thought on, and for the want whereof this nation perishes, I had not yet at this time been induced but by your earnest entreaties and serious conjurements, as having my mind for the present half diverted in the pursuance of some other assertions, the knowledge and the use of which cannot but be a great furtherance both to the enlargement of truth and honest living, with much more peace. Nor should the laws of any private friendship have prevailed with me to divide thus or transpose my former thoughts, but that I see those aims, those actions which have won you with me the esteem of a person sent hither by some good providence from a far country, to be the occasion and the incitement of great good to this island.[5] And, as I hear, you have obtained the same repute with men of most approved wisdom, and some of highest authority, among us—not to mention the learned correspondence which you hold in foreign parts, and the extraordinary

as lawfully permitted by the magistrate to Christians as they were to Jews.' Fagius, Professor of Hebrew at Cambridge at his death in 1549, was a famous reformer, almost a Protestant martyr, since, like Bucer's, his body was exhumed and burned as that of an heretic in Mary's reign.—Masson, *Life*, Vol. III, pp.256–257.

5 Hartlib, a London merchant and an enthusiastic educational theorist, was the Prussian-born son of a Polish merchant. His mother was English.

pains and diligence which you have used in this matter both here and beyond the seas,[6] either by the definite will of God so ruling, or the peculiar sway of nature, which also is God's working. Neither can I think, that so reputed and so valued as you are, you would to the forfeit of your own discerning ability impose upon me an unfit and over-ponderous argument, but that the satisfaction which you profess to have received from those incidental discourses which we have wandered into hath pressed and almost constrained you into a persuasion that what you require from me in this point I neither ought nor can in conscience defer beyond this time both of so much need at once and so much opportunity, to try what God hath determined. I will not resist therefore whatever it is either of divine or human obligement that you lay upon me, but will forthwith set down in writing, as you request me, that voluntary Idea, which hath long in silence presented itself to me, of a better education, in extent and comprehension far more large, and yet of time far shorter, and of attainment far more certain, than hath been yet in practice. Brief I shall endeavour to be, for that which I have to say, assuredly this nation hath extreme need should be done sooner than spoken. To tell you therefore what I have benefited herein among old renowned authors, I shall spare; and to search what many modern Januas and didactics more than ever I shall read have projected, my inclination leads me not. But if you can accept of these few observations which have flowered off, and are, as it were, the burnishing of many studious and contemplative years altogether spent in the search of religious and civil knowledge, and such as pleased you so well in the relating, I here give you them to dispose of.

82. From the *Judgement of Martin Bucer concerning Divorce.* 1644.

I leave him[7] also as my complete surety and testimonial, if truth be not the best witness to itself, that what I formerly presented to

6 The reference is to Hartlib's efforts to introduce into the English universities, and of course to further elsewhere, the educational reforms advocated by Comenius, whose works Hartlib published in England.—Masson, *Life*, Vol. III, pp.193–255.

7 I.e. Martin Bucer.

your reading on this subject,[8] was good, and just, and honest, not licentious. Not that I have now more confidence by the addition of these great authors to my party; for what I wrote was not my opinion, but my knowledge—even then when I could trace no footstep in the way I went—; nor that I think to win upon your apprehensions with numbers and with names rather than with reasons; yet certainly the worst of my detractors will not except against so good a bail of my integrity and judgement as now appears for me. They must else put in the fame of Bucer and of Fagius as my accomplices and confederates into the same indictment;[9] they must dig up the good name of these prime worthies (if their names could be ever buried), they must dig them up and brand them as the Papists did their bodies;[10] and those their pure unblamable spirits, which live not only in Heaven, but in their writings, they must attaint with new attaintures which no Protestant ever before aspersed them with. Or if perhaps we may obtain to get our appeachment new drawn a writ of error, not of libertinism, that those two principal leaders of reformation may not come now to be sued in a bill of licence, to the scandal of our church, the brief result will be that for the error, if their own works be not thought sufficient to defend them, there lives yet who will be ready, in a fair and Christianly discussive way, to debate and sift this matter to the utmost ounce of learning and religion, in him that shall lay it as an error either upon Martin Bucer or any other of his opinion. If this be not enough to qualify my traducers, and that they think it more for the wisdom of their virulence not to recant the injuries they have bespoke me, I shall not for much more disturbance than they can bring me intermit the prosecution of those thoughts which may render me best serviceable, either to this age, or if it so happen, to posterity, following the fair path which your illustrious exploits, honoured Lords and Commons, against the breast of tyranny have opened, and depending so on your happy successes in the hopes that I have conceived either of myself or of

8 In the *Doctrine and Discipline of Divorce*, 1643.
9 Milton often takes satisfaction in finding his name in the company of great names; e.g. in the *Second Defence* (extract 127).
10 See note 4 above.

the nation as must needs conclude me one who most affectionately wishes and awaits the prosperous issue of your noble and valorous counsels.

John Milton.

83. From *Areopagitica*. 1644.

This is the opening paragraph of the *Areopagitica*, described by Milton as 'a speech . . . to the Parliament of England,' and written in the form of a classical oration.

They who to states and governors of the commonwealth direct their speech, high court of Parliament, or wanting such access in a private condition write that which they foresee may advance the public good, I suppose them as at the beginning of no mean endeavour, not a little altered and moved inwardly in their minds: some with doubt of what will be the success, others with fear of what will be the censure; some with hope, others with confidence of what they have to speak. And me perhaps each of these dispositions, as the subject was whereon I entered, may have at other times variously affected, and likely might in these foremost expressions now also disclose which of them swayed most, but that the very attempt of this address thus made, and the thought of whom it hath recourse to, hath got the power within me to a passion far more welcome than incidental to a preface. Which though I stay not to confess ere any ask, I shall be blameless if it be no other than the joy and gratulation which it brings to all who wish and promote their country's liberty, whereof this whole discourse proposed will be a certain testimony, if not a trophy.

84. From *Areopagitica*. 1644.

And lest some should persuade ye, Lords and Commons, that these arguments of learned men's discouragement at this your order, are mere flourishes, and not real, I could recount what I have seen and heard in other countries, where this kind of inquisition tyrannizes, when I have sat among their learned men (for that honour I had) and been counted happy to be born in such a place of philosophic freedom as they supposed England was, while themselves did nothing but bemoan the servile condition into which learning amongst them was brought: that this was it which had damped the glory of Italian wits; that nothing had been there written now these many years but flattery and fustian. There it was that I found and visited the famous Galileo grown old,[11] a prisoner to the Inquisition for thinking in astronomy otherwise than the Franciscan and Dominican licencers thought. And though I knew that England then was groaning loudest under the prelatical yoke, nevertheless I took it as a pledge of future happiness that other nations were so persuaded of her liberty. Yet was it beyond my hope that those worthies were then breathing in her air who should be her leaders to such a deliverance as shall never be forgotten by any revolution of time that this world hath to finish. When that was once begun, it was as little in my fear that what words of complaint I heard among learned men of other parts uttered against the Inquisition, the same I should hear by as learned men at home uttered in time of parliament against an order of licensing; and that so generally that when I had disclosed myself a companion of their discontent, I might say, if without envy, that he whom an honest quæstorship had endeared to the Sicilians was not more by them importuned against Verres than the favourable opinion which I had among many who honour ye, and are known and respected by ye, loaded me with entreaties and persuasions that I would not despair to lay together that which just reason should bring into my mind toward the removal of an undeserved thraldom upon learning. That this is not therefore the disburdening of a particular fancy, but the common grievance of all those who had prepared their minds and studies above the vulgar pitch to advance truth in others, and from others to entertain it, thus much may satisfy. And in their name I shall for neither friend nor foe conceal what the general murmur is: that if it come to inquisitioning again, and licensing, and that we are so timorous of ourselves and so suspicious of all men, as to fear each book, and the

11 See Introduction, pp.xxxv–xxxvi.

shaking of every leaf, before we know what the contents are; if some who but of late were little better than silenced from preaching shall come now to silence us from reading except what they please, it cannot be guessed what is intended by some but a second tyranny over learning: and will soon put it out of controversy that bishops and presbyters are the same to us both name and thing.[12]

85. From a volume of tracts presented to Patrick Young, the King's Librarian. 1645.

From the Latin.

To the most learned man, Patrick Young, John Milton sends these works of his, bound in one volume, content with readers of this sort though few.[13]

86. From a volume of tracts presented to John Rouse for the Bodleian Library. 1646.

From the Latin.

To the most learned man and upright judge of books, John Rouse, Librarian of Oxford University (who said this would please him), John Milton gladly sends these his pamphlets, to be received into that most ancient and celebrated library as into a temple of immortal fame and a vacation (as he hopes) exempt from envy and calumny, if Truth and Good Fortune alike be propitious. The titles follow. . . .

87. From the *Tenure of Kings and Magistrates.* 1649.

A statement of his aims in the particular work.

Another sort there is, who, coming in the course of these affairs to have their share in great actions above the form of law or custom— at least to give their voice and approbation—, begin to swerve and

12 Cf. *On the New Forces of Conscience under the Long Parliament,* l.20:
New presbyter is but old priest writ large.
13 See section IX, note 7.

almost shiver at the majesty and grandeur of some noble deed, as if they were newly entered into a great sin, disputing presidents, forms, and circumstances, when the commonwealth nigh perishes for want of deeds in substance, done with just and faithful expedition. To these I wish better instruction, and virtue equal to their calling, the former of which, that is to say instruction, I shall endeavour, as my duty is, to bestow on them, and exhort them not to startle from the just and pious resolution of adhering with all their strength and assistance to the present parliament and army in the glorious way wherein justice and victory hath set them—the only warrants through all ages, next under immediate revelation, to exercise supreme power—in those proceedings which hitherto appear equal to what hath been done in any age or nation heretofore, justly or magnanimously.

88. From *Eikonoklastes*. 1649.

To descant on the misfortunes of a person fallen from so high a dignity, who hath also payed his final debt both to nature and his faults, is neither of itself a thing commendable, nor the intention of this discourse. Neither was it fond ambition, or the vanity to get a name, present, or with posterity, by writing against a king: I never was so thirsty after fame, nor so destitute of other hopes and means better and more certain to attain it. For kings have gained glorious titles from their favourers by writing against private men, as Henry the Eighth did against Luther; but no man ever gained much honour by writing against a king, as not usually meeting with that force of argument in such courtly antagonists which to convince might add to his reputation. Kings most commonly, though strong in legions, are but weak at arguments, as they who ever have accustomed from the cradle to use their will only as their right hand, their reason always as their left. Whence, unexpectedly constrained to that kind of combat, they prove but weak and puny adversaries. Nevertheless for their sakes who through custom, simplicity, or want of better teaching, have not more seriously considered kings than in the gaudy name of majesty, and admire them and their doings as if they breathed not the same breath with other mortal men, I shall make no scruple to take up (for it seems to be the challenge both of him and all his party) to take up this gauntlet, though a king's, in the behalf of liberty and the commonwealth.

And further, since it appears manifestly the cunning drift of a factious and defeated party to make the same advantage of his book which they did before of his regal name and authority, and intend it not so much the defence of his former actions as the promoting of their own future designs, making thereby the book their own rather than the King's, as the benefit now must be their own more than his, now the third time to corrupt and disorder the minds of weaker men by new suggestions and narrations, either falsely or fallaciously representing the state of things to the dishonour of this present government and the retarding of a general peace, so needful to this afflicted nation, and so nigh obtained, I suppose it no injury to the dead, but a good deed rather to the living, if by better information given them, or, which is enough, by only remembering them the truth of what they themselves know to be here misaffirmed, they may be kept from entering the third time unadvisedly into war and bloodshed. For as to any moment of solidity in the book itself, save only that a king is said to be the author[14]—a name, than which there needs no more among the blockish vulgar,[15] to make it wise, and excellent, and admired, nay to set it next the Bible, though otherwise containing little else but the common grounds of tyranny and popery dressed up the better to deceive in a new Protestant guise, and trimly garnished over—or as to any need of answering in respect of staid and well-principled men, I take it on me as a work assigned rather than by me chosen or affected.[16] Which was the cause both of beginning it so late and finishing it so leisurely, in the midst of other employments and diversions. And though well it

---

14 Milton is here apparently doubtful of the King's authorship of *Eikon Basilike*. See Introduction, p.xxviii.
15 See section IX, note 7, and below in the present extract for Milton's opinion of the 'blockish vulgar.' In *Eikonoklastes* he is avowedly addressing them.
16 Assigned by the Council of State.

might have seemed in vain to write at all, considering the envy and almost infinite prejudice likely to be stirred up among the common sort against whatever can be written or gainsaid to the King's book, so advantageous to a book it is only to be a king's, and though it be an irksome labour to write with industry and judicious pains that which, neither weighed nor well read, shall be judged without industry or the pains of well judging by faction and the easy literature of custom and opinion, it shall be ventured yet, and the truth not smothered, but sent abroad in the native confidence of her single self, to earn, how she can, her entertainment in the world, and to find out her own readers—few perhaps, but those few such of value and substantial worth as truth and wisdom, not respecting numbers and big names, have been ever wont in all ages to be contented with.

89. From *Eikonoklastes*. 1649.

Another statement of a particular aim in a particular work.

What the King wrote to his son as a father concerns not us; what he wrote to him as a king of England concerns not him, God and the Parliament having now otherwise disposed of England. But because I see it done with some artifice and labour, to possess the people that they might amend their present condition by his or by his son's restorement, I shall show point by point, that although the King had been reinstalled to his desire, or that his son admitted should observe exactly all his father's precepts, yet that this would be so far from conducing to our happiness, either as a 'remedy to the present distempers, or a prevention of the like to come,' that it would inevitably throw us back again into all our past and fulfilled miseries, would force us to fight over again all our tedious wars, and put us to another fatal struggling for liberty and life more dubious than the former. In which as our success hath been no other than our cause, so it will be evident to all posterity that his 'misfortunes' were the mere consequence of his perverse 'judgement.'

90. From *Eikonoklastes*. 1649.

The discussion of the relationship of truth to justice which is so large
a part of the following extract is necessary to the understanding of
Milton's statement at the end of his hope 'to set free the minds of
English men from longing to return poorly under that captivity of
kings from which the strength and supreme sword of justice hath
delivered them.'

It happened once, as we find in Esdras and Josephus, authors not
less believed than any under sacred, to be a great and solemn debate in the court of Darius, what thing was to be counted strongest
of all other. He that could resolve this, in reward of his excelling
wisdom, should be clad in purple, drink in gold, sleep on a bed of
gold, and sit next Darius. None but they doubtless who were reputed wise had the question propounded to them. Who, after some
respite given them by the King to consider, in full assembly of all
his lords and gravest counsellors, returned severally what they
thought. The first held that wine was strongest; another that the
King was strongest. But Zorobabel, Prince of the captive Jews and
heir to the crown of Judah, being one of them, proved women to be
stronger than the King, for that he himself had seen a concubine
take his crown from off his head to set it upon her own: and others
besides him have lately seen the like feat done, and not in jest. Yet
he proved on, and it was so yielded by the King himself, and all his
sages, that neither wine nor women, nor the King, but truth, of all
other things was the strongest. For me, though neither asked, nor in
a nation that gives such rewards to wisdom, I shall pronounce my
sentence somewhat different from Zorobabel, and shall defend, that
either truth and justice are all one, for truth is but justice in our
knowledge, and justice is but truth in our practice, and he indeed
so explains himself in saying that with truth is no accepting of persons, which is the property of justice; or else, if there be any odds,
that justice, though not stronger than truth, yet by her office is to
put forth and exhibit more strength in the affairs of mankind. For
truth is properly no more than contemplation, and her utmost effi-
ciency is but teaching: but justice in her very essence is all strength

and activity, and hath a sword put into her hand to use against all violence and oppression on the earth. She it is most truly who accepts no person and exempts none from the severity of her stroke. She never suffers injury to prevail but when falsehood first prevails over truth; and that also is a kind of justice done on them who are so deluded. Though wicked kings and tyrants counterfeit her sword, as some did that buckler fabled to fall from heaven into the Capitol, yet she communicates her power to none but such as like herself are just, or at least will do justice. For it were extreme partiality and injustice, the flat denial and overthrow of herself, to put her own authentic sword into the hand of an unjust and wicked man, or so far to accept and exalt one mortal person above his equals that he alone shall have the punishing of all other men transgressing, and not receive like punishment from men when he himself shall be found the highest transgressor.

We may conclude therefore that justice, above all other things, is and ought to be the strongest: she is the strength, the kingdom, the power and majesty of all ages. Truth herself would subscribe to this, though Darius and all the monarchs of the world should deny. And if by sentence thus written it were my happiness to set free the minds of English men from longing to return poorly under that captivity of kings from which the strength and supreme sword of justice hath delivered them, I shall have done a work not much inferior to that of Zorobabel, who by well praising and extolling the force of truth, in that contemplative strength conquered Darius, and freed his country and the people of God from the captivity of Babylon. Which I shall yet not despair to do if they in this land whose minds are yet captive be but as ingenuous to acknowledge the strength and supremacy of justice as that heathen king was to confess the strength of truth: or let them but as he did, grant that, and they will soon perceive that truth resigns all her outward strength to justice: justice therefore must needs be strongest, both in her own and in the strength of truth. But if a king may do among men whatsoever is his will and pleasure, and notwithstanding be unaccountable to men, then contrary to this magnified wisdom of Zorobabel, neither truth nor justice, but the king, is strongest of all other things—which that Persian monarch himself in the midst of all his pride and glory durst not assume.

91. From the *First Defence*. 1651.

From the Latin.

> Milton states his aim in the *First Defence*, anticipating the estimate of it in the *Second Defence* (extract 129) upon the basis of which Grierson observes that Milton regarded the controversial writings as the fulfilment of his ambition to write a national epic. See also the epilogue to the second edition of the *First Defence* (extract 120) and Introduction, pp.xvii–xxi.

If I be as copious of words and empty of matter in my defence of the people of England as most men think Salmasius has been in his defence of the King, I fear that I shall apparently have deserved to be called a defender at once wordy and silly. Yet no man thinks he must make such haste, even in handling any ordinary subject, as not to employ an opening worthy of its importance. In handling well-nigh the greatest of all subjects then, if I neither omit an introduction, nor overdo it, I am in hopes of attaining two things, both of which I earnestly desire: the one, that I be nowise wanting, as far as in me lies, to this cause, most renowned and most worth the remembrance of all the generations of men; the other, that I myself be yet deemed to have avoided the silliness and verbosity which I blame in my antagonist.

For I shall relate no common things, or mean; but how a most puissant king, when he had trampled upon the laws, and stricken down religion, and was ruling at his own lust and wantonness, was at last subdued in the field by his own people, who had served a long term of slavery; how he was thereupon put under guard, and when he gave no ground whatever, by either word or action, to hope better things of him, was finally by the highest council of the realm condemned to die, and beheaded before his very palace gate. I shall likewise relate (which will much conduce to the easing men's minds of a great superstition) under what system of laws, especially what laws of England, this judgement was rendered and executed, and shall easily defend my valiant and worthy countrymen, who have extremely well deserved of all subjects and nations in the world, from the most wicked calumnies of both domestic and foreign railers, and chiefly from the reproaches of this utterly empty sophister who sets up to be captain and ringleader of all the rest.[17] For what king's majesty high enthroned ever shone so bright as did the people's majesty of England, when, shaking off that age-old superstition which had long prevailed, they overwhelmed with judgement their very king (or rather him who from their king had become their enemy), ensnared in his own laws him who alone among men claimed by divine right to go unpunished, and feared not to inflict upon this very culprit the same capital punishment which he would have inflicted upon any other.

Yet why do I proclaim as done by the people these actions, which themselves almost utter a voice, and witness everywhere the presence of God? Who, as often as it hath seemed good to His infinite wisdom, useth to cast down proud unbridled kings, puffed up above the measure of mankind, and often uprooteth them with their whole house. As for us, it was by His clear command we were on a sudden resolved upon the safety and liberty that we had almost lost; it was He we followed as our leader, and revered His divine footsteps imprinted everywhere; and thus we entered upon a path not dark but bright, and by His guidance shown and opened to us. I should be much in error if I hoped that by my diligence alone, such as it is, I might set forth all these matters as worthily as they deserve, and might make such records of them as, haply, all nations and all ages would read. For what eloquence can be august and magnificent enough, what man has parts sufficient, to undertake so great a task? Yea, since in so many ages as are gone over the world there has been but here and there a man found able to recount worthily the actions of great heroes and potent states, can any man have so good an opinion of himself as to think that by any style or language of his own he can compass these glorious and wonderful works—not of men, but, evidently, of almighty God?

17 Salmasius.

Yet such is the office which the most eminent men of our commonwealth have by their influence prevailed upon me to undertake, and have wished this next best task assigned to me of defending their deeds from envy and calumny, against which steel and the furniture of war avail not—of defending, I say, with far other arms and other weapons the works which under God's guidance they had gloriously wrought. Their decision, certainly, I count a great honour to myself—that they voted me before all others the one to render this never-to-be-regretted assistance to the valiant liberators of my country. And indeed from my youth upward I had been fired with a zeal which kept urging me, if not to do great deeds myself, at least to celebrate them.[18] Yet, mistrusting these advantages, I have

---

18 In the *Reason of Church Government* Milton says he has applied himself to the resolution 'to fix all the industry and art I could unite to the adorning of my native tongue . . . to be an interpreter and relater of the best and sagest things among mine own citizens throughout this island, in the mother dialect,' in order that he might do for England 'what the greatest and choicest wits of Athens, Rome, or modern Italy, and those Hebrews of old, did for their country . . .' (extract 1). Frequently throughout his works he speaks of the recorder of great deeds as, as truly to be called great as the doer of them. In the *Second Defence*, for example, he says that 'he alone deserves the appellation of great who either achieves great things himself, or teaches how they may be achieved, or who describes with suitable dignity the great achievements of others' (Columbia *Milton*, Vol. VIII, pp.95–97). Also in the *Second Defence*: 'I thought, therefore, that if it were the will of God those men should perform such gallant exploits, it must be likewise His will, that, when performed, there should be others to set them forth with becoming dignity and ornament' (extract 124). Alexander More did not miss the implication of these sentences; consequently in the *Defence of Himself* (extract 43) Milton finds it necessary to quote More's response and to exclaim upon it: 'What says our professor to this? That is, he remarks, who teaches great things "like Milton on the subject of divorce"; or who describes them with suitable dignity, "like the same Milton in his defence of the people; and he is here doubly great." A shrewd interpretation, More, no doubt, and evidently of a piece with your interpretation of that passage of the Gospel concerning divorce, which was given, however, not in words but in deeds.' Whereupon Milton returns to the Pontia episode.
   See also section VI, note 12.
   Cf. also the lines spoken by Christ in *Paradise Regained*, Book I, ll.201–207:

> When I was yet a child, no childish play
> To me was pleasing, all my mind was set
> Serious to learn and know, and thence to do,

recourse to the divine assistance, and pray the great and holy God, dispenser of all gifts: even as successfully and piously as those our glorious guides to freedom crushed in battle the royal insolence and tyranny uncontrolled, and then at last by a memorable punishment utterly ended them; even as easily as I, single-handed, lately refuted and set aside the King himself when he, as it were, rose from the grave and in that book published after his death tried to cry himself up before the people with new verbal sleights and harlotries;[19] so, I pray, may I now as auspiciously and as truly refute and demolish this outlandish rhetorician's wanton lies.

Foreign born as he is, and (though he deny it a thousand times) a mere grammarian, yet, not satisfied with the grammarian's dole, he has chosen to mind everybody's business, and has presumed to mix in an affair of state, a foreign state at that, though he brings to the task neither moderation, nor understanding, nor anything else that so grand a judge would surely need, save his presumption and his grammar. Indeed if he had published here, and in English, the same things as he now has writ in Latin (such as it is), I think scarce any man would have thought it worth while to return an answer to them, but would partly despise them as common and exploded over and over already, and partly (even one who sided with the King) abhor them as foul despotic maxims, hardly to be endured by the most worthless of slaves. But as he undertakes to puff his portentous sheet among outsiders, who are quite ignorant of our affairs, they, who thus get an utterly false notion of them, certainly ought to be fully informed; and he, who is so very forward to speak ill of others, should be treated in his own kind.

If haply anyone wonder why, then, we all have suffered him so

> What might be public good; myself I thought
> Born to that end, born to promote all truth,
> All righteous things: therefore above my years,
> The Law of God I read, and found it sweet. . . .

19 Throughout *Eikonoklastes*, and in other passages—e.g. in the *Second Defence* (extract 2)—, Milton expresses the doubts which he and his party had of the King's authorship of *Eikon Basilike*. In other places, here, occasionally in *Eikonoklastes*, and elsewhere, he accepts the fiction of the King's authorship and makes good use of it to enhance the seeming importance of his own work in answer to it.

long to strut unharmed, swollen in triumph at our silence, I know
not what others may say, but for myself I can boldly declare that I
had neither words nor arguments long to seek for the defence of so
good a cause, had I but found leisure and such health as could bear
the toil of writing. Yet as I still possess but slender strength, I am
forced to write by piecemeal, and break off almost every hour,
though the subject be such as requires unremitted study and attention.[20] If for this reason it be not given me to clarion with right he-
raldry, befitting their praises, those glorious fellow citizens of mine,
their country's saviours, whose deathless deeds already ring round
the world, yet I hope it will not be difficult for me to defend, at
least, and justify them, against the impertinence of this bore of a
pedant, and the squallings of his professorial tongue. Nature and
laws would be in ill case if slavery were eloquent and liberty mute; if
tyrants should find defenders, and they that are potent to master
and vanquish tyrants should find none. And it were deplorable indeed, if the reason mankind is endued withal, which is God's gift,
should not furnish more arguments for men's preservation, for
their deliverance, and, as much as the nature of the thing will bear,
for their equality, than for their oppression and utter ruin under
one man's dominion. Let me therefore enter upon this noble cause
with cheerfulness grounded upon the assurance that on the other
side are cheating, and trickery, and ignorance, and outlandishness,
and on my side the light of truth and reason, and the practice and
theory of the best historic ages.[21]

20 It was the writing of the *First Defence*, from which this extract is taken,
that finally completed Milton's blindness. His health was otherwise bad
also.
21 Extravagant as they are, the expressions in this passage of Milton's enthusiasm for his cause and of his pride in the part he played in it are more
moderate than many other similar expressions; e.g. in the epilogue to the
second edition of the *First Defence* (extract 120) and in the *Second Defence* (extracts 124 and 129). The despair that came to Milton in the failure
of the Commonwealth is given less explicit if not briefer statement, but
may be inferred from Milton's exultation during its successes and read between the lines of the great poems. It may also be found occasionally in
the letters and late pamphlets; e.g. in the *Ready and Easy Way to Establish a Free Commonwealth* (extracts 100 and 134) and in Familiar Letter
31, to Peter Heimbach (extract 157).

92. From the *Defence of Himself*. 1655.

From the Latin.

At the time when I first undertook to vindicate the cause of liberty [22]
I thought it would be no unheard of accident, nor from the very beginning was it at all foreign to my expectation, if I, who above the
rest had publicly applauded my fellow citizens as the deliverers of
their country, and had confounded the unlimited and mischievous
prerogative of tyrants, should have the hatred of all the unprincipled accumulated almost upon me alone. Englishmen! I foresaw,
likewise, that your contest with the enemy would not be long; but
that mine with the fugitives and their hirelings would be only not
everlasting; because those from whose hands you had wrested their
arms would therefore with the greater bitterness shower their curses
and their reproaches upon me. Against you, then, the fury and violence of the enemy have abated. To me, it seems, alone it remains to
terminate this war. These concluding attacks are indeed most con-
temptible; but like those from most low animals, they are full of
venom. As all who are over-curious about other people's concerns,
all who are mischievous and corrupt, whether among our own profligate citizens or among foreigners, fly upon me, who attend my
own duty only, upon me will they point their venom and their
stings. Whence it happens that I am not at liberty on the present
occasion to imitate the common practice of writers, with whom it is
usual to premise something in commendation of their work, with a
view to procure a favourable hearing, and thus to raise themselves
by degrees from what may be low or ordinary in their subjects to
those topics which may be of the greatest weight and importance.
On the contrary, I am now obliged to stoop from recounting achievements the most lofty and glorious to things of no note or lustre—to
trace out the lurking holes of the nameless, and the haunts and the
crimes of an adversary of the basest kind. Although this may appear
little creditable to one who is making a beginning, and still less

22 I.e. in the two defences of the people of England.

suited to gain the attention of the reader, yet, when we consider that the same thing has happened to the best and most illustrious of men, my situation, by presenting a parallel, is not without its circumstances of consolation. Even Scipio Africanus himself, after he had performed those exploits, than which nothing in that line of glory could be greater or more fortunate, after his affairs began to wane, which they continued to do without interruption, he seems always to have fed upon the substance of his own worth. At the outset of his career he was the first of generals, superior even to Hannibal; afterwards he was sent to combat the Syrian, an unwarlike enemy; then he was harassed by the insolence of the tribunes; and last of all he was constrained to fortify his own villa at Liternum against thieves and robbers: yet, throughout this decline of his fortune he is said to have been always the same, always equal to himself. Hence I am taught, as likewise from lessons derived from other sources, not to despise any condition or any office that may be allotted me by God, however humble it may be, or however inferior to what I before enjoyed. But as a good general (for why should we not imitate the good in every kind of excellence?) will do the duty of a good general against an enemy of any description; or, if this comparison be too invidious, as a good shoemaker (for thus philosophized a wise man of ancient times) will make the best shoe he is able of the leather he may happen to have in hand, so I will try, if, out of this shoe (for when I had resolved on it, I was ashamed to call it an argument), though now worn and unsewn, I cannot patch up something, at least, which the ears of my readers may not disdain. Still, I should have spared myself altogether this trouble if my enemy had not thrown out against me accusations and lies of such a nature as I could not endure should adhere as a stain and a suspicion to my character. Forced then of necessity to undertake this task, I trust I shall be pardoned by all, if, as heretofore I was not found wanting to the people and to the commonwealth, I shall now show that I am not wanting to myself.

93. From the *Defence of Himself*. 1655.

From the Latin.

The application of this passage is more particular than most of Milton's statements of literary aims, applying almost exclusively to his reasons for undertaking the *Defence of Himself*, not like the preceding extract upon the same subject to more general ambitions.

Hence, by stoutly denying that the book is yours, you [23] thought that my credit with respect to the other parts of your conduct would also be invalidated, at least for people at a distance, and that, on account of my credulity, and of the rash and injurious manner in which I had assailed you, your ignominy would in a great measure be removed. But if you failed in getting through with your denial as to the libel, you foresaw that the only alternative left you, however tart, however much against the grain, would be to return an answer, and that no very slight and superficial one, concerning your manners and scandalous behaviour. Nevertheless, if I cannot prove, if I cannot make it plain, either that you were the author of that notorious libel against us, or that you have given sufficient cause for being deservedly considered as the author, I refuse not to acknowledge myself vanquished by you in this cause, and ingloriously to retire with shame and dishonour. I do not even deprecate the imputation of any offence, whether it be of imprudence, of rashness, or of slander.

It is now two years since was published the opprobrious book entitled *The Cry of the Royal Blood to Heaven against the English Parricides*. In this book, the Commonwealth of England, and Cromwell in particular (who was at that time the leader of our armies, but who is now the first man in the state), are loaded with the grossest calumnies of which language can be the interpreter. Next after Cromwell (for thus it seemed good to the anonymous scribbler) the largest share of the abuse falls upon me. The book was scarcely complete in sheets before it was put into my hands in the Council. Soon after

23 Alexander More, denying the authorship of the *Cry*, in the *Public Faith of Alexander More*.

that sitting another copy is sent me by the person who was then president,[24] accompanied with the intimation that the Commonwealth expected my services to stop the mouth of this importunate crier. But at that time, in an especial manner, I was oppressed with concerns of a far different nature. My health was infirm, I was mourning the recent loss of two relatives,[25] the light had now utterly vanished from my eyes. Besides, my old adversary abroad,[26] a far more desirable one than the present, hovered for an attack, and now daily threatened to descend upon me with all his force. But considering myself relieved from a certain portion of my task by his sudden death, and being somewhat re-established in health by its being in part restored and in part desperate, that I might not appear as disappointing altogether the expectation of persons of the first consequence, and amid so many calamities to have abandoned all regard for reputation, as soon as an opportunity was given me of collecting any certain information concerning this anonymous crier, I commence my attack upon him.

94. From the *Defence of Himself*. 1655.

From the Latin.

Nor is it only a satire (as you call it) on you that I have written; but that all men may perceive how much more ready and studious I am to praise the good than to blame the bad, I have everywhere intermingled and copiously set forth the praises of some names of the highest renown, who by their arms and counsels had either wrought the signal deliverance of their country, or at least had shown favour to me when defending their achievements; for this also might serve to dignify the cause. Nor, moreover, will you ever be able to show, because I bestowed upon the most serene Queen of Sweden not praises indeed, but thanks rather, that this had nothing to do with the defence of the people of England, which she was reputed to hold

24 Colonel Purefoy.
25 Masson identifies the two as Milton's wife (Mary Powell) and his only
   son, John, then in his second year. *Life*, Vol. IV, p.468.
26 Salmasius.

in high estimation.[27] And what, lastly (which you object to me), if in a brief digression I should have praised myself? Who is there who would refuse to acknowledge that such times and very often such reasons may exist as would render self-commendation not unbecoming men of the most sanctified purity and modesty—and that it was never considered as unbecoming? Were I disposed to illustrate this fertile topic by an accumulation of examples, it would be an easy matter for me to prove this point to the satisfaction of mankind and to your confusion. But I have nowhere commended myself; nor will you anywhere find, what you have laid to my charge, that I have pronounced a panegyric on myself.[28] It is a singular favour of the divinity towards me that I above others was chosen out to defend the cause of liberty, which had been maintained with such dauntless valour; and this favour I must affirm I acknowledged; nor can the time ever come when it will cease to be my duty to acknowledge it; and that I took hence, which in my judgement can hardly be imputed to me as a fault, the noble matter of my exordium. And when assailed by that royal cry with every species of insult and calumny, being handled even as one of the lowest of the rabble, I defended myself not with commendations (though that had been no crime) against my contemptuous adversaries, but contented myself with a naked and simple narrative of facts.[29] Of what moment it was to the people of England, in whose defence I had enlisted myself, that I should not utterly neglect my reputation, and leave it to any, whoever they may be, to be disparaged and spurned, I was careful to show in my preface,[30] before I said anything of my-

---

27 The eulogy of Christina is in the *Second Defence*. See extract 126 and note 70 below.

28 Cf. the *Second Defence* (extract 124). There as here Milton tries to avoid the charge of writing a panegyric on himself by expressing his estimate of himself and his work in the form of thanks to God for his gifts and opportunities, and for his achievement: 'I return thanks to God that in a task so arduous, so full of expectation, I neither disappointed the hopes nor the opinions of my fellow citizens nor failed to satisfy no small number of foreigners. . . .' Much of the rest of the passage is devoted to the indirect explanation of how high the hopes and opinions of his fellow citizens were.   29 In the *Second Defence* (extract 2).

30 Extract 124. See also Introduction, pp.xvii–xviii.

self; and lastly, lest I should happen to give offence to any in this particular, I was at no small pains to obviate the cause. If, by reason of your envy and malice, you choose either not to read or not to remember these things, what remains for you but to raise a clamour? No other lie will be found in the title-page but what has been forged by your malice and slander. How much blacker a lie is the *Public Faith of Alexander More*! Do you presume to say that you wrote every part of your book as influenced by the public faith? You must of necessity assert this, or there is 'no faith in the front' of that book. Thus, what with your affectation in respect of your own title, and your malice in regard to mine, either the public faith through your fault has lost its front, or your front has lost its faith.

95. From *Of Civil Power in Ecclesiastical Causes*. 1659.

I have prepared, supreme Council, against the much expected time of your sitting, this treatise; which, though to all Christian magistrates equally belonging, and therefore to have been written in the common language of Christendom, natural duty and affection hath confined and dedicated first to my own nation: and in a season wherein the timely reading thereof to the easier accomplishment of your great work may save you much labour and interruption: of two parts usually proposed, civil and ecclesiastical, recommending civil only to your proper care, ecclesiastical to them only from whom it takes both that name and nature. Yet not for this cause only do I require or trust to find acceptance, but in a twofold respect besides: first, as bringing clear evidence of Scripture and Protestant maxims to the Parliament of England, who in all their late acts upon occasion have professed to assert only the true Protestant Christian religion as it is contained in the Holy Scriptures: next, in regard that your power being but for a time, and having in yourselves a Christian liberty of your own which at one time or other may be oppressed, thereof truly sensible, it will concern you while you are in power so to regard other men's consciences as you would your own should be regarded in the power of others, and to consider that any law against conscience is alike in force against any conscience, and so may one way or other justly redound upon your-selves. One advantage I make no doubt of, that I shall write to many eminent persons of your number already perfect and resolved in this important article of Christianity. Some of whom I remember to have heard often for several years, at a council next in authority to your own, so well joining religion with civil prudence, and yet so well distinguishing the different power of either, and this not only voting, but frequently reasoning why it should be so, that if any there present had been before of an opinion contrary, he might doubtless have departed thence a convert in that point, and have confessed that then both commonwealth and religion will at length, if ever, flourish in Christendom, when either they who govern dis-cern between civil and religious, or they only who so discern shall be admitted to govern. Till then nothing but troubles, persecutions, commotions can be expected: the inward decay of true religion among ourselves, and the utter overthrow at last by a common en-emy. Of civil liberty I have written heretofore by the appointment and not without the approbation of civil power:[31] of Christian liberty I write now, which others long since having done with all freedom under heathen emperors, I should do wrong to suspect that I now shall with less under Christian governors, and such especially as profess openly their defence of Christian liberty; although I write this not otherwise appointed or induced than by an inward persua-sion of the Christian duty which I may usefully discharge herein to the common Lord and Master of us all, and the certain hope of His approbation, first and chiefest to be sought: in the hand of whose providence I remain, praying all success and good event on your public councils to the defence of true religion and our civil rights.

John Milton.

96. From the *Likeliest Means to Remove Hirelings out of the Church*. 1659.

In the address to Parliament here, written in August 1659, is almost

31 In *Eikonoklastes*, the *Tenure of Kings and Magistrates*, and the three de-fences.

the last note in Milton of a genuine hope of the good time coming. By October, in the *Letter to a Friend concerning the Ruptures of the Commonwealth*, his hopes are definitely waning (extract 98), and in March 1660, in the *Ready and Easy Way to Establish a Free Commonwealth*, he has come to regard the days before the inevitable Restoration as a 'shroving-time' before a 'long Lent of servitude' (extract 100).

Owing to your protection, supreme Senate, this liberty of writing which I have used these eighteen years on all occasions to assert the just rights and freedoms both of church and state, and so far approved as to have been trusted with the representment and defence of your actions to all Christendom against an adversary of no mean repute,[32] to whom should I address what I still publish on the same argument but to you whose magnanimous councils first opened and unbound the age from a double bondage under prelatical and regal tyranny, above our own hopes heartening us to look up at last like men and Christians from the slavish dejection wherein from father to son we were bred up and taught, and thereby deserving of these nations, if they be not barbarously ingrateful, to be acknowledged next under God the authors and best patrons of religious and civil liberty that ever these islands brought forth. The care and tuition of whose peace and safety, after a short but scandalous night of interruption,[33] is now again by a new dawning of God's miraculous providence among us revolved upon your shoulders. And to whom more appertain these considerations which I propound than to yourselves and the debate before you, though I trust of no difficulty, yet at present of great expectation, not whether ye will gratify (were it no more than so) but whether ye will hearken to the just petition of many thousands best affected both to religion and to this your return, or whether ye will satisfy, which you never can, the covetous

32 Salmasius. Milton is writing of the three defences, perhaps particularly of the *First Defence*, which was specifically in reply to Salmasius.
33 The dissolution of Richard Cromwell's Parliament by the army, April 22, 1659. The Rump Parliament was restored May 7. Milton is here hailing the restoration of the Rump as a happy delivery from two weeks of military despotism.—Masson, *Life*, Vol. V, pp.605ff.

pretences and demands of insatiable hirelings, whose disaffection ye well know both to yourselves and your resolutions. That I, though among many others in this common concernment, interpose to your deliberations what my thoughts also are, your own judgement and the success thereof hath given me the confidence, which requests but this: that if I have prosperously, God so favouring me, defended the public cause of this commonwealth to foreigners,[34] ye would not think the reason and ability whereon ye trusted once, and repent not, your whole reputation to the world, either grown less by more maturity and longer study, or less available in English than in another tongue, but that if it sufficed some years past to convince and satisfy the unengaged of other nations in the justice of your doings, though then held paradoxal, it may as well suffice now against weaker opposition in matters, except here in England with a spiritualty of men devoted to their temporal gain, of no controversy else among Protestants. Neither do I doubt, seeing daily the acceptance which they find who in their petitions venture to bring advice also and new models of a commonwealth, but that you will interpret it much more the duty of a Christian to offer what his conscience persuades him may be of moment to the freedom and better constituting of the church: since it is a deed of highest charity to help undeceive the people, and a work worthiest your authority, in all things else authors, asserters, and now recoverers, of our liberty, to deliver us, the only people of all Protestants left still undelivered, from the oppressions of a simonious decimating clergy, who shame not, against the judgement and practice of all other churches reformed, to maintain, though very weakly, their Popish and oft refuted positions, not in a point of conscience, wherein they might be blameless, but in a point of covetousness and unjust claim to other men's goods—a contention foul and odious in any man, but most of all in ministers of the Gospel, in whom contention, though for their own right, scarce is allowable. Till which grievances be removed and re-

---

34 Again the reference is to the defences. It is almost impossible to over-estimate how highly Milton thought of them, how great a patriotic contribution he considered them.

ligion set free from the monopoly of hirelings, I dare affirm that
no model whatsoever of a commonwealth will prove successful or
undisturbed, and so persuaded, implore divine assistance on your
pious councils and proceedings to unanimity in this and all other
truth.

John Milton.

97. From the *Likeliest Means to Remove Hirelings out of the
Church.* 1659.

Another passage rather particular than general in its application.

The former treatise, which leads in this, began with two things ever
found working much mischief to the church of God and the advancement of truth: force on the one side restraining, and hire on
the other side corrupting, the teachers thereof.[35] The latter of these
is by much the more dangerous: for under force, though no thank to
the forcers, true religion oft-times best thrives and flourishes; but
the corruption of teachers, most commonly the effect of hire, is the
very bane of truth in them who are so corrupted. Of force not to be
used in matters of religion, I have already spoken, and so stated
matters of conscience and religion in faith and divine worship, and
so severed them from blasphemy and heresy, the one being such
properly as is despiteful, the other such as stands not to the rule of
Scripture, and so both of them not matters of religion, but rather
against it, that to them who will yet use force, this only choice can
be left: whether they will force them to believe to whom it is not
given from above, being not forced thereto by any principle of the
Gospel, which is now the only dispensation of God to all men; or
whether being Protestants, they will punish in those things wherein

35 In *Of Civil Power in Ecclesiastical Causes*: 'Two things there be which
have been ever found working much mischief to the church of God and
the advancement of truth: force on the one side restraining, and hire on
the other side corrupting, the teachers thereof. . . . The former shall be
at this time my argument; the latter as I shall find God disposing me,
and opportunity inviting.'—Columbia *Milton*, Vol. VI, p.4.

the Protestant religion denies them to be judges either in themselves infallible or to the consciences of other men; or whether, lastly, they think fit to punish error, supposing they can be infallible that it is so, being not wilful, but conscientious, and, according to the best light of him who errs, grounded on Scripture—which kind of error all men religious, or but only reasonable, have thought worthier of pardon, and the growth thereof to be prevented by spiritual means and church discipline, not by civil laws and outward force, since it is God only who gives as well to believe aright, as to believe at all, and by those means which He ordained sufficiently in His church to the full execution of His divine purpose in the Gospel. It remains now to speak of hire, the other evil so mischievous in religion, whereof I promised then to speak further when I should find God disposing me and opportunity inviting. Opportunity I find now inviting, and apprehend therein the concurrence of God disposing, since the maintenance of church-ministers, a thing not properly belonging to the magistrate, and yet with such importunity called for and expected from him, is at present under public debate. Wherein lest anything may happen to be determined and established prejudicial to the right and freedom of church, or advantageous to such as may be found hirelings therein, it will be now most seasonable, and in these matters wherein every Christian hath his free suffrage, no way misbecoming Christian meekness to offer freely, without disparagement to the wisest, such advice as God shall incline him and enable him to propound—since heretofore in commonwealths of most fame for government civil laws were not established till they had been first for certain days published to the view of all men, that who so pleased might speak freely his opinion thereof, and give in his exceptions, ere the law could pass to a full establishment. And where ought this equity to have more place than in the liberty which is unseparable from Christian religion? This, I am not ignorant, will be a work unpleasing to some: but what truth is not hateful to some or other, as this, in likelihood, will be to none but hirelings. And if there be among them who hold it their duty to speak impartial truth as the work of their ministry though not performed without money, let them not envy others who think the same no less their duty by the general office of Christianity, to speak truth, as in all reason may be thought, more impartially and unsuspectedly without money.

98. From the *Letter to a Friend concerning the Ruptures of the Commonwealth.* 1659.

Upon the sad and serious discourse which we fell into last night concerning these dangerous ruptures of the Commonwealth, scarce yet in her infancy, which cannot be without some inward flaw in her bowels, I began to consider more intensely thereon than hitherto I have been wont, resigning myself to the wisdom and care of those who had the government, and not finding that either God or the public required more of me than my prayers for them that govern.[36] And since you have not only stirred up my thoughts by acquainting me with the state of affairs more inwardly than I knew before, but also have desired me to set down my opinion thereof, trusting to your ingenuity, I shall give you freely my apprehension, both of our present evils, and what expedients, if God in mercy regard us, may remove them.

99. From the *Letter to a Friend concerning the Ruptures of the Commonwealth.* 1659.

The conclusion of the letter.

But unless these things which I have above proposed, one way or other be once settled, in my fear, which God avert, we instantly

---

36 Milton's political and ecclesiastical pamphlets were usually written in response to attacks upon himself, at the command of the Council, or at the call of conscience interpreted to be the command of God. It is as interesting to find Milton explaining that he has not written earlier because he has felt no 'call' as to find him, as elsewhere frequently, explaining that he writes in response to a call. Cf. *Of Civil Power* (extract 95), written in the same year. The occasion for the composition of the essay *Of Education* is exactly parallel to this, it also growing out of a conversation with a friend, Samuel Hartlib, and being written at the friend's request (extract 81). The present 'letter' was not published until 1698; the friend to whom it was addressed is unknown.

ruin, or at best become the servants of one or other single person, the secret author and fomenter of these disturbances. You have the sum of my present thoughts, as much as I understand of these affairs, freely imparted, at your request, and the persuasion you wrought in me that I might chance hereby to be some way serviceable to the Commonwealth in a time when all ought to be endeavouring what good they can, whether much or but little. With this you may do what you please, put out, put in, communicate or suppress: you offend not me, who only have obeyed your opinion that in doing what I have done I might happen to offer something which might be of some use in this great time of need. However, I have not been wanting to the opportunity which you presented before me of showing the readiness which I have in the midst of my unfitness to whatever may be required of me as a public duty.

October 20, 1659.

100. From the *Ready and Easy Way to Establish a Free Commonwealth*. 1660.

Although since the writing of this treatise the face of things hath had some change, writs for new elections have been recalled, and the members at first chosen readmitted from exclusion,[37] yet not a little rejoicing to hear declared the resolution of those who are in power, tending to the establishment of a free commonwealth, and to remove, if it be possible, this noxious humour of returning to bondage instilled of late by some deceivers and nourished from bad principles and false apprehensions among too many of the people, I thought best not to suppress what I had written, hoping that it may now be of much more use and concernment to be freely published in the midst of our elections to a free parliament or their sitting to consider freely of the government, whom it behoves to have

37 The *Ready and Easy Way* appeared in February 1660, though dated March 3, just after General Monk had cancelled the writ for a new election and reshaped the Long Parliament by restoring the members excluded in 1648. Milton had written before this restoration, which was a great blow to his own hopes for the future of the Commonwealth, but published his pamphlet nevertheless, sending it to General Monk.

all things represented to them that may direct their judgement
therein; and I never read of any state, scarce of any tyrant grown so
incurable, as to refuse counsel from any in a time of public delibera-
tion, much less to be offended. If their absolute determination be
to enthral us, before so long a Lent of servitude they may permit us
a little shroving-time first, wherein to speak freely and take our
leaves of liberty. And because in the former edition through haste
many faults escaped, and many books were suddenly dispersed ere
the note to mend them could be sent, I took the opportunity from
this occasion to revise and somewhat to enlarge the whole discourse,
especially that part which argues for a perpetual senate.[38] The treatise thus revised and enlarged is as follows.

101. From *Brief Notes upon a Sermon*, '*The Fear of God and the
King.*' 1660.

The *Brief Notes* appeared in April 1660, the same month as the second
edition of the *Ready and Easy Way*, in answer to a Royalist sermon
preached by Dr. Matthew Griffith and published with a dedication
to General Monk urging him that 'it is a greater honour to make a
king than to be one.' Griffith was given the double punishment of
imprisonment in Newgate because his publication was unauthor-
ized and ill-timed and therefore embarrassing to General Monk,
and of Milton's *Brief Notes* because Milton needed a whipping-
boy for a last attack upon the kingship. The time was so confused
that anti-Royalist pamphlets like Milton's were equally likely to
endanger their authors.

I affirmed in the preface of a late discourse, entitled *The Ready Way
to Establish a Free Commonwealth, and the Dangers of Readmitting
Kingship in this Nation*, that 'the humour of returning to our old
bondage was instilled of late by some deceivers'; and to make good
that what I then affirmed was not without just ground, one of those
deceivers I present here to the people: and if I prove him not such,
refuse not to be so accounted in his stead.

38 The present extract is from the second edition of the *Ready and Easy
Way*, published in April 1660, and addressed not to General Monk but
to the parliament that in less than a month was to vote the restoration of

102. From the *Christian Doctrine*. 1655–1660.

From the Latin.

Perhaps no other passage in Milton reveals so unselfconsciously his awareness of his high mission and of the visiting spirit of prophecy as the address to the world prefixed to the *Christian Doctrine*. Saurat, who makes more than enough of Milton's egotism, observes 'that Milton will end by identifying himself with God, being the spokesman and indeed a very part of the Divinity.'[39]

John Milton, Englishman, to all the churches of Christ and to all who profess the Christian faith throughout the world: peace, and the recognition of the truth, and eternal salvation in God the Father, and in our Lord Jesus Christ.

Since the commencement of the last century, when religion began to be restored from the corruptions of more than thirteen hundred years to something of its original purity, many treatises of theology have been published, conducted according to sounder principles, wherein the chief heads of Christian doctrine are set forth sometimes briefly, sometimes in a more enlarged and methodical order. I think myself obliged, therefore, to declare in the first instance why, if any works have already appeared as perfect as the nature of the subject will admit, I have not remained contented with them— or, if all my predecessors have treated it unsuccessfully, why their failure has not deterred me from attempting an undertaking of a similar kind.

If I were to say that I had devoted myself to the study of the Christian religion because nothing else can so effectually rescue the lives and minds of men from those two detestable curses, slavery and superstition, I should seem to have acted rather from a regard to my highest earthly comforts than from a religious motive.

But since it is only to the individual faith of each that the Deity

the Stuarts. Milton is quite aware of the futility of writing, and later in the pamphlet (extract 134) shows that he is aware also of the danger.
39 Denis Saurat, *Milton: Man and Thinker*, p.48, New York, 1935.

has opened the way of eternal salvation, and as He requires that he who would be saved should have a personal belief of his own, I resolved not to repose on the faith or judgement of others in matters relating to God; but on the one hand, having taken the grounds of my faith from divine revelation alone, and on the other, having neglected nothing which depended on my own industry, I thought fit to scrutinize and ascertain for myself the several points of my religious belief by the most careful perusal and meditation of the Holy Scriptures themselves.

If therefore I mention what has proved beneficial in my own practice, it is in the hope that others who have a similar wish of improving themselves, may be thereby invited to pursue the same method. I entered upon an assiduous course of study in my youth, beginning with the books of the Old and New Testament in their original languages, and going diligently through a few of the shorter systems of divines, in imitation of whom I was in the habit of classing under certain heads whatever passages of Scripture occurred for extraction, to be made use of hereafter as occasion might require. At length I resorted with increased confidence to some of the more copious theological treatises and to the examination of the arguments advanced by the conflicting parties respecting certain disputed points of faith. But, to speak the truth with freedom as well as candour, I was concerned to discover in many instances adverse reasonings either evaded by wretched shifts or attempted to be refuted rather speciously than with solidity by an affected display of formal sophisms or by a constant recourse to the quibbles of the grammarians, while what was most pertinaciously espoused as the true doctrine seemed often defended with more vehemence than strength of argument by misconstructions of Scripture or by the hasty deduction of erroneous inferences. Owing to these causes, the truth was sometimes as strenuously opposed as if it had been an error or a heresy—while errors and heresies were substituted for the truth, and valued rather from deference to custom and the spirit of party than from the authority of Scripture.

According to my judgement, therefore, neither my creed nor my hope of salvation could be safely trusted to such guides; and yet it appeared highly requisite to possess some methodical tractate of Christian doctrine, or at least to attempt such a disquisition as might be useful in establishing my faith or assisting my memory. I deemed it therefore safest and most advisable to compile for myself, by my own labour and study, some original treatise, which should be always at hand, derived solely from the word of God itself, and executed with all possible fidelity, seeing that I could have no wish to practice any imposition on myself in such a matter.

After a diligent perseverance in this plan for several years, I perceived that the strongholds of the reformed religion were sufficiently fortified as far as it was in danger from the Papists, but neglected in many other quarters—neither competently strengthened with works of defence, nor adequately provided with champions. It was also evident to me that, in religion as in other things, the offers of God were all directed, not to an indolent credulity, but to constant diligence and to an unwearied search after truth, and that more than I was aware of still remained which required to be more rigidly examined by the rule of Scripture and reformed after a more accurate model. I so far satisfied myself in the prosecution of this plan as at length to trust that I had discovered, with regard to religion, what was matter of belief and what only matter of opinion. It was also a great solace to me to have compiled, by God's assistance, a precious aid for my faith—or rather to have laid up for myself a treasure which would be a provision for my future life and would remove from my mind all grounds for hesitation as often as it behoved me to render an account of the principles of my belief.

If I communicate the result of my inquiries to the world at large; if, as God is my witness, it be with a friendly and benignant feeling towards mankind that I readily give as wide a circulation as possible to what I esteem my best and richest possession, I hope to meet with a candid reception from all parties, and that none at least will take unjust offence, even though many things should be brought to light which will at once be seen to differ from certain received opinions. I earnestly beseech all lovers of truth, not to cry out that the church is thrown into confusion by that freedom of discussion and inquiry which is granted to the schools, and ought certainly to be refused to no believer, since we are ordered 'to prove all things,' and since the daily progress of the light of truth is productive far less of disturbance to the church, than of illumination and edification. Nor do I see how the church can be more disturbed by the investigation of truth than were the Gentiles by the first promulgation of the Gospel, since so far from recommending or imposing anything on my own authority, it is my particular advice that everyone should suspend his opinion, on whatever points he may not feel himself fully satisfied, till the evidence of Scripture prevail and persuade his reason into assent and faith. Concealment is not my object; it is to the learned that I address myself, or if it be thought that the learned are not the best umpires and judges of such things, I should at least wish to submit my opinions to men of a mature and manly understanding, possessing a thorough knowledge of the doctrines of the Gospel, on whose judgements I should rely with far more confidence than on those of novices in these matters. And whereas the greater part of those who have written most largely on these subjects have been wont to fill whole pages with explanations of their own opinions, thrusting into the margin the texts in support of their doctrine with a summary reference to the chapter and verse, I have chosen, on the contrary, to fill my pages even to redundance with quotations from Scripture, that so as little space as possible might be left for my own words, even when they arise from the context of revelation itself.

It has also been my object to make it appear from the opinions I shall be found to have advanced, whether new or old, of how much consequence to the Christian religion is the liberty not only of winnowing and sifting every doctrine, but also of thinking and even writing respecting it, according to our individual faith and persuasion: an inference which will be stronger in proportion to the weight and importance of those opinions, or rather in proportion to the authority of Scripture, on the abundant testimony of which they rest. Without this liberty there is neither religion nor Gospel—force

alone prevails, by which it is disgraceful for the Christian religion to
be supported. Without this liberty we are still enslaved, not indeed,
as formerly, under the divine law, but, what is worst of all, under
the law of man, or to speak more truly, under a barbarous tyranny.
But I do not expect from candid and judicious readers a conduct so
unworthy of them—that like certain unjust and foolish men they
should stamp with the invidious name of heretic or heresy whatever appears to them to differ from the received opinions without
trying the doctrine by a comparison with Scripture testimonies. According to their notions, to have branded anyone at random with
this opprobrious mark is to have refuted him without any trouble,
by a single word. By the simple imputation of the name of heretic,
they think that they have dispatched their man at one blow. To men
of this kind I answer, that in the time of the apostles, ere the New
Testament was written, whenever the charge of heresy was applied
as a term of reproach, that alone was considered as heresy which
was at variance with their doctrine orally delivered—and that those
only were looked upon as heretics who according to Rom. xvi, 17,
18, 'caused divisions and offences contrary to the doctrine' of the
apostles, 'serving not our Lord Jesus Christ, but their own belly.'
By parity of reasoning therefore, since the compilation of the New
Testament, I maintain that nothing but what is in contradiction to it
can properly be called heresy.

For my own part, I adhere to the Holy Scriptures alone—I follow no other heresy or sect. I had not even read any of the works of
heretics, so called, when the mistakes of those who are reckoned for
orthodox, and their incautious handling of Scripture, first taught me
to agree with their opponents whenever those opponents agreed
with Scripture. If this be heresy, I confess with St. Paul, Acts xxiv,
14, 'that after the way which they call heresy, so worship I the God
of my fathers, believing all things which are written in the law and
the prophets'—to which I add, whatever is written in the New Testament. Any other judges or paramount interpreters of the Christian
belief, together with all implicit faith, as it is called, I, in common
with the whole Protestant Church, refuse to recognize.

For the rest, brethren, cultivate truth with brotherly love. Judge of my present undertaking according to the admonishing of the Spirit of God—and neither adopt my sentiments nor reject them, unless every doubt has been removed from your belief by the clear testimony of revelation. Finally, live in the faith of our Lord and Saviour Jesus Christ. Farewell.

J.M.

Milton also discusses his aims and motives as prose-writer and pamphleteer in extracts 1, 2, 43, 46, 65, 71, 72, 103–105, 107, 109, 111–113, 119, 123–126, 131, *and* 134.

B. METHODS AND PRACTICES

Of mere necessity.

103. From *Of Reformation in England.* 1641.

Although anticipated by the apology for vulgarity in the Sixth Prolusion (extract 38), this is the first of Milton's many apologies for
violence in his pamphlets. It is the type and pattern of them all; he
writes as he does 'of mere necessity,' in order 'to vindicate the
spotless truth.'

AND herewithal I invoke the immortal Deity, Revealer and Judge of secrets, that wherever I have in this book plainly and roundly (though worthily and truly) laid open the faults and blemishes of fathers, martyrs, or Christian emperors, or have otherwise inveighed against error and superstition with vehement expressions, I have done it neither out of malice, nor list to speak evil, nor any vain-glory, but of mere necessity, to vindicate the spotless truth from an ignominious bondage. . . .

104. From *Animadversions upon the Remonstrant's Defence against Smectymnuus.* 1641.

The preface.

Although it be a certain truth that they who undertake a religious cause need not care to be men-pleasers, yet because the satisfaction of tender and mild consciences is far different from that which is called men-pleasing, to satisfy such, I shall address myself in few words to give notice beforehand of something in this book which to some men perhaps may seem offensive, that when I have rendered a lawful reason of what is done, I may trust to have saved the labour of defending or excusing hereafter. We all know that in private and personal injuries, yea in public sufferings for the cause of Christ, His rule and example teaches us to be so far from a readiness to speak evil as not to answer the reviler in his language though never so much provoked. Yet in the detecting and convincing of any notorious enemy to truth and his country's peace, especially that is conceited to have a voluble and smart fluence of tongue, and in the vain confidence of that, and out of a more tenacious cling to worldly respects, stands up for all the rest to justify a long usurpation and convicted pseudepiscopy of prelates, with all their ceremonies, liturgies, and tyrannies, which God and man are now ready to explode and hiss out of the land, I suppose and more than suppose, it will be nothing disagreeing from Christian meekness to handle such a one in a rougher accent, and to send home his haughtiness well bespurted with his own holy water. Nor to do thus are we unauthoritied either from the moral precept of Solomon to answer him thereafter that prides him in his folly, nor from the example of Christ and all His followers in all ages, who in the refuting of those that resisted sound doctrine and by subtle dissimulations corrupted the minds of men, have wrought up their zealous souls into such vehemencies as nothing could be more killingly spoken: for who can be a greater enemy to mankind, who a more dangerous deceiver, than he who defending a traditional corruption uses no common arts, but with a wily stratagem of yielding to the time a greater part of his cause, seeming to forego all that man's invention hath done therein, and driven from much of his hold in Scripture, yet leaving it hanging by a twined thread, not from divine command but from apostolical prudence or assent, as if he had the surety of some rolling trench, creeps up by this means to his relinquished fortress of divine authority again; and still hovering between the confines of that which he dares not be openly, and that which he will not be sincerely, trains on the easy Christian insensibly within the close ambushment of worst errors, and with a sly shuffle of counterfeit principles chopping and changing till he have gleaned all the good ones out of their minds, leaves them at last, after a slight resemblance of sweeping and garnishing under the sevenfold possession of a desperate stupidity. And therefore they that love the souls of men, which is the dearest love and stirs up the noblest jealousy, when they meet with such collusion cannot be blamed though they be transported with the zeal of truth to a well-heated fervency; especially, seeing they which thus offend against the souls of their brethren, do it with delight to their great gain, ease, and advancement in this world, but they that seek to discover and oppose their false trade of deceiving, do it not without a sad and unwilling anger, not without many hazards, but without all private and personal spleen, and without any thought of earthly reward, whenas this very course they take stops their hopes of ascending above a lowly and unenviable pitch in this life. And although in the serious uncasing of a grand imposture (for to deal plainly with you, readers, prelatry is no better) there be mixed here and there such grim laughter as may appear at the same time in an austere visage, it cannot be taxed of levity or insolence: for even this vein of laughing (as I could produce out of grave authors) hath oft-times a strong and sinewy force in teaching and confuting; nor can there be a more proper object of indignation and scorn together than a false prophet taken in the greatest, dearest, and most dangerous cheat, the cheat of souls: in the disclosing whereof if it be harmful to be angry, and withal to cast a louring smile, when the properest object calls for both, it will be long enough ere any be able to say why those two most rational faculties of human intellect, anger and laughter, were first seated in the breast of man. Thus much, readers, in favour of the softer spirited Christian; for other exceptioners there was no thought taken. Only if it be asked why this close and succinct manner of coping with the adversary was rather chosen, [40] this was the reason, chiefly that the ingenuous reader without further amusing himself in the labyrinth of controversal antiquity, may come the speediest way to see the truth vindicated and sophistry taken short at the first false bound. Next that the remonstrant himself as oft as he pleases to be frolic and brave it with others may find no gain of money, and may learn not to insult in so bad a cause. But now he begins.

105. From *An Apology for Smectymnuus*. 1642.

If, readers, to that same great difficulty of well doing what we certainly know, were not added in most men as great a carelessness of knowing what they and others ought to do, we had been long ere this, no doubt but all of us, much farther on our way to some degree of peace and happiness in this kingdom. But since our sinful neglect of practising that which we know to be undoubtedly true and good hath brought forth among us, through God's just anger, so great a difficulty now to know that which otherwise might be soon learned, and hath divided us by a controversy of great importance indeed, but of no hard solution, which is the more our punishment, I resolved (of what small moment soever I might be thought) to stand on that side where I saw both the plain authority of Scripture leading and the reason of justice and equity persuading, with this opinion which esteems it more unlike a Christian to be a cold neuter in the cause of the church, than the law of Solon made it punishable after a sedition in the state. And because I observe that fear and dull disposition, lukewarmness and sloth, are not seldomer wont to cloak themselves under the affected name of moderation than true and lively zeal is customably disparaged with the term of indiscretion, bitterness, and choler, I could not, to my thinking, honour a good cause more from the heart than by defending it earnestly as oft as I could judge it to behove me, notwithstanding any false name

40 Milton's method in the *Animadversions* is to quote out of context sentences and fragments from Hall's *Defence of the Humble Remonstrance against the Frivolous and False Exceptions of Smectymnuus* and attach to each quotation some sarcastic or merely insulting remark.

that could be invented to wrong or undervalue an honest meaning. Wherein, although I have not doubted to single forth more than once such of them as were thought the chief and most nominated opposers on the other side, whom no man else undertook, if I have done well either to be confident of the truth, whose force is best seen against the ablest resistance, or to be jealous and tender of the hurt that might be done among the weaker by the entrapping authority of great names titled to false opinions, or that it be lawful to attribute somewhat to gifts of God's imparting, which I boast not, but thankfully acknowledge, and fear also lest at my certain account they be reckoned to me many rather than few, or if lastly it be but justice not to defraud of due esteem the wearisome labours and studious watchings wherein I have spent and tired out almost a whole youth, I shall not distrust to be acquitted of presumption. Knowing that if heretofore all ages have received with favour and good acceptance the earliest industry of him that hath been hopeful, it were but hard measure now if the freedom of any timely spirit should be oppressed merely by the big and blunted fame of his elder adversary, and that his sufficiency must be now sentenced, not by pondering the reason he shows, but by calculating the years he brings.[41] However, as my purpose is not, nor hath been formerly, to look on my adversary[42] abroad through the deceiving glass of other men's great opinion of him, but at home, where I may find him in the proper light of his own worth, so now against the rancour of an evil tongue, from which I never thought so absurdly as that I of all

41 Here, as in the *Reason of Church Government*, also written when Milton was thirty-three, Milton is concerned to anticipate objections to his fitness for his task because of his youth. There is no recurrence of his own dismay at his 'late flowering.' Even though in the *Reason of Church Government* (extract 1; see also extract 70) he speaks of himself as writing out of his own season, before he has completed the full circle of his studies, he 'complains not of any insufficiency to the matter in hand,' and here he is confident of the fruit of a youth spent in 'wearisome labours and studious watchings.' Below in the present extract Milton observes that the office of protesting against such deceivers as the prelates 'goes not by age or youth, but to whomsoever God shall give apparently the will, the spirit, and the utterance.' It is only for his appointed work as epic poet that Milton is yet unready.

42 Bishop Hall. See headnote, extract 41.

men should be exempt, I must be forced to proceed from the unfeigned and diligent inquiry of mine own conscience at home (for
better way I know not, readers) to give a more true account of myself abroad than this modest confuter, as he calls himself, hath
given of me. Albeit that in doing this I shall be sensible of two
things which to me will be nothing pleasant: the one is that not un-
likely I shall be thought too much a party in mine own cause, and
therein to see least; the other, that I shall be put unwillingly to mo-
lest the public view with the vindication of a private name; as if it
were worth the while that the people should care whether such a
one were thus, or thus. Yet those I entreat who have found the
leisure to read that name, however of small repute, unworthily defamed, would be so good and so patient as to hear the same person
not unneedfully defended. I will not deny but that the best apology
against false accusers is silence and sufferance, and honest deeds set
against dishonest words. And that I could at this time most easily
and securely, with the least loss of reputation, use no other defence,
I need not despair to win belief. Whether I consider both the foolish
contriving and ridiculous aiming of these his slanderous bolts, shot
so wide of any suspicion to be fastened on me that I have oft with
inward contentment perceived my friends congratulating themselves in my innocence, and my enemies ashamed of their partner's
folly; or whether I look at these present times wherein most men,
now scarce permitted the liberty to think over their own concern-
ments, have removed the seat of their thoughts more outward to the
expectation of public events; or whether the examples of men, either
noble or religious, who have sat down lately with a meek silence and
sufferance under many libellous endorsements, may be a rule to
others, I might well appease myself to put up any reproaches in
such an honourable society of fellow-sufferers, using no other defence. And were it that slander would be content to make an end
where it first fixes, and not seek to cast out the like infamy upon
each thing that hath but any relation to the person traduced, I
should have pleaded against this confuter by no other advocates
than those which I first commended, silence, and sufferance, and

speaking deeds against faltering words. But when I discerned his intent was not so much to smite at me, as through me to render odious the truth which I had written, and to stain with ignominy that evangelic doctrine which opposes the tradition of prelaty, I conceived myself to be now not as mine own person, but as a member incorporate into that truth whereof I was persuaded and whereof I had declared openly to be a partaker.[43] Whereupon I thought it my duty, if not to myself, yet to the religious cause I had in hand, not to leave on my garment the least spot or blemish in good name so long as God should give me to say that which might wipe it off; lest those disgraces which I ought to suffer, if it so befall me, for my religion, through my default, religion be made liable to suffer for me. And whether it might not something reflect upon those reverent men whose friend I may be thought in writing the *Animadversions*,[44] was not my last care to consider; if I should rest under these reproaches, having the same common adversary with them, it might be counted small credit for their cause to have found such an assistant as this babbler hath devised me. What other thing in his book there is of dispute or question, in answering thereto I doubt not to be justified; except there be who will condemn me to have wasted time in throwing down that which could not keep itself up. As for others who notwithstanding what I can allege have yet decreed to misinterpret the intents of my reply, I suppose they would have found as many causes to have misconceived the reasons of my silence.

To begin therefore an apology for those animadversions which I writ against the remonstrant in defence of Smectymnuus, since the preface which was purposely set before them is not thought apologetical enough,[45] it will be best to acquaint ye, readers, before other things, what the meaning was to write them in that manner which I did. For I do not look to be asked wherefore I writ the book, it being no difficulty to answer that I did it to those ends which the best men

43 See Introduction, pp.xvii–xviii.
44 The Smectymnuans, Young and his collaborators.
45 Extract 104.

propose to themselves when they write. But wherefore in that manner neglecting the main bulk of all that specious antiquity which
might stun children, but not men, I chose rather to observe some
kind of military advantages, to await him at his foragings, at his
waterings, and whenever he felt himself secure to solace his vein in
derision of his more serious opponents. And here let me have pardon, readers, if the remembrance of that which he hath licensed
himself to utter contemptuously of those reverend men provoke me
to do that over again which some expect I should excuse as too
freely done; since I have two provocations, his latest insulting in his
short answer, and their final patience. I had no fear but that the
authors of *Smectymnuus*, to all the show of solidity which the remonstrant could bring, were prepared both with skill and purpose
to return a sufficing answer, and were able enough to lay the dust
and pudder in antiquity which he and his, out of stratagem, are
wont to raise; but when I saw his weak arguments headed with
sharp taunts, and that his design was, if he could not refute them,
yet at least with quips and snapping adages to vapour them out,
which they bent only upon the business were minded to let pass, by
how much I saw them taking little thought for their own injuries, I
must confess I took it as my part the less to endure that my respected friends through their own unnecessary patience should thus
lie at the mercy of a coy flirting style, to be girded with frumps and
curtal gibes by one who makes sentences by the statute, as if all
above three inches long were confiscate. To me it seemed an indig-
nity, that whom his whole wisdom could not move from their place,
them his impetuous folly should presume to ride over. And if I were
more warm than was meet in any passage of that book, which yet I
do not yield, I might use therein the patronage of no worse an
author than Gregory Nyssen, who mentioning his sharpness against
Eunomius in the defence of his brother Basil, holds himself irre-
provable in that it 'was not for himself, but in the cause of his
brother; and in such cases,' saith he, 'perhaps it is worthier pardon
to be angry, than to be cooler.' And whereas this confuter taxes the
whole discourse of levity, I shall show ye, readers, wheresoever it

shall be objected in particular that I have answered with as little lightness as the remonstrant hath given example. I have not been so light as the palm of a bishop, which is the lightest thing in the world when he brings out his book of ordination: for then, contrary to that which is wont in releasing out of prison, anyone that will pay his fees is laid hands on.[46] Another reason (it would not be amiss though the remonstrant were told) wherefore he was in that unusual manner beleaguered—and this was it: to pluck out of the heads of his admirers the conceit that all who are not prelatical are gross-headed, thick witted, illiterate, shallow. Can nothing then but episcopacy teach men to speak good English, to pick and order a set of words judiciously? Must we learn from canons and quaint sermonings interlined with barbarous Latin to illumine a period, to wreathe an enthymeme with masterous dexterity? I rather incline— as I have heard it observed that a Jesuit's Italian when he writes is ever naught, though he be born and bred a Florentine—so to think that from like causes we may go near to observe the same in the style of a prelate. For doubtless that indeed according to art is most eloquent which returns and approaches nearest to nature from whence it came; and they express nature best who in their lives least wander from her safe leading, which may be called regenerate reason. So that how he should be truly eloquent who is not withal a good man, I see not.[47] Nevertheless as oft as is to be dealt with men who pride themselves in their supposed art, to leave them unexcusable wherein they will not be bettered, there be of those that esteem prelaty a figment who yet can pipe, if they can dance, nor will be unfurnished to show that what the prelates admire and have not, others have and admire not. The knowledge whereof, and not of that only, but of what the Scripture teacheth us how we ought to withstand the perverters of the Gospel, were those other motives

46 The remark is personal; the 'Modest Confuter,' is a bishop.
47 Cf. elsewhere in *An Apology for Smectymnuus* (extract 41): '. . . he who would not be frustrate of his hope to write well hereafter in laudable things, ought himself to be a true poem, that is, a composition and pattern of the best and honourablest things. . . .' See also section VI, note 12.

which gave the animadversions no leave to remit a continual vehemence throughout the book. For as in teaching, doubtless the
spirit of meekness is most powerful, so are the meek only fit persons
to be taught: as for the proud, the obstinate, and false doctors of
men's devices, be taught they will not; but discovered and laid open
they must be. For how can they admit of teaching who have the con-
demnation of God already upon them for refusing divine instruction; that is, to be 'filled with their own devices,' as in the Proverbs
we may read; therefore we may safely imitate the method that God
uses; 'with the froward to be froward, and to throw scorn upon the
scorner,' whom if anything, nothing else will heal. And if 'the
righteous shall laugh at the destruction of the ungodly,' they may
also laugh at their pertinacious and incurable obstinacy, and at the
same time be moved with detestation of their seducing malice, who
employ all their wits to defend a prelaty usurped and to deprave that
just government which pride and ambition, partly by fine fetches
and pretences, partly by force, hath shouldered out of the church.
And against such kind of deceivers openly and earnestly to protest,
lest anyone should be inquisitive wherefore this or that man is for-
warder than others, let him know that this office goes not by age or
youth, but to whomsoever God shall give apparently the will, the
spirit, and the utterance.[48] Ye have heard the reasons for which I
thought not myself exempted from associating with good men in
their labours toward the church's welfare: to which if anyone
brought opposition, I brought my best resistance. If in requital of
this and for that I have not been negligent toward the reputation of
my friends, I have gained a name bestuck, or as I may say, bedecked
with the reproaches and reviles of this modest confuter, it shall be
to me neither strange nor unwelcome, as that which could not come
in a better time.

106. From the *Judgement of Martin Bucer concerning Divorce*. 1644.

Thus far Martin Bucer, whom, where I might without injury to
either part of the cause, I deny not to have epitomized, in the rest

48 See note 41 above.

observing a well-warranted rule, not to give an inventory of so many words, but to weigh their force. I could have added that eloquent and right Christian discourse written by Erasmus on this argument, not disagreeing in effect from Bucer. But this, I hope, will be enough to excuse me with the mere Englishman to be no forger of new and loose opinions. Others may read him in his own phrase on the first to the Corinthians, and ease me who never could delight in long citations, much less in whole traductions—[49] whether it be natural disposition or education in me, or that my mother bore me a speaker of what God made mine own, and not a translator. There be others also whom I could reckon up, of no mean account in the church (and Peter Martyr among the first), who are more than half our own in this controversy. But this is a providence not to be slighted, that as Bucer wrote this tractate of divorce in England and for England, so Erasmus professes he begun here among us the same subject, especially out of compassion for the need he saw this nation had of some charitable redress herein, and seriously exhorts others to use their best industry in the clearing of this point, wherein custom hath a greater sway than verity. That therefore which came into the mind of these two admired strangers to do for England, and in a touch of highest prudence, which they took to be not yet recovered from monastic superstition, if I a native am found to have done for mine own country, altogether suitably and conformly to their so large and clear understanding, yet without the least help of theirs, I suppose that henceforward among conscionable and judicious persons, it will no more be thought to my discredit or at all to this nation's dishonour. And if these their books, the one shall be printed often, with best allowance in most religious cities, the other with express authority of Leo the Tenth, a pope, shall for the propagating of truth be published and republished, though against the received opinion of that church, and mine containing but the same thing, shall in a time of reformation, a time of free speaking, free

49 In *An Apology for Smectymnuus* (extract 150): 'Be not deceived, readers, by men that would overawe your ears with big names and huge tomes that contradict and repeal one another, because they can cram a margent with citations.'

writing, not find a permission to the press, I refer me to wisest men, whether truth be suffered to be truth, or liberty to be liberty now among us, and be not again in danger of new fetters and captivity after all our hopes and labours lost: and whether learning be not (which our enemies too prophetically feared) in the way to be trodden down again by ignorance.[50] Whereof while time is, out of the faith owing to God and my country, I bid this kingdom beware, and doubt not but God, who hath dignified this parliament already to so many glorious degrees, will also give them (which is a singular blessing) to inform themselves rightly in the midst of an unprincipled age, and to prevent this working mystery of ignorance and ecclesiastical thraldom which under new shapes and disguises begins afresh to grow upon us.

107. From *Tetrachordon*. 1645.

That which I knew to be the part of a good magistrate, aiming at true liberty through the right information of religious and civil life, and that which I saw and was partaker of, your vows and solemn covenants, Parliament of England, your actions also manifestly tending to exalt the truth, and to depress the tyranny of error and ill custom, with more constancy and prowess than ever yet any since that parliament which put the first sceptre of this kingdom into his hand whom God and extraordinary virtue made their monarch, were the causes that moved me, one else not placing much in the eminence of a dedication, to present your high notice with a discourse, conscious to itself of nothing more than of diligence and firm affection to the public good. And that ye took it so as wise and impartial men obtaining so great power and dignity are wont to accept in matters both doubtful and important what they think offered them well meant, and from a rational ability, I had no less

50 The *Judgement of Martin Bucer* appeared in July 1644, the *Areopagitica* in November. The writing of both, perhaps, grew out of the attacks upon the *Doctrine and Discipline of Divorce*, published in August 1643, and in a second edition in February 1644. This passage suggests that Milton is already contemplating the *Areopagitica*, as indeed in the *Second Defence* he implies that it was part of a larger plan. (See extract 2 and Introduction, pp.xv–xvi.)

than to persuade me. And on that persuasion am returned, as to a famous and free port, myself also bound by more than a maritime law, to expose as freely what fraughtage I conceive to bring of no trifles. For although it be generally known how and by whom ye have been instigated to a hard censure of that former book, entitled the *Doctrine and Discipline of Divorce,* an opinion held by some of the best among reformed writers without scandal or confutement, though now thought new and dangerous by some of our severe gnostics, whose little reading and less meditating holds ever with hardest obstinacy that which it took up with easiest credulity, I do not find yet that aught, for the furious incitements which have been used, hath issued by your appointment that might give the least interruption or disrepute either to the author or to the book. Which he who will be better advised than to call your neglect or connivance at a thing imagined so perilous, can attribute it to nothing more justly than to the deep and quiet stream of your direct and calm deliberations, that gave not way either to the fervent rashness or the immaterial gravity of those who ceased not to exasperate without cause. For which uprightness and incorrupt refusal of what ye were incensed to, Lords and Commons, (though it were done to justice, not to me, and was a peculiar demonstration how far your ways are different from the rash vulgar) besides those allegiances of oath and duty which are my public debt to your public labours, I have yet a store of gratitude laid up which cannot be exhausted; and such thanks perhaps they may live to be as shall more than whisper to the next ages. Yet that the author may be known to ground himself upon his own innocence and the merit of his cause, not upon the favour of a diversion or a delay to any just censure, but wishes rather he might see those his detractors at any fair meeting, as learned debatements are privileged with a due freedom under equal moderators, I shall here briefly single one of them[51] (because he hath

51 Herbert Palmer, President of Queen's College, Cambridge, by appointment of the Earl of Manchester in the purge of Cambridge in February 1644. Palmer preached a sermon on the dangers of toleration before the two houses of Parliament on August 13, 1644 in which he referred to the *Doctrine and Discipline of Divorce* as 'a wicked book . . . abroad and

obliged me to it) who I persuade me having scarce read the book nor knowing him who writ it, or at least feigning the latter, hath not forborne to scandalize him, unconferred with, unadmonished, undealt with by any pastorly or brotherly convincement, in the most open and invective manner, and at the most bitter opportunity that drift or set design could have invented. And this, whenas the canon law, though commonly most favouring the boldness of their priests, punishes the naming or traducing of any person in the pulpit, was by him made no scruple. If I shall therefore take licence by the right of nature and that liberty wherein I was born to defend myself publicly against a printed calumny, and do willingly appeal to those judges to whom I am accused, it can be no immoderate or unallowable course of seeking so just and needful reparations. Which I had done long since, had not these employments, which are now visible, deferred me. It was preached before ye, Lords and Commons, in August last upon a special day of humiliation,[52] that 'there was a wicked book abroad,' and ye were taxed of sin that it was yet 'uncensured, the book deserving to be burnt'; and 'impudence' also was charged upon the author, who durst 'set his name to it, and dedicate it to yourselves.' First, Lords and Commons, I pray to that God, before whom ye then were prostrate, so to forgive ye those omissions and trespasses which ye desire most should find forgiveness, as I shall soon show to the world how easily ye absolve yourselves of that which this man calls your sin, and is indeed your wisdom and your nobleness, whereof to this day ye have done well not to repent. He terms it 'a wicked book,' and why but 'for allowing other causes of divorce than Christ and his apostles mention'; and with the same censure condemns of wickedness not only Martin Bucer, that elect instrument of reformation, highly honoured and had in reverence by Edward the Sixth and his whole Parliament, whom also I had published in English by a good providence about a

uncensured, though deserving to be burnt, whose author hath been so impudent as to set his name to it and dedicate it to yourselves.'

52 The sermon was preached on a day set aside by order of Parliament as an 'extraordinary day of humiliation,' one of many days of solemn fast by similar order.

week before this calumnious digression was preached—[53] so that if
he knew not Bucer then, as he ought to have known, he might at
least have known him some months after, ere the sermon came in
print,[54] wherein notwithstanding he persists in his former sentence
and condemns again of wickedness, either ignorantly or wilfully,
not only Martin Bucer and all the choicest and holiest of our re-
formers, but the whole Parliament and Church of England in those
best and purest times of Edward the Sixth. All which I shall prove
with good evidence at the end of these explanations. And then let
it be judged and seriously considered with what hope the affairs of
our religion are committed to one among others who hath now only
left him which of the twain he will choose, whether this shall be his
palpable ignorance, or the same wickedness of his own book, which
he so lavishly imputes to the writings of other men: and whether
this of his that thus peremptorily defames and attaints of wickedness
unspotted churches, unblemished parliaments, and the most eminent restorers of Christian doctrine, deserve not to be burned first.
And if his heat had burst out only against the opinion, his wonted
passion had no doubt been silently borne with wonted patience.
But since against the charity of that solemn place and meeting, it
served him further to inveigh opprobriously against the person,
branding him with no less than impudence, only for setting his
name to what he had written, I must be excused not to be so wanting to the defence of an honest name or to the reputation of those
good men who afford me their society, but to be sensible of such a
foul endeavoured disgrace, not knowing aught either in mine own
deserts or the laws of this land, why I should be subject in such a
notorious and illegal manner to the intemperancies of this man's
preaching choler. And indeed to be so prompt and ready in the
midst of his humbleness to toss reproaches of this bulk and size,
argues as if they were the weapons of his exercise—I am sure not of
his ministry or of that day's work. Certainly to subscribe my name

53 The *Judgement of Martin Bucer* was entered in the Stationer's Register as
   of July 15, 1644.
54 The sermon, preached August 13, was not printed until September or
   October, although then at the request of Parliament.

at what I was to own was what the state had ordered and requires. And he who lists not to be malicious would call it ingenuity, clear conscience, willingness to avouch what might be questioned or to be better instructed. And if God were so displeased with those (Isa. 58) who 'on the solemn fast were wont to smite with the fist of wickedness,' it could be no sign of his own humiliation accepted which disposed him to smite so keenly with a reviling tongue. But if only to have writ my name must be counted 'impudence,' how doth this but justify another who might affirm with as good warrant that the late discourse of *Scripture and Reason*,[55] which is certain to be chiefly his own draft, was published without a name out of base fear and the sly avoidance of what might follow to his detriment if the party at court should hap to reach him. And I, to have set my name where he accuses me to have set it, am so far from recanting that I offer my hand also if need be to make good the same opinion which I there maintain by inevitable consequences drawn parallel from his own principal arguments in that of *Scripture and Reason*; which I shall pardon him if he can deny without shaking his own composition to pieces. The 'impudence' therefore, since he weighed so little what a gross revile that was to give his equal, I send him back again for a phylactery to stitch upon his arrogance, that censures not only before conviction so bitterly without so much as one reason given, but censures the congregation of his governors to their faces for not being so hasty as himself to censure.

And whereas my other crime is that I addressed the dedication of what I had studied to the Parliament, how could I better declare the loyalty which I owe to that supreme and majestic tribunal, and the opinion which I have of the high-entrusted judgement and personal worth assembled in that place? With the same affections, therefore, and the same addicted fidelity, Parliament of England, I here again have brought to your perusal on the same argument these following expositions of Scripture. The former book, as pleased

---

55 The work which Milton is here attributing chiefly to Palmer, *Scripture and Reason*, was described on its title-page as 'by divers Reverend and Learned Divines.'

some to think who were thought judicious, had of reason in it to a sufficiency; what they required was that the Scriptures there alleged might be discussed more fully. To their desires, thus much further hath been laboured in the Scriptures. Another sort also, who wanted more authorities and citations, have not been here unthought of. If all this attain not to satisfy them, as I am confident that none of those our great controversies at this day hath had a more demonstrative explaining, I must confess to admire what it is, for doubtless it is not reason nowadays that satisfies or suborns the common credence of men to yield so easily and grow so vehement in matters much more disputable and far less conducing to the daily good and peace of life.

108. From *Tetrachordon*. 1645.

But God, I solemnly attest him, withheld from my knowledge the consenting judgement of these men so late, until they could not be my instructors, but only my unexpected witnesses to partial men, that in this work I had not given the worst experiment of an industry joined with integrity and the free utterance though of an unpopular truth.[56]

109. From *Colasterion*. 1645.

Colasterion was written in reply to *An Answer to a Book, Intituled, the Doctrine and Discipline of Divorce . . .*, published anonymously in November 1644.

But as I still was waiting when these light-armed refuters would have done pelting at their three lines uttered with a sage delivery of no reason, but an impotent and worse than Bonner-like censure to burn that which provokes them to a fair dispute, at length a book was brought to my hands, entitled *An Answer to the Doctrine and Discipline of Divorce*. Gladly I received it, and very attentively composed myself to read, hoping that now some good man had vouchsafed the pains to instruct me better than I could yet learn out of all the volumes which for this purpose I had visited. Only this I

56 See section II, note 17.

marvelled, and other men have since, whenas I, in a subject so new to this age and so hazardous to please, concealed not my name, why this author, defending that part which is so creeded by the people, would conceal his.

110. From *Colasterion*. 1645.

In the meanwhile it shall be seen I refuse no occasion and avoid no adversary, either to maintain what I have begun or to give it up for better reason.

111. From *Colasterion*. 1645.

And for this, for I affirm no more than Bucer, what censure do you think, readers, he hath condemned the book to? To a death no less infamous than 'to be burnt by the hangman.' Mr. Licenser, for I deal not now with this caitiff, never worth my earnest and now not seasonable for my jest, you are reputed a man discreet enough, religious enough, honest enough—that is, to an ordinary competence in all these. But now your turn is to hear what your own hand hath earned ye, that when you suffered this nameless hangman to cast into public such a despiteful contumely upon a name and person deserving of the church and state equally to yourself, and one who hath done more to the present advancement of your own tribe than you or many of them have done for themselves, you forgot to be either honest, religious, or discreet.[57] Whatever the state might do concerning it, supposed a matter to expect evil from, I should not doubt to meet among them with wise, and honourable, and knowing men. But as to this brute libel, so much the more impudent and lawless for the abused authority which it

57 The licenser, Joseph Caryl, invited this, his share of the chastisement of *Colasterion*, by prefixing to the anonymous answer to the *Doctrine and Discipline of Divorce* the following note: 'To preserve the strength of the Marriage-bond and the Honour of that estate\against those sad breaches and dangerous abuses of it which common discontents (on this side Adultery) are likely to make in unstaid minds and men given to change, by taking in or grounding themselves upon the opinion answered and with good reason confuted in this Treatise, I have approved the printing and publishing of it.—November 14, 1644. Joseph Caryl.'

bears, I say again that I abominate the censure of rascals and their licensers.

With difficulty I return to what remains of this ignoble task, for the disdain I have to change a period more with the filth and venom of this gourmand swelled into a confuter. Yet for the satisfaction of others I endure all this.

112. From *Colasterion*. 1645.

The conclusion of the pamphlet.

I have now done that which for many causes I might have thought could not likely have been my fortune, to be put to this under-work of scouring and unrubbishing the low and sordid ignorance of such a presumptuous losel. Yet Hercules had the labour once imposed upon him to carry dung out of the Augean stable. At any hand I would be rid of him: for I had rather, since the life of man is likened to a scene, that all my entrances and exits might mix with such persons only whose worth erects them and their actions to a grave and tragic deportment, and not to have to do with clowns and vices. But if a man cannot peaceably walk into the world, but must be infested, sometimes at his face with dors and horseflies, sometimes beneath with bawling whippets and shin-barkers, and these to be set on by plot and consultation with a junto of clergymen and licensers, commended also and rejoiced in by those whose partiality cannot yet forgo old papistical principles, have I not cause to be in such a manner defensive as may procure me freedom to pass more unmolested hereafter by these encumbrances, not so much regarded for themselves as for those who incite them? And what defence can properly be used in such a despicable encounter as this, but either the flap or the spurn? If they can afford me none but a ridiculous adversary, the blame belongs not to me, though the whole dispute be strewed and scattered with ridiculous. And if he have such an ambition to know no better who are his mates, but among those needy thoughts which, though his two faculties of servingman and solicitor should compound into one mongrel, would be but thin and meagre, if in this penury of soul he can be possible to have the lustiness to think of fame, let him but send me how he calls him-self, and I may chance not fail to endorse him on the backside of posterity, not a golden, but a brazen ass. Since my fate extorts from me a talent of sport, which I had thought to hide in a napkin, he shall be my Batrachomyomachia, my Bavius, my Calandrino, the common adagy of ignorance and over-weening. Nay perhaps, as the provocation may be, I may be driven to curl up this gliding prose into a rough Sotadic, that shall rhyme him into such a condition, as instead of judging good books to be burned by the executioner, he shall be readier to be his own hangman. Thus much to this nuisance.

But as for the subject itself which I have writ and now defend according as the opposition bears, if any man equal to the matter shall think it appertains him to take in hand this controversy, either excepting against aught written, or persuaded he can show better how this question of such moment to be thoroughly known may re-ceive a true determination, not leaning on the old and rotten sugges-tions whereon it yet leans, if his intents be sincere to the public and shall carry him on without bitterness to the opinion or to the person dissenting, let him not, I entreat him, guess by the handling which meritoriously hath been bestowed on this object of contempt and laughter, that I account it any displeasure done me to be contra-dicted in print: but as it leads to the attainment of anything more true, shall esteem it a benefit, and shall know how to return his civility and fair argument in such a sort as he shall confess that to do so is my choice, and to have done thus was my chance.

113. From *Eikonoklastes*. 1649.

The present extract is concerned exclusively with the presence in *Eikon Basilike* of the 'Pamela Prayer' from the *Arcadia*. The pos-sibility that Milton, not the King or his friends, was responsible for its presence 'in all the best editions' has been given brief dis-cussion in the Introduction, p.xxviii.

They who are yet incredulous of what I tell them for a truth, that this Philippic prayer is no part of the King's goods, may satisfy their own eyes at leisure in the third book of Sir Philip's *Arcadia*, p.248, comparing Pamela's prayer with the first prayer of His Majesty, delivered to Dr. Juxton immediately before his death, and entitled, 'A Prayer in Time of Captivity,' printed in all the best editions of his book. And since there be a crew of lurking railers, who in their libels and their fits of railing up and down, as I hear from others, take it so currishly that I should dare to tell abroad the secrets of their Egyptian Apis, to gratify their gall in some measure yet more, which to them will be a kind of alms (for it is the weekly vomit of their gall which to most of them is the sole means of their feeding) that they may not starve for me, I shall gorge them once more with this digression somewhat larger than before: nothing troubled or offended at the working upward of their sale-venom thereupon, though it happen to asperse me; being, it seems, their best livelihood and the only use or good digestion that their sick and perishing minds can make of truth charitably told them. However, to the benefit of others much more worth the gaining, I shall proceed in my assertion: that if only but to taste wittingly of meat or drink offered to an idol be in the doctrine of St. Paul judged a pollution, much more must be his sin who takes a prayer, so dedicated, into his mouth and offers it to God.

114. From *Eikonoklastes*. 1649.

Milton is writing here of the claim of kingly virtue put forward in the *Eikon* on the ground that Charles had not dissolved a hostile parliament. The passage is included here for Milton's handling of the lawyers, who are dismissed almost as curtly as the 'councilists' are dismissed in the ecclesiastical pamphlets, e.g. in *An Apology for Smectymnuus* (extract 150).

It appears then that if this Bill of not dissolving were an unparalleled act, it was a known and common right which our ancestors under other kings enjoyed as firmly as if it had been graven in marble, and that the infringement of this king first brought it into a written Act, who now boasts that as a great favour done us which his own less fidelity than was in former kings constrained us only of an old undoubted right to make a new written Act. But what needed written Acts, whenas anciently it was esteemed part of his crown oath not to dissolve parliaments till all grievances were considered; whereupon, the old *Modi* of parliament calls it flat perjury if he dissolve them before, as I find cited in a book mentioned at the beginning of this chapter, to which and other law tractates I refer the more lawyerly mooting of this point, which is neither my element nor my proper work here, since the book which I have to answer pretends reason, not authorities and quotations: and I hold reason to be the best arbitrator and the law of law itself.

115. From the *Defence of Himself*. 1655.

From the Latin.

An account of Milton's reception of More's assurances, through Nieuport, that he was not the author of the *Cry* and of his reasons for refusing Nieuport's request that he refrain from publishing the *Second Defence*.[58]

At last, you seem inclined to be serious. 'You will give neither rumours nor common talk but letters, in proof that I was forewarned not to fall foul of an innocent man.' Pray then let us have a sight of the letter you produce, which was written to you by 'His Excellency D. Nieuport, Ambassador of the United Provinces,' and which you have brought forward, it appears, not for its weight of evidence, of which it has nothing, but merely out of ostentation. The Ambassador—a circumstance which shows the exemplary humanity of that dignified personage (for what would he not do for a good man, when he exerts himself so strenuously for you who are totally unworthy of it?)—the Ambassador went and communicated your letter to Mr. Secretary Thurlow. But finding that he made no progress with him, he dispatches two noble friends of mine with the same letter to me. What do these gentlemen do? After reading to me More's letter, they make a request, affirming at the same time that the Ambassador Nieuport joined in the request, that I would give

58 See Introduction, pp.xxiii–xxix, above, and Masson, *Life*, Vol. IV, pp.632ff.

credit to this your letter, in which you denied yourself to be the author of the *Cry of the Royal*. I replied that what they required was unreasonable; that More was neither worthy of such credit, nor was it agreeable to any usage to give credit to merely a letter of an adversary under accusation making a denial relating to himself, in contradiction to common report and to the result of an investigation sufficiently satisfactory. The messengers having nothing to say in answer to this give up the parley. If you do not believe this account, pray run over the Ambassador's letter, which I now make use of as evidence against you. 'He desired him not to publish the book';—but this was at my own option, and in my own power—'that he might avoid doing you the injury of imputing to you that work.' But he does not say that it was plain to him, or whence could it be plain to him, that the injury would be precisely my imputing the book to you. At least that, 'I would insert nothing which could touch you.' And why should not that touch you which relates to you? unless he had shown that it did not relate to you. That he could not do this, it is a most clear proof that in a second attempt to prevail with Mr. Secretary Thurlow he had nothing to send him but that very same copy of your letter, from which it may further be easily seen that those 'reasons' alleged to me 'for which he desired' I would not publish that book possessed nothing connected with the reasons of the republic. Don't corrupt now the Ambassador's letter. There is nothing there about 'a hostile spirit,' nothing about 'an unseasonable time.' He only writes, 'he is grieved that I would not, at his request, show the slightest moderation': that is, that I would not, at his private request, do a favour to you, who are a public enemy—namely, recall and compose anew a work already printed and on the eve of being published. That 'dignified personage' must excuse me, and the more because he is an ambassador, if I neither would nor could pardon public injuries for private intercessions—and far less those injuries of the *Cry of the Royal*, which had no sort of connection with the war, nor with the peace, which has been recently concluded.

116. From the *Defence of Himself*. 1655.

From the Latin.

> This is one of the most laboured of Milton's attempts to justify the occasional vulgarity of his controversial writings, here, as usually, upon the authority of classical, Biblical, and patristic precedent. The apology generously repeats the offence, assuring More that whoever speaks of him 'cannot choose but speak obscenely.'

You say I promised the Ambassador [59] 'that nothing indecorous should fall from my pen'—and I have not deceived him; or if I have at all offended in this respect, I have offended against myself only, while employed in shaking off those loathsome odours of yours, and in handling your pollutions: and, as I said before in my preface, I considered less what might most become me than what was best suited to you. Yet, after all, have I inveighed with greater indecorum and bitterness against you than those grave orators of old, in their harangues made in the place and the assembly of highest honour in the city, as likewise in their published writings, were accustomed to use against all scoundrels and miscreants?

But I come now to that which has given offence to the sanctified More—that prodigy of the age for chastity. 'I employ (it seems) language of unwashed foulness, words naked and indelicate.' O shameful, prostituted man! And do you censure words as foul, who without a blush can be guilty of deeds of unequalled foulness? Indeed, it would not repent me now, had I been a little more liberal of my words of this kind, had it been only to elicit this scoundrelly dissimulation, and hence openly to expose you (masked as you are to the eyes of the world) as the worst of hypocrites! But what expression, what word, will you point out to me, in any part of the book, more foul than the word *Morus* itself? Yet it is neither in the word nor in the thing, but in yourself, exists all vice and all obscenity. Lewder than any faun or naked satyr, your manners have converted words of chastest meaning into words of naked ribaldry. No shade could veil your filthiness, not even that notable fig-tree. Whoever speaks of you and of your debaucheries cannot choose but speak

59 Nieuport.

obscenely. And if I have uttered naked words in your reproach, I should be at no loss to defend myself by the practice of gravest authors, who have always been of opinion that words naked and plain, indignantly uttered, have a meaning far different from obscenity—that they express the utmost vehemence of reproof. Whoever imputed it as a crime to Piso, the writer of the annals, who for his virtue and modest manners obtained the surname of *Frugi*, that in those annals he complained—'*Adolescentes peni deditos esse*'? Whoever censured Sallust, a very serious writer, for saying even in his history—'*Ventre, manu, pene, alea, bona patria dilacerari*': not to mention Herodotus, Seneca, Suetonius, Plutarch, the gravest of authors? and with whom you sufficiently proclaim your non-acquaintance if you deny that they intermix, on divers occasions, words more than indelicate indeed, and subjects abundantly gross, with matters of greater seriousness. If this be indecorous at all times and places, how often will you have to charge with a writ of indecency and obscenity, Erasmus, that miracle of learning, whose brazen statue stands at Rotterdam; how often our own Thomas More, whose name you dishonour by pronouncing it at the same time with your own; lastly, how often the ancient fathers of the Church, Clemens Alexandrinus, Arnobius, Lactantius, Eusebius, when they uncover and cast derision upon the obscene mysteries of the old religions! But perhaps, as hypocrites are usually austere in words, though in things unclean, you will not suffer even Moses himself to escape unimpeached of this crime: for, as is usual with him in various other places, so, if we are to believe the Hebrews, it is especially remarkable in the passage where he speaks without any disguise of the very part where the spear of Phinehas transfixed the woman. You will not spare even Job, most modest and patient of men, while in naked and homely phrase he imprecates on himself the curse of a harlot-wife if he had ever lain in wait for the wife of another. Not the writings of Solomon the elegant, nor even of the prophets, could escape your proscription of every petty indelicacy, indeed sometimes even of broad obscenity, whenever the Masoretes and rabbins think proper to write their marginal *Keri*, to note the eloquent plainness of the text. As for me, I should choose rather to be plain-spoken with the sacred writers than delicate with the futile rabbins. In vain will you call Marcus Tullius to your aid; for if he in that 'golden book of offices,' which you quote, deems of this kind of raillery as elegant, urbane, ingenious, witty, and of which not only Plautus and the ancient Attic comedy, but even the books of the Socratic philosophers, are full, as you might there have seen —it is not he who will be found to confine decorum within limits so narrow and strict that it should be difficult for anyone to restrain himself, and especially for me to restrain myself, within those limits. Let us hear no more then, most polluted man, of your trifling about the honourable and the becoming; believe me, this becomes not you; nay, be assured, there is nothing less becoming, nothing more foreign to the very nature of decorum, than for such a one as you to usurp the language of purity or to censure that which is foul.

117. From the *Defence of Himself*. 1655.

From the Latin.

But you were hastening, I think, to another part of your proposed task—to my calumnies: for you have before given us to understand that you have at last done with the subject of lies—by far the greatest part of your work—of which, nevertheless, the only one was that I pronounced you the author of the *Cry*. Now, as my imputing of this book to you, though even with some wrong bias upon my mind, may be justly regarded by anyone as a matter of trifling moment, since, in other respects, you neither disapproved the book, nor was it unworthy of your reputation—why, with such a host of words, such fury of passion, such indignant scorn of a thing in itself most insignificant, you should thus exaggerate, thus emblazon one only offence, as if that alone comprehended all impiety and all crime— this, if not already explained by me, would be more to be wondered at. But the truth is that this was your only fortress, in which you had placed all your hope. If you had succeeded in persuading the majority of mankind that you were not the author of the *Cry*, and

that I was a liar, you had the hope that in the other part, which you
entitle 'Of Calumnies,' and on which topic you have absolutely
nothing to say for yourself—you had the hope, I say, that your defence against me, previously convicted of lying, would be an easy
matter, and that you, as it respected people at a distance and those
to whom you were unknown, would by this artifice come off scot-
free, and wash out every stain of your past life. But contrary to what
you hoped and to what you believed, as I, in spite of your subter-
fuges and of your denials, have fairly proved you to be the author
of the *Cry*, I do not doubt that I shall obtain entire credit with impartial judges of things, as to your debaucheries also; and which you
in more cautious phrase, according as the thing may bear, could
wish should be called calumnies.

118. From *Of Civil Power in Ecclesiastical Causes*. 1659.

> Milton here concludes an argument from Scriptural sources that the
> ten commandments were never given into the hands of civil magis-
> trates for enforcement and were never meant to be, with a defence
> of his plainness and brevity, eschewing 'pomp and ostentation of
> reading' as admirable only to the vulgar.

But of these things perhaps more some other time; what may serve
the present hath been above discoursed sufficiently out of the Scriptures: and to those produced might be added testimonies, examples,
experiences of all succeeding ages to these times, asserting this doctrine: but having herein the Scripture so copious and so plain, we
have all that can be properly called true strength and nerve; the
rest would be but pomp and encumbrance. Pomp and ostentation of
reading is admired among the vulgar; but doubtless in matters of
religion he is learnedest who is plainest. The brevity I use, not ex-
ceeding a small manual, will not therefore, I suppose, be thought
the less considerable, unless with them perhaps who think that
great books only can determine great matters. I rather chose the
common rule, not to make much ado where less may serve. Which
in controversies and those especially of religion, would make them

less tedious, and by consequence read ofter, by many more, and with more benefit.

119. From *Of True Religion, Heresy, Schism, Toleration, and the Growth of Popery.* 1673.

This extract is the introductory paragraph of Milton's last ecclesiastical pamphlet, almost his last utterance. The application of the passage is to the particular pamphlet, which is itself of little interest, but it is another significant commentary upon the limits of Milton's own capacity for toleration.

It is unknown to no man who knows aught of concernment among us that the increase of Popery is at this day no small trouble and offence to greatest part of the nation, and the rejoicing of all good men that it is so—the more their rejoicing, that God hath given a heart to the people to remember still their great and happy deliverance from Popish thraldom, and to esteem so highly the precious benefit of His Gospel, so freely and so peaceably enjoyed among them. Since therefore some have already in public with many considerable arguments exhorted the people to beware the growth of this Romish weed, I thought it no less than a common duty to lend my hand, how unable soever, to so good a purpose. I will not now enter into the labyrinth of councils and fathers, an entangled wood which the Papist loves to fight in, not with hope of victory, but to obscure the shame of an open overthrow—which yet in that kind of combat, many heretofore, and one of late, hath eminently given them.[60] And such manner of dispute with them, to learned men is useful and very commendable. But I shall insist now on what is plainer to common apprehension, and what I have to say, without longer introduction.

Further explanation of or apology for Milton's methods and practices in controversy will be found in extracts 1, 2, 41, 43, 65, 72, 79–82, 91, 92, 94, 96, 100–102, 122–124, 126, 128, 130, 134, 152, *and* 154.

60 Cf. the *Judgement of Martin Bucer* (extract 106) and section X, note 49.

C. ACHIEVEMENTS AND REWARDS

My zealous labour's fruit.

120. Epilogue to the second edition of the *First Defence*. 1658.

From the Latin.

This epilogue to the second edition of the *First Defence* issued seven years after its first publication is here put out of its normal chronological order among Milton's estimates of his achievement as a prose writer because it is one of the most deliberate and considered of Milton's appraisals of the prose work he considered most important and his greatest contribution to liberty's defence, his noble task.

IT is now several years since I published the foregoing, in haste, as reason of state then required, for I kept thinking that if ever I might take it in hand again at leisure, as occasionally happens, I might thereupon smooth out, or remove, maybe, or add somewhat. This I now judge that I have accomplished, though more briefly than I used to count upon doing it: a memorial which, such as it is, I see will not easily perish. Though someone may be found who may have defended civil freedom more freely than here it is defended, yet there shall hardly be found anyone who hath defended it in a greater and more glorious example. If, then, an action of example so high and illustrious is believed to have been as successfully accomplished as not without God's prompting undertaken, let this be reason good for thinking that in these my praises too it hath even by the same might and inspiration been glorified and defended. Indeed I had much rather all men thought so, than that any other success, whether of wit or judgement or industry, were allowed me. Yet, as that famous Roman consul upon retiring from office swore in the popular assembly that the state and the city owed their safety to his single efforts, even so, as I now put the last touches to this work, so much only I dare assert, calling God and man to witness: that in this book I have indicated and brought to light, from the highest authors of wisdom both divine and human, matters whereby, I trust, not only the English people has been adequately defended in this cause, to the everlasting reputation of its posterity, but numerous other human beings as well, hitherto deluded by foul ignorance of their right and by false show of religion—multitudes of men, I say, except such as themselves prefer and deserve to be slaves—have been quite set free. Now the oath of that consul, great as were its claims, was in that same assembly ratified by oath of the whole Roman people with one mind and one voice; this conviction of mine, I have long understood, is fully ratified by the most excellent not only of my fellow citizens, but of foreigners too, with the loud voice of nations everywhere.

This my zealous labour's fruit—the highest that I for my part have set before me in this life—I gratefully enjoy; yet therewith too consider chief how I may bear best witness—not only to my own country, to which I have paid the highest I possessed, but even to men of whatever nation, and to the cause of Christendom above all —that I am pursuing after yet greater things if my strength suffice (nay, it will if God grant), and for their sake meanwhile am taking thought and studying to make ready.

121. Sonnet XI. 1645.

This and Sonnet XII are Milton's most telling comment upon the reception of the divorce pamphlets.

> A Book was writ of late called *Tetrachordon*,
>> And woven close, both matter, form, and style;
>> The subject new: it walked the town a while,
>> Numbring good intellects; now seldom pored on.
> Cries the stall-reader, 'bless us! what a word on
>> A title-page is this!' and some in file
> Stand spelling false, while one might walk to Mile-
>> End Green. Why is it harder, sirs, than Gordon,
> Colkitto, or Macdonnel, or Galasp?
>> Those rugged names to our like mouths grow sleek,
>> That would have made Quintilian stare and gasp.

Thy age, like ours, O soul of Sir John Cheek,
 Hated not learning worse than toad or asp,
 When thou taught'st Cambridge, and King Edward, Greek.[61]

122. Sonnet XII. 1645.

 I did but prompt the age to quit their clogs
  By the known rules of ancient liberty,
  When straight a barbarous noise environs me
 Of owls and cuckoos, asses, apes and dogs,
 As when those hinds that were transformed to frogs
  Railed at Latona's twin-born progeny,
  Which after held the Sun and Moon in fee.
 But this is got by casting pearl to hogs,
 That bawl for freedom in their senseless mood,
  And still revolt when truth would set them free.
  Licence they mean when they cry liberty;
 For who loves that must first be wise and good:
  But from that mark how far they rove we see,
  For all this waste of wealth, and loss of blood.

123. From the *First Defence*. 1651.

From the Latin.

And now I think, through God's good help, I have finished the work I undertook at the beginning, namely to defend both at home and abroad the noble actions of my countrymen against the brain-sick envious rage of this mad sophist,[62] and to assert the people's common rights against the unrighteous despotism of kings—and this not out of any hatred of kings, but of tyrants. Nor have I knowingly

61 The fair copy of this sonnet in the Trinity College Manuscript has the title, 'On the Detraction which followed upon my writing certain treatises,' and the rougher copy has an interesting variant of the first lines:

 I writ a book of late called *Tetrachordon*,
 And weaved it close, both matter, form, and style.

This reading is cancelled even in the earlier draft for the less personal present reading.
62 Salmasius.

left unanswered any argument or example or document alleged by my adversary that seemed to possess any solid substance or power to convince. Perhaps I have been nearer the opposite fault, that by rather too often answering also his sillinesses and threadbare quibbles as if they were arguments, I may seem to have given them an importance that they nothing deserved.

124. From the *Second Defence*. 1654.

From the Latin.

> After another statement of the value of the *First Defence*, of his gratitude to the Council for the opportunity of writing it, and of the unparalleled importance and nobility of the action with which it, his prose epic, is concerned, Milton gives an account of its reception in Europe and of the effect it had upon the reputation and fortunes of Salmasius. He reaffirms also his confidence that he writes under special favour of God. Nowhere does Milton express greater enthusiasm for his party's cause nor for his contribution to it.

As it is the first of duties throughout the life of man, and in every condition, to be ever thankful to God and mindful of His benefits; and as it should be our earliest and especial care when events have been prosperous beyond our hopes and even our wishes, to return, on that account, our peculiar and solemn thanks—this I now feel incumbent on myself; and chiefly for three reasons. First, that I was born in those times of my country when the effulgent virtue of its citizens—when their magnanimity and steadiness, surpassing the highest praise of their ancestors, under the inspection of God first implored, and under His manifest guidance, setting examples and performing deeds of valour, the greatest since the foundation of the world—delivered the commonwealth from a grievous domination, and religion from a most debasing thraldom. And secondly, when there suddenly appeared many who as is customary with the vulgar hatefully calumniated deeds nobly done, and when one above the rest, inflated and confident with literary pride and with the opinion entertained of him by those of his own herd, nefariously undertook the defence of all tyrants in a book beyond example scanda-

lous, levelled against us—that I, rather than another, deemed not
unequal to an adversary of so great a name,[63] nor to speaking on so
great a subject, accepted of those very deliverers of the country, and
by general consent, the part spontaneously assigned me: namely,
to defend publicly (if anyone ever did) the cause of the people of
England, and thus of liberty itself. Lastly, I return thanks to
God, that in a task so arduous, so full of expectation, I neither
disappointed the hopes nor the opinions of my fellow citizens,
nor failed to satisfy no small number of foreigners, as well among
the learned as among persons conversant with public affairs;
that I even so completely routed my adversary, though of the most
audacious order, that he retired with his spirit broken, his reputation shattered; and for the three years which he afterwards lived,
much as in his rage he threatened, he gave us no farther trouble
than to solicit for his support the secret services of certain persons
of the vilest character,[64] and to suborn I know not what senseless
and unconscionable applauders, to patch up if possible his unexpected and recent ignominy. This will immediately appear. As I
conceived these fortunate and even great events to have happened
to me from above, and indeed that they were particularly suited not
only to discharge my debt of gratitude to the Deity, but to supply
the most favourable omen for my proposed work, I thought it behoved me to begin, as I do, with the reverend mention of them.
And who is there who considers not the honourable achievements
of his country as his own? And what can be more for the honour or
glory of any country than liberty restored alike to civil life and to
divine worship? What nation, what city has struggled for it, in both
kinds, more successfully or more courageously? Indeed, as courage
shines out not exclusively in war and arms, but displays its intrepid
power equally against every species of fear, those Greeks and Romans whom we most admire brought along with them for the expulsion of tyrants from their states scarcely any other virtue but
zeal for liberty accompanied with ready arms and eager hands. The

63 Salmasius.
64 E.g. Alexander More, Vlaccus, etc.

rest they achieved from the impulse thence derived, amid the general shout, applause, and joyous circumstance. They were even less eager for dangerous and uncertain enterprise than for the trial of virtue fair and glorious, and for rewards and crowns, and the certain hope of immortal fame. For the sovereign authority was not yet consecrated to tyrants. Tyrants, suddenly transformed into viceroys, forsooth, and vicars of Christ, could not yet exercise their power through royal grace, had not yet fortified themselves by the blind superstition of the vulgar. The lower orders, stupefied by the wicked arts of priests, had not yet degenerated into a barbarism viler than what disgraces the Indians, dullest of mortals: for these merely worship as gods those malignant demons they are unable to put to flight; while those, that they might not cashier tyrants when they had it in their power, exalted them into gods most impotent to rule over them—deifying the pests of the human race for their own destruction. Now against all these close embattlements of long-received opinions, religions, slanders, and terrors, more dreaded far by others than the enemy himself, had Englishmen to contend; and being better taught, and without doubt inspired from heaven, such was their confidence in their cause, such their firmness and strength of mind, that all these they overcame. Hence, though in number they were indeed a great people, yet were they in spirit so erect and lofty that they were no longer a mere populace; even Britain herself, which heretofore has been said to be a land fruitful in tyrants, shall henceforth deserve the perpetual celebration of succeeding ages as a country far more fruitful in deliverers. These men were never let loose by a contempt or violation of the laws to an unreigned licence; they were inflamed by no delusive vision of virtue and of glory or by any foolish emulation of the ancients for the empty name of liberty; they were taught the straight and only way to true liberty, by innocence of life and sanctity of manners; they were compelled by necessity to arm in the just defence of the laws and of religion. Thus, confident of the divine aid, they drove out slavery in their glorious warfare. Of this glory, though I claim no share for myself, it is easy for me to defend myself against the charge, if any such be brought against me, either of timidity or of cowardice. For if I avoided the toils and the perils of war, it was only that I might earnestly toil for my fellow citizens in another way, with much greater utility, and with no less peril. In doubtful postures of our affairs, my mind never betrayed any symptom of despondence, nor was I more afraid than became me of malice, or even of death. Devoted even from a child to the more humanizing studies, and always stronger in mind than in body, I set an inferior value upon the service of the camp, in which I might have been easily surpassed by any ordinary man of a more robust make, and betook myself to those occupations where my services could be of more avail; that, if I were wise, I might contribute my utmost power, from the higher and more excellent, not from the lower, parts of my nature, to the designs of my country, and to this transcendent cause. I thought, therefore, that if it were the will of God those men should perform such gallant exploits, it must be likewise His will, that, when performed, there should be others to set them forth with becoming dignity and ornament,[65] and that the truth, after being defended by arms, should be alike defended by reason— the only defence which is truly and properly human. Hence it is that while I admire those men unconquered in the field, I complain not of the part allotted to myself; nay, I may rather congratulate myself, and once again return my highest thanks to the heavenly bestower of gifts, that such a lot has fallen to me as may be viewed with much greater reason as a subject of envy to others than in any way as a cause of repentance to myself. It is not my wish, however, to make a comparison of myself with anyone, not even with the humblest; nor is it from any arrogant feeling that I have spoken a single word in my own behalf. But when I turn my mind to that cause of all others the most noble and most renowned, and to this splendid office of defending even the defenders—an office assigned me by their own suffrages and judgements—I confess it is with difficulty I restrain myself from soaring to a more daring height than is suitable to the purpose of an exordium and from casting

65 See section X, note 18 and section VI, note 12.

about for something of more grandeur to which I may give utterance: for, to whatever degree I am surpassed (of which there can be little doubt) by the ancient, illustrious orators, not only as an orator, but also as a linguist (and particularly in a foreign tongue, which I employ of necessity, and in which I am often very far from satisfying myself), I shall surpass no less the orators of all ages in the nobleness and in the instructiveness of my subject. This it is which has imparted such expectation, such celebrity to this theme, that I now feel myself not in the forum or on the rostrum, surrounded by a single people only, whether Roman or Athenian, but, as it were, by listening Europe, attending, and passing judgement. I feel that I addressed myself in my former defence, and that I shall again address myself in this, to all sittings and assemblies, wherever are to be found men of the highest authority, wherever there are cities and nations. I imagine myself to have set out upon my travels, and that I behold from on high, tracts beyond the seas, and wide-extended regions; that I behold countenances strange and numberless, and all in feelings of mind my closest friends and neighbours. Here is presented to my eyes the manly strength of the Germans, disdainful of slavery; there the lively and generous impetuosity of the Franks, worthily so called; on this side, the considerate virtue of the Spaniards; on that, the sedate and composed magnanimity of the Italians.[66] Wherever there are natures free, ingenuous, magnanimous, either they are prudently concealed or openly professed. Some favour in silence, others give their suffrages in public; some hasten to receive me with shouts of applause, others, in fine, vanquished by truth, surrender themselves captive. Encompassed by such countless multitudes, it seems to me that from the columns of Hercules to the farthest borders of India, that throughout this vast expanse, I am bringing back, bringing home to every nation, liberty, so long driven out, so long an exile; and as is recorded of Tripto-

---

66 Cf. Sonnet XXII, to Mr. Cyriack Skinner upon his Blindness (extract 48),

> In liberty's defence, my noble task,
> Of which all Europe talks from side to side.

lemus of old, that I am importing fruits for the nations from my
own city, but of a far nobler kind than those fruits of Ceres; that I
am spreading abroad among the cities, the kingdoms, and nations,
the restored culture of citizenship and freedom of life. But if I am
he who laid low that redoubted satellite of tyrants, hitherto deemed
invincible in the general opinion and in his own conceit; if I am he,
who, when he disdainfully defied us and our embattled might (and
our chief men turning their eyes first upon me), engaged him in
single combat, and with this stylus, the weapon of his choice,
stabbed the reviler to the heart, and bore off abundant spoils—unless I should choose to discredit and wholly to disparage the estimates and opinions of hosts of intelligent readers on all sides, far
from being devoted or under obligations to me; if I am he, I say,
I shall return as one not utterly unknown, perhaps even not unwelcome.[67] That all this is true, without any extravagant talking, is
most clearly proved even from the following circumstances: when
Salmasius, or Salmasia (for of what sex he was, was rendered extremely doubtful from his being plainly ruled by his wife, alike in
matters regarding his reputation and in his domestic concerns)
when Salmasius, or Salmasia, then, had indeed the honour of being
invited by the most serene, the Queen of Sweden (than whom there
lives not, I think, nor has ever lived one who has more studiously
cultivated the liberal arts, or who is a more generous patroness of
men of letters), and when arrived in that country, of being treated,
though a foreigner, with great distinction, he was there surprised,
while dreaming of no such thing, by our *Defence*—an event which I
must think could not have happened but by the will of God. Here
it was immediately perused by no small number; and the Queen,
who was among its first readers, attentive only to what became her

---

67 Du Moulin, in the *Cry of the Royal Blood*, tried to discount the importance of the *First Defence* by gibes at Milton's lack of reputation. Later in
  the *Second Defence* (extract 2), Milton explains that his obscurity was a
  matter of choice, that he had carried silently in his own breast what would
  long since have gained him a name had he chosen to bring it forth. Now
  the *First Defence* itself has brought him fame and a welcome throughout
  Europe.

own dignity, remitted nothing, indeed, of her former grace and munificence towards her guest. For the rest, if it be allowable to disclose what I have often heard, and which is no secret, so remarkable a change was suddenly wrought in the sentiments of people, that the man who of yesterday blossomed in the meridian beams of favour is today almost withered; and on his leaving Sweden, which he did with good leave not long after, it became a matter of doubt with many persons whether his arrival was attended with more honour or his departure with more contempt. It sufficiently appears also that his reputation sustained no less injury in other places. But as to all these matters, I am not so situated as to be forced to trumpet my own praises. This is not at all necessary. I would only show more clearly that I had no light reasons for beginning, as I did, with giving my especial thanks to God most high and most excellent; I would show that this proem—in which I am able to evince by so many proofs that I and my concerns (though in no wise free from the ills of humanity) are under the care of the Deity—must redound to my honour and fair fame; I would show that I am aided by the divine favour and help in undertakings of the greatest magnitude, planned for the needed service of my country, and tending to be of the highest use to society and to religion, not in respect of one people only, much less of one unprincipled man, but rather of the universal race of man, against the enemies of man's freedom—addressing myself, as it were, to the multitudes of all nations gathered together and crowded into one vast congregation. It is not possible for me, nor can it ever be my desire, to ascribe to myself anything greater or more glorious. Wherefore I implore the same immortal God, that as upheld solely by His wonted aid and goodness I have both justly and intrepidly defended deeds hitherto unparalleled, I may not be deficient in vindicating with the same or even greater integrity, diligence, fidelity, and even success, the authors, and myself also, conjoined as I am with so many others in unmerited reproach and calumny for purposes of ignominy instead of honour. And if there be anyone who thinks that these things would have been better passed over in contempt, I do not dispute it, admitting these things to have been scattered among those who have understood us rightly; but how shall it be made appear at last to the rest of mankind that the lies which our adversary has told are not truths? Yet, as we shall do our endeavour, which is no more than just, that however far slander has gone before, so far the avenger truth shall follow after, it is my belief that those who have been deceived will cease to think wrongfully of us, and that the adversary will peradventure be ashamed of his lies; and if he is not ashamed, that then it would at last be better to treat him with contempt. Meanwhile, I should have prepared a suitable reply to him with more dispatch, if he had not all along entrenched himself in delusive rumours, giving out every now and then his menacing warnings that Salmasius was sweating at the anvil and fabricating new volumes against us which he was even on the point of publishing. By all this he merely effected that the punishment he would suffer for his slanderous tongue should be deferred: for I thought it behoved me to wait, that I might reserve my strength entire against the more potent adversary. But with Salmasius I imagine my battling is now at an end, for he is among the dead. And how he died I shall not undertake to say: for I will not impute to him his death as a crime, as he did to me my blindness. There are not wanting, however, those who lay the guilt of his death upon me, and upon those stings of mine which were but too sharp—and which by resisting he caused to sink the deeper. And while he saw the work he had in hand advance slower and slower; saw that the time for reply was gone by; saw that the grace of his work was no more: stung, moreover, by the recollection that his fame, his estimation, had perished; in fine, that the favour shown him by princes had abated by reason of his poor defence of the royal cause—he is said, after three years of chagrin, to have died, worn away by sickness of mind more than from any bodily disease. But however this may be, if I must engage him a second time—if I must wage even a posthumous war with an enemy who is now sufficiently well known to me, as I have found no difficulty in sustaining the ferocity of his most vigorous charge, I can have no reason to dread his feeble and dying efforts.

125. From the *Second Defence*. 1654.

From the Latin.

> Milton translates the judgement expressed in the *Cry of the Royal Blood* that he is among the worst of his party, second in evil only to Cromwell, coming from an enemy as it does, into a glorious tribute to his worth and to the importance of his work.

Go on and revile me in this way, as being, in your eyes, 'worse than Cromwell': for it is impossible for you to bestow upon me higher praise. But am I to consider you as a friend, or as a blockhead, or as an insidious enemy? That you are not a friend is certain: for your words betray you for an enemy. How then came you to be so great a blockhead as to take it into your head to prefer me for your accusation to so great a personage? Do you imagine that what you do not comprehend, I also do not comprehend?—namely, that the more inveterate you discover your hatred to be against me, the greater do you proclaim my merits to be towards the commonwealth?—that with my own party your manifold reproaches do but declare my praise? For if you hate me to a degree beyond all others, it is plain that I, of all others, have galled you the most severely; that it is I who have the most humbled you; that it is I who have done the most mischief to your cause. If this be the fact, then it is I also who have deserved the most highly of my fellow citizens: for the testimony or judgement of an enemy, though in other respects abundantly trivial, is the weightiest of all on the subject of his own pain. Do you not remember, when Ajax and Ulysses contended for the arms of the dead Achilles, that the poet by the counsel of Nestor chose the judges not from among the Greeks, who were their countrymen, but from the Trojans, who were their enemies?

Hence let the impartial Trojans judge the strife. And a little after:

> Now they a righteous judgement will declare,
> As nor to one nor t'other love they bear;
> For all the Greeks they hold in equal hate;
> Darkly remembering their ruined state.

Thus far the Smyrnæan, or Calaber. It follows, then, that you must be insidious, and labour to cast an odium upon me, since, by wicked arts, and with the purpose of inflicting a deeper injury, you pervert and deprave that kind of judgement which is usually un-biassed and sincere in an enemy: hence you are not merely the most depraved of men, but the most depraved of enemies. But my good man! I will render frustrate none of your endeavours: for though I could most ardently wish that I were Ulysses, that is, that I had deserved the most highly of all of my country, yet I covet not the arms of Achilles; I seek not to carry before me the heavens painted on my shield, which others may look to in a contest, though I do not; it is my endeavour to bear on my shoulders a real not a painted burden, to be felt by myself, rather than by others. Indeed, as I have no private malice or enmity against any man, nor, as far as I know, has any man against me, I am the less concerned at the tor-rent of abuse which is cast upon me, at the numberless reproaches which are hurled against me, as I bear all this not for myself, but for the sake of the commonwealth. Nor do I complain that by far the least share of the reward, and of the advantages thence proceeding, and that by far the greatest share of the reproach, have attached to me, content to have had in view and to have prosecuted without re-ward those things which were honourable to be done for their own sakes alone. This is what others should look to; and as for yourself, know that I have not so much as touched those 'good things,' 'that wealth' with which you reproach me, nor am made one halfpenny the richer by that name on account of which you bring your chief accusations against me.

126. From the *Second Defence*. 1654.

From the Latin.

Another statement of the effect of the *First Defence* upon the respective reputations of Milton and Salmasius, and then the famous tribute to the Queen of Sweden. The *Second Defence* was published in May 1654; Christina did not abdicate her throne until June 6, 1654.

Now I do not deny that after the publication of that book [68] Sal-masius was in everybody's mouth, and that he pleased the Royalists to a miracle; that 'he was invited, and amply rewarded, by the most august the Queen of Sweden'; nay, that in the whole of that contest Salmasius had everything in his favour, and I almost everything against me. In the first place, of his erudition, the opinion of man-kind could go no higher, which opinion he had been collecting for many previous years by writing a multitude of books, and of no small bulk; not books of general utility, but on the abstrusest sub-jects, and stuffed with scraps of citation from eminent authors, than which nothing sooner excites the wonderment of the literary vulgar. On the contrary, who I was, scarcely anyone in those parts had ever heard.[69] He, by applying a more than ordinary diligence to the work, the subject being of such magnitude, had awakened in re-spect of himself great expectation, while it was not in my power to awaken any. Nay, as I should be a raw recruit engaging with a veteran, there were many who dissuaded me from the undertaking, partly out of envy, lest whatever the issue I should gain glory from a contest with an enemy so illustrious, partly from apprehension for me and for the cause, lest I should retire vanquished, to the heavy disgrace of both. Lastly the specious and plausible nature of his cause, the rooted opinion of the vulgar, or which is more properly called superstition, and the prepossession in favour of the royal name, had given additional vigour and spirit to Salmasius—circum-stances which all made against me. Hence when our defence soon after made its appearance, it is less to be wondered at that it was seized with avidity by most persons (as they had an eager curiosity to see who could be so rash as to presume to enter the lists with Salmasius) than that it should give such pleasure and satisfaction to many; insomuch that as respect was no longer had to the author, but to truth itself, Salmasius, who was lately seated on the summit of honour, now, as if the mask which disguised him had been taken off, suddenly fell from his renown and from his confidence; and

68 The *Defence of Kings*.
69 Cf. elsewhere in the *Second Defence* (extracts 2 and 124) and note 67 above.

though he strained every nerve to recover himself, he was unable to accomplish it as long as he lived.

But you, most serene Queen of the Swedes! [70] and that nice discernment of yours, he could not long deceive. You have stood forth the princess and the authoress little less (shall I say?) than heavenly, of preferring truth to the partialities of faction. For although you invited and loaded with honours the man who at that time was celebrated above his fellows for pre-eminent learning, and for his defence of the royal cause, yet, after that answer had appeared, which was perused by you with singular equanimity, and you had discovered that Salmasius was convicted of talking to no purpose, and of palpable misrepresentation, that he had said many things which are frivolous, many which are extravagant, some which are false, others which go against himself and are contrary to his former sentiments, and that when called into your presence, as the report goes, he could give no satisfactory reasons for all this—your mind underwent so visible a change that from that time it was plain to everybody that you neither paid the same attention to the man as before, nor made much account of his genius and learning; and what was altogether unexpected, showed an evident inclination to favour his adversary. For you denied that what was spoken against tyrants could have any reference whatever to you; and by this you gained, with yourself the fruit, with others the reputation, of a most upright conscience. As it is sufficiently plain from your actions that you are no tyrant, this open declaration of your sentiments shows in a still clearer light that you are utterly unconscious of the thing. Happy am I! happy even beyond my highest hope! (for I boast of no other eloquence than that persuasion which is inherent in truth itself) who, when I had fallen upon those times of my country in

70 Since it was the official answer of the Commonwealth to Salmasius, since Salmasius was so distinguished a man, and since it was addressed to all Europe, the *First Defence* not unnaturally made a great impression upon Europe. That it should have been read eagerly in Stockholm, where Salmasius was a guest of the Queen of Sweden, is even less surprising. Milton was quite apparently delighted by the Queen's approval, rewarding her, Masson says, with 'the most hyperbolic eulogy on anything called woman that ever came from Milton's pen.'—*Life*, Vol. IV, pp.597–598.

which I was constrained of necessity to engage in a cause at once so
arduous and invidious that I must seem to impugn all regal right,
have found a witness and an interpreter of my integrity so illustrious, so truly royal, as to interpret and bear witness for me that I
have spoken not a syllable against kings, but against the undermin-
ers and pests of kings—against tyrants only. But how magnanimous,
Augusta, how secure on all sides must you be, fortified as you are
with a virtue and wisdom clearly divine! when you could not only
peruse with such equanimity, such calmness, with a candour of
mind so unexampled, with a serenity of countenance so perfect,
what might have seemed written against your own right and dignity; but could adopt an opinion of this nature against your own
advocate himself, so as to be commonly thought even to award the
palm to his adversary! In what honour, in what veneration, must
you ever be held by me, when your exalted virtue and greatness of
spirit, not only glorious to yourself, but auspicious and fortunate
for me, have freed me, as it respects other kings, from all suspicion
and disgrace, and by this signal and immortal benefit have bound
me to you for ever! With what favour must foreigners have thought,
with what favour must your own people have both thought and
hoped of your equity and impartiality, when at a time in which your
own concerns, in which your majesty itself seemed to be the subject
of contention, they saw you delivering your judgement with as little
emotion, with no less composure, on your own rights, than you had
been accustomed to do on the rights of the people! Besides, it was
for no idle purpose that you collected from all parts such multitudes
of choice volumes, so many monuments of learning! It was not that
from these things yourself might learn anything, but that from them
your own citizens might learn to know you, that they might be able
to contemplate the pre-eminence of your virtue and of your wisdom; and unless the very image of the goddess of wisdom had sat
before your inmost spirit, unless she had appeared, as it were, in a
visible form before your eyes, she could never have raised in you,
by any book-learning, such an ardent love of herself. This makes
us admire the more your vigour of mind manifestly ethereal, as if

the purest particle of the breath divine had fallen upon those remote regions—a particle which that melancholy and cloudy sky,
with its freezing cold, could neither extinguish nor oppress; nor
could that horrid and rugged soil, which is wont to harden also the
minds of its inhabitants, create in you anything unequal or rough;
nay, this very land, so fertile in divers metals, though to others a
stepmother, being certainly to you a fostering parent, seems to have
exerted her utmost powers to produce you entirely of gold. I would
address you as the daughter of Adolphus, as the only descendant of
that invincible and famous king, if, Christina, you did not outshine
him as much as wisdom exceeds strength, as much as the arts of
peace surpass the stratagems of war. Henceforward, not the Queen
of the South alone shall be celebrated in story. The North has now
also his queen, and worthy too, not merely to go and listen to that
wisest King of the Jews, or to any other, should any ever more arise
like him, but to be herself the heroine to be visited by others, flock-
ing from all quarters as to the brightest pattern of royal virtue; and
who should confess that there is no dignity upon earth equal to her
praises and merits, of which they would see that the least is, that
she is a queen—the monarch of so many nations. Again, it is not
the least that she herself thinks this the least of her honours, and
meditates upon something far greater and more sublime than to
reign, meriting to be valued, on this very account, above innumerable kings. Hence she may abdicate the kingdom, should such a
misfortune await the Swedish nation; but that she who has proved
herself worthy of the empire not of Sweden only, but of the world,
should divest herself of the queen can never be in her power!

There is no one I trust, who, so far from blaming, would not
commend me for this digression to an eulogium of the Queen so
well deserved; an eulogium which, though others were silent, I
could not omit without a heavy charge of ingratitude; since, I know
not by what chance, though certainly by a most happy one, or
whether by some hidden consent or guidance of the stars, or of
spirits, or of things—I, who the least of all men expected,
who the most of all wished such a thing, have found in the

remotest regions an arbitress so illustrious, so impartial and favourable to me.

127. From the *Second Defence*. 1654.

From the Latin.

> After a discussion of the burning of the *First Defence* in Paris and in Toulouse, and a statement of his unconcern, Milton again gives an account of the world-wide approval given the *First Defence*, enforcing what he has to say by an account of the congratulations he received upon it from the various ambassadors resident in London at the time of its publication. He is again addressing Alexander More as author of the *Cry of the Royal Blood*.

'The infamous pages of Milton are strewn with sesamum and poppy of a like description.' [71] You always join me with some illustrious colleague, and in this affair you make me evidently Cromwell's equal, sometimes even his superior—a name by which, above all others, I think you honour me most, if anything honourable can proceed from you.—'But those pages (you say) were burned by the hangman at Paris, by order of the parliament.' So far from this being the work of the parliament, I find it was done by one of the city officers (and whether he held a civil or an uncivil office I know not) at the instigation of some of the clergy, those laziest of animals, who from scattered and distant auguries prognosticated for their own bellies what I pray may one day fall upon them.[72] Do you

71 The reference is to Cromwell's letter to Walter Dundas, Governor of Edinburgh Castle, September 12, 1650, shortly after the battle of Dunbar, September 3: 'Now if the civil Authority, or that part of it which continued faithful to their trust, and true to the ends of the Covenant, did in answer to their consciences, turn out a tyrant, in a way in which the Christians in aftertimes will mention with honour, and all tyrants in the world look at with fear; and if while many thousands of saints in England rejoice to think of it, and have received from the hand of God a liberty from the fear of like usurpations, . . . will this be found a "personal persecution?" '

72 'The fame of Milton's Answer to Salmasius had been steadily on the increase. In France, more particularly, it had been greatly promoted by the public burning of the book by the hands of the hangman at Paris and Toulouse. As far as Milton himself could learn, the burning at Paris . . . had not been the act of the Government, but only of some city official, stimulated by the clergy.'—Masson, *Life*, Vol. IV, p.341.

imagine that we also could not have burned, in our turn, the royal defence of Salmasius? If I had thought such an insult deserving of any other revenge than contempt, I could myself have easily obtained this from our magistrates. In your hurry to put out one fire by another, you have raised an Herculean pile, from which I may rise up in greater brightness. We have more wisely thought that the chilliness of the royal defence should not be warmed. But this I wonder at, that the people of Toulouse should have become so unlike their ancestors (for I find I have been also burned at Toulouse) as now to burn the defence of liberty and religion in the very city in which under the counts of Raimond both liberty and religion had been before so signally defended. 'Would! (you exclaim) that the writer also had been burned!' And is this indeed your wish, slave? You have taken especial care that I shall not return you a like compliment, as you have been long since consuming in far blacker flames. You are burned by your adulteries, you are burned by your fornications, you are burned by your perjuries, by the aid of which perjuries you perfidiously shook off the woman who became betrothed to you by the sacrifice of her honour; you are burned by your outrageous madness, which has impelled you, miscreant as you are, to covet the holiest of functions, and as a priest to pollute with adulterous hands the undiscerned body of the Lord. Under the pretence of sanctity also, you would denounce in this cry of yours, everything that is direful against pretenders to sanctity, though you must bring your own accursed head into the snare, as being condemned even by your own sentence. With these crimes, with these infamies are you all on fire; in these furious flames are you scorching day and night, and suffering a punishment for us, than which no enemy could imprecate on you one more grievous. Meanwhile, these burnings of yours injure not, they touch not me; and against such disgraces I have many things to oppose which are grateful, which are delightful to my spirit. Under the influence of bad auspices, I have been burned by one court, perhaps by a single Parisian executioner. But in spite of this, how many excellent and learned men are there, throughout all France, who read, approve, embrace?

How many throughout the spacious tracts of Germany, the domicile, as it were, of liberty, and in other regions, wherever any traces of liberty are yet visible: and even Greece herself—Athens the eye of Greece, revived as it seems once more—has contributed her applause by the voice of one of her sons, the noble Philaras.[73] This, moreover, I can truly say; at the time when our defence was first published and readers were all glowing with attention to it, there was not an ambassador from any prince or state at that time in the city, who did not congratulate me either on an accidental meeting, who did not desire my company at his own house, or who did not visit me at mine. But it were an injury to forget your departed spirit, Adrian Pauw, who, with the high dignity of ambassador to us, and the glory and ornament of Holland, were solicitous to make known to me by frequent messages, though I never happened to see you, your great and distinguished kindness towards me. It is also pleasing to me to dwell frequently upon the circumstance, and which, it is my belief, could never have happened without the especial favour of God, that I, who, as it seemed, had been writing in opposition to kings, have obtained the approving nod even of royal majesty itself, and its testimony, only not divine, to my integrity and to the superior truth of my opinion. And why should I scruple to say this as often as I think of that most august queen whose high praises are the theme of every tongue? Indeed, not even that wisest Athenian, between whom and myself, however, I make no comparison, can I think more graced by the testimony of the Pythian himself, than me by her opinion. And if I had happened to have written what I have, when a young man, and the same liberty were allowed to orators as to poets, I should in truth not have hesitated to prefer my fortune to that of some among the gods; forasmuch as they, being gods, contended only for beauty, or in music, before a human arbiter; and I, being a man, with a goddess for my arbitress, have come off victorious in the noblest far of all contests. Thus highly honoured, no one but an executioner would dare to treat me with disrespect, whether by ordering it to be done, or by doing it himself.

73 See Familiar Letter 12 (extract 153).

128. From the *Second Defence*. 1654.

From the Latin.
  Specific comment upon the *Tenure of Kings and Magistrates* in
  response to gibes in the *Cry*.

But as you are so courageous a fellow, what has checked your
late violence? 'Unless (you say) I had been religiously scrupulous
not to invade the province of the great Salmasius, to whom shall
be left the substantial part of the victory over his great adversary,
forsooth.' Since you now seem to think *me* great as well as him, I
shall perhaps be found to be a province the more difficult to be invaded, especially as he is dead. I am little solicitous about the victory, provided only truth be the victor.—Meanwhile, you pursue
your clamour: 'They convert parricide into a doctrine; and this
they would fain do with the consent of the reformed churches; they
dare not defend it openly. This was the opinion also, says Milton,
of the most eminent divines, the very authors of the reformation in
the church.' It was, I say; and this I have shown abundantly in the
book, in our own tongue, entitled the *Tenure of Kings and Magistrates*, second edition; and in other places. What I have done so
often, I feel a reluctance to do again. In that work, I have cited word
for word the very passages from Luther, Zuinglius, Calvin, Bucer,
Martyr, Pareus, and lastly from that Knox, 'the only Scot (you say)
I have of my side, and who was condemned, as to this matter, by all
the Protestants of that age, especially by the French.'

129. From the *Second Defence*. 1654.

From the Latin.
  The most pointed suggestion that Milton regarded the defences
  as his patriotic epic.

As for myself, to whatever state things may return, I have performed, and certainly with a good will, I hope not in vain, the service which I thought would be of most use to the commonwealth.
It is not before our own doors alone that I have borne my arms in
defence of liberty; I have wielded them on a field so wide that the

justice and reason of these which are no vulgar deeds shall be explained and vindicated alike to foreign nations and to our own countrymen; and by all good men shall no doubt be approved; and shall remain to the matchless renown of my fellow citizens, and as the brightest example for after-ages. If our last actions should not be sufficiently answerable to the first, it is for themselves to see to it. I have celebrated, as a testimony to them, I had almost said, a monument, which will not speedily perish, actions which were glorious, lofty, which were almost above all praise; and if I have done nothing else, I have assuredly discharged my trust. But as the poet who is styled epic, if he adhere strictly to established rules, undertakes to embellish not the whole life of the hero whom he proposes to celebrate in song, but usually one particular action of his life, as for example, that of Achilles at Troy, or the return of Ulysses, or the arrival of Æneas in Italy, and leaves alone the rest, so likewise will it suffice for my duty and excuse that I have at least embellished one of the heroic actions of my countrymen. The rest I pass by: for who could do justice to all the great actions of an entire people? [74]

130. Familiar Letter 16, to Leo Van Aizema. 1654/5.

From the Latin.

> Milton replies to a letter from Van Aizema, whom he had no doubt known from the time of Van Aizema's appointment in 1652 as resident ambassador in London from the Hanse towns. Van Aizema writes from the Hague, January 29, 1654/5, as follows: 'Partly because Morus, in his book, has made some aspersions on you for your English Book on Divorce, partly because many have been inquiring eagerly about the arguments with which you support your opinion, I have, most honoured and esteemed Sir, given your little work entire to a friend of mine to be translated into Dutch, with a desire to have it printed soon. Not knowing, however, whether you would like anything corrected therein or added, I take the liberty to give you this notice, and to request you to let me know your mind on the subject.' [75]

74 See Introduction, pp.xix–xxi, and the *First Defence* (extracts 91 and 120).
75 Masson's translation, *Life*, Vol. V, p.170.

Van Aizema seems not to have kept to his intention; at any rate
I am unable to find any trace of the translation.

It is very gratifying to me that you retain the same amount of recollection of me as you very politely showed of good will by once
and again visiting me while you resided among us. As regards the
book on divorce, which you tell me you have given to someone to
be turned into Dutch, I would rather you had given it to be turned
into Latin.[76] For my experience in those books of mine has now
been that the vulgar still receive according to their wont, opinions
not already common. I wrote a good while ago, I may mention,
three treatises on the subject: the first, in two books, in which the
Doctrine and Discipline of Divorce (for that is the title of the book) is
contained at large; a second, which is called *Tetrachordon*, and in
which the four chief passages of Scripture concerning that doctrine
are explicated; the third called *Colasterion*, in which answer is made
to a certain sciolist. Which of these treatises you have given to be
translated, or what edition, I do not know: the first of them was
twice issued, and was much enlarged in the second edition. Should
you not have been made aware of this already, or should I understand that you desire anything else on my part, such as sending you
the more correct edition or the rest of the treatises, I shall attend to
the matter carefully and with pleasure. For there is not anything at
present that I should wish changed in them or added. Therefore,
should you keep to your intention, I earnestly hope for myself a
faithful translator and for you all prosperity.

Westminster: February 5, 1654/5.

131. From the *Defence of Himself*. 1655.

From the Latin.

After another apology for his entrance into personal controversy,
Milton expresses a judgement that in his reproof of a 'common adversary almost of all men' he has done a work acceptable to God,

76 Cf. the *Second Defence* (extract 2): 'I could wish only that I had not written
in the vernacular tongue, for I had not fallen upon vernacular readers,
with whom it is usual to be unconscious of their own good fortune and to

salutary to the church, and useful to the commonwealth. The passage is also interesting for its commentary upon education and its proper uses.

It is true, that in that former defence[77] to which I was called by a public order and by private injury, as it was the cause of my country as well as my own, I performed the common task with zealous diligence: and who will say I ought to have chosen rather to lose by silence the honest reputation I might have gained by speaking, and to leave it, as it were, without a possessor, to be invaded and oppressed by lies? And being now under a heavy accusation, by the same person,[78] of having defamed forsooth by scandal and falsehood an innocent and unoffending man, that I might confound his impudence and vindicate my own innocence, and further (if I have hitherto written anything well, or shall hereafter write what may be of utility) that I may be able to obtain, if not the praise of learning and of genius, at least a fame untainted by dishonour, with the credit of being an adorer of truth—I have stooped again to this contention, necessary indeed, though in itself most ungrateful. Nor, if these inducements were wanting, should I myself have any reason to repent of this undertaking; nor would anyone else, unless conscious of guilt, have any cause for sorrow. Indeed, as the reproof of the bad is meant as a most serious punishment, so is the commendation of the good intended as the noblest reward; it is not merely just—it goes near to the perfection of justice: we may add that in the just regulation of life we see they are both almost of equal efficacy. In effect, these two things are so closely allied that they are accomplished by one and the same act: for when we blame the bad we may be considered in some sort as praising the good. But that each may have its peculiar province, and reason, and use, they are not alike in point of favour; for he who blames another has to sustain at once the burden and the envy of two very serious things: namely, the burden

ridicule the misfortune of others.' In prose as in verse Milton has come to seek 'fit audience though few.'

77 The *Second Defence*.

78 This time Alexander More, in the *Public Faith of Alexander More*, and not the 'same person' that had attacked him in the *Cry*, Peter Du Moulin.

of accusing another, and the envy which is the consequence of his having a good opinion of himself. Hence it is that both the good and the bad readily bestow praise, and with little distinction, upon the worthy and the unworthy; but no one, except the upright alone, openly and fearlessly either presumes, or has the authority, to accuse. We, who as boys are accustomed under so many masters to sweat in the shade at eloquence, and who are convinced that its persuasive power consists in censure no less than in applause, may, it is true, safely and valiantly batter the names of ancient tyrants: and as it happens, we kill Mezentius over again in stale antitheses; or, in the rueful bellowing of enthymemes, we roast, with a daintiness more exquisite than in his own bull, the Agrigentine Phalaris. I allude to those who were trained in the public walks and schools of exercise: for such are the men whom in a republic we most delight to honour and adore—such we fondly style most potent and most magnificent and most august! But yet, it was expected that those who thus spent a good part of their prime in mere pastime in the shade, should, at some after period, when the country, when the republic, stood in need of their services, throw aside their foils, and dare the sun and the dust and the field; that they should at last have the courage to use in their contests hands and arms of flesh and blood, to brandish real weapons, to encounter a real enemy. We persecute, with no small hostility indeed, some, the Suffenuses and sophists; some, the Pharisees, the Simons, the Hymenæuses, the Alexanders: for all these are ancients. But when we find them brought to life again, and appearing in the modern church, then we club our eulogies for them and honour them, with stipends and professorial chairs, as patterns of all excellence, as prodigies of learning, as mirrors of sanctity. Should we ever go so far as to censure; should the mask and the fair outside happen to be torn away from one of this sort; should he prove to be foul within, nay plainly, manifestly villainous, there are yet not wanting those who (influenced by what consideration, by what fear, I know not) would rather choose for him to be defended by public testimonies than branded with his merited reproof. My way of thinking is, I confess, far enough removed from this, as I have shown by my conduct on more occasions than one. If as a boy in the above mentioned recreations of learning I have profited anything from the precepts of the learned, or from my own lucubrations, it is my purpose, as far as my infirmity will permit, and if I may hope to perform anything on so wide a field, to contribute the whole to increase the welfare of life and of humankind. And if even from private enmities public offences are sometimes reproved and often corrected; if impelled by every motive to inflict reproof so well deserved upon an adversary now become not mine alone, but the common adversary almost of all men, upon a character outrageously scandalous, the disgrace of the reformed religion and above all of the holy order, the blot of letters, the fatal preceptor of youth, the preacher impure in sacred things—whether I shall have done this with all that effect which it ought to have, it is their business to see whom it most concerns to make an example of him. As for me, I have the hope (for why shall I have any mistrust?) that I have performed an office neither unacceptable to God, unsalutary to the church, or without its utility to the commonwealth.

132. From Familiar Letter 28, to Jean Labadie, Minister of Orange. 1659.

From the Latin.

The letter of which this is a part is an invitation to Labadie, a Catholic priest turned Protestant, and a charlatan, to settle in London. Milton was fortunate that the invitation was not accepted, for he might well have found himself befriending a man of whom were said things very like those he himself urged against More.[79]

If I answer you rather late, distinguished and reverend sir, our common friend Durie,[80] I believe, will not refuse to let me transfer the

79 Masson, *Life*, Vol. V, pp.592–595.
80 John Durie, who translated Milton's *Eikonoklastes* into French, was the friend who told More of Milton's purposed publication of the *Second Defence*, attributing the *Cry* to More. In More's behalf Durie wrote two letters to Milton telling him that More denied authorship and that two of More's friends had assured him that More was not the author.

blame of the late answer from myself to him. For now that he has communicated to me that paper which you wished read to me, on the subject of your doings and sufferings in behalf of the Gospel, I have not deferred preparing this letter for you, to be given to the first carrier, being really anxious as to the interpretation you may put upon my long silence. I owe very great thanks meanwhile to your Du Moulin of Nîmes,[81] who by his speeches and most friendly talk concerning me has procured me the good will of so many good men in those parts. And truly, though I am not ignorant that, whether from the fact that I did not when publicly commissioned decline the contest with an adversary of such name, or on account of the celebrity of the subject, or, finally, on account of my style of writing, I have become sufficiently known far and wide, yet my feeling is that I have real fame only in proportion to the good esteem I have among good men. That you also are of this way of thinking I see plainly. . . .

133. From Familiar Letter 29, to Henry Oldenburg. 1659.

From the Latin.
      The letter is eloquent of Milton's disappointment in the course of the events leading up to the Restoration.

That forgiveness which you ask for *your* silence you will give rather to *mine*; for, if I remember rightly, it was my turn to write to you. By no means has it been any diminution of my regard for you (of this I would have you fully persuaded) that has been the impediment, but only my employments or domestic cares; or perhaps it is mere sluggishness to the act of writing that makes me guilty of the intermitted duty. As you desire to be informed, I am, by God's mercy, as well as usual. Of any such work as compiling the history of our political troubles, which you seem to advise, I have no thought whatever: they are worthier of silence than of commemoration.

81 Peter Du Moulin the elder, a French Protestant clergyman, whose son of the same name was the actual author of the *Cry*.

134. From the *Ready and Easy Way to Establish a Free Common-wealth*. 1660.

Even the tone of what Milton writes upon the eve of the Restoration is significant.

However, with all hazard I have ventured what I thought my duty to speak in season, and to forewarn my country in time: wherein I doubt not but there be many wise men in all places and degrees, but am sorry the effects of wisdom are so little seen among us. Many circumstances and particulars I could have added in those things whereof I have spoken; but a few main matters now put speedily in execution will suffice to recover us and set all right: and there will want at no time who are good at circumstances; but men who set their minds on main matters and sufficiently urge them, in these most difficult times I find not many. What I have spoken is the language of that which is not called amiss 'the good old cause': if it seem strange to any, it will not seem more strange, I hope, than convincing to backsliders. Thus much I should perhaps have said though I were sure I should have spoken only to trees and stones, and had none to cry to but with the prophet, 'O earth, earth, earth!' to tell the very soil itself what her perverse inhabitants are deaf to— nay though what I have spoke should happen (which Thou suffer not, who didst create mankind free; nor Thou next, who didst redeem us from being servants of men!) to be the last words of our expiring liberty.[82] But I trust I shall have spoken persuasion to abundance of sensible and ingenuous men—to some perhaps whom God may raise of these stones to become children of reviving liberty —and may reclaim, though they seem now choosing them a captain back for Egypt, to bethink themselves a little and consider whither they are rushing; to exhort this torrent also of the people, not to be so impetuous, but to keep their due channel; and at length recovering and uniting their better resolutions, now that they see already how open and unbounded the insolence and rage is of our common enemies, to stay these ruinous proceedings, justly and timely fear-

82 Milton's last before the Restoration.

ing to what a precipice of destruction the deluge of this epidemic
madness would hurry us through the general defection of a misguided and abused multitude.

*Milton's achievements in prose and his reward for them will be found
mentioned further in extracts* 1, 2, 43, 46, 48, 65, 71, 79, 91, 92, 95–
97, 111, *and* 112.

XI. THE SECRETARYSHIP

Some sudden pieces of business.

135. From the Orders of the Council. 1649/50.

At various times during his secretaryship Milton took the oath of
secrecy, at least once in this form—on February 23, 1649/50.

THAT Mr. John Milton . . . did this day take the Engagement following: 'I, being nominated by this Council to be . . . for the
year to come, do promise in the sight of God that, through His
grace, I will be faithful in the performance of the trust committed
to me, and not reveal or disclose anything, in whole or in part, directly or indirectly, that shall be debated or resolved upon in the
Council and ordered to be kept secret by the said Council, without
the command, direction, or allowance of the Parliament or Council.'

136. Milton to Mylius. 1651.

From the Latin.
   The length of the correspondence between Milton and Mylius,
   the extravagance of Mylius' flattery of Milton, and the disproportionate pains that Milton expended in return for it upon an unimportant errand for a comparatively unimportant stranger, suggest that except for his literary services Milton was not a very
   efficient secretary, that he was too wasteful of his energies to be a
   really capable man of affairs.

Most noble sir, I have received from you now three letters, filled
with all courtesy and the greatest kind feeling toward myself, in the
first two of which you signify in most friendly fashion that you desire to meet me. I am indeed sorry that partly because of business
with which I am at present much distracted, and partly because of
ill health, I have been unable as yet to receive a gentleman and visi-

tor so full of regard for me, and certainly I cannot longer refrain from replying by letter at least, if I may not do so in person, to your distinguished civility to me. The drafts of which you speak have been sent to me, and, so far as I could command the time, I have gone through them with some care. But, while in view of their tenor I cannot readily foresee what you are likely to secure for your Count from our people,[1] I can say this, that you have overlooked nothing in this matter which might pertinently have been said to gain your end. And I hope that a reply in harmony with your desire will shortly be given to you. For I know the men to whom this affair has been referred have this in view. Meanwhile the drafts, read through as I say, I return to you, and I place at your disposal all my good offices in this and any other matter, with all possible faith and respect. Your most zealous and attached,

John Milton.

London: November 7, 1651.

[1] Among the letters of state, which as Latin Secretary it was Milton's duty to write, is one as follows to the Count of Oldenburgh:

'Most Illustrious Lord,

'The Parliament of the Commonwealth of England have received an extraordinary congratulation from Your Excellency most kindly and courteously delivered to us by word of mouth by Herman Mylius, your counsellor and doctor of laws, who wished all things lucky and prosperous in your name to the Parliament and English interest and desired that the friendship of this republic might remain inviolable within your territories. He also desired letters of safe-conduct, to the end your subjects may the more securely trade and sail from place to place, together with our orders to our public ministers abroad to be aiding and assisting to Your Excellency and your interests with their good offices and counsels. To which requests of his we willingly consented, and granted both our friendship, the letters desired, and our orders to our public ministers under the seal of the Parliament. And though it be some months ago since your public minister first came to us, however that delay neither arose from any unwillingness on our part to assent to the request made in Your Excellency's name, or that your deputy was at any time wanting in his sedulity (whose solicitations were daily and earnest with all the diligence and importunity that became him, to the end he might be dispatched), but only it happened so, that at that time the greatest and most weighty affairs of the republic were under debate and serious negotiation. Of which we thought meet to certify Your Illustrious Lordship lest anybody, through a false construction of this delay, should think those favours unwillingly or hardly obtained which

137. Milton to Mylius. 1651/2.

From the Latin.

Before I reply, most noble Hermann, to your letter to me of the seventeenth of December, I must first of all, lest you should perchance consider me the person responsible for so long a silence, explain why I did not reply sooner. Understand then that a first cause of delay was poor health, a thing that is now almost a perpetual enemy of mine; next, on account of my health, there was a sudden and unavoidable removal to another house,[2] and I had begun the same, as it chanced, on the very day on which your letter was brought me; finally, I was, in truth, ashamed at then having nothing to report on your business that I thought would be agreeable to you. For, when, the day after, I met Mr. Frost[3] accidentally, and carefully inquired of him whether any answer was yet under resolution for you (for in my invalid state I was often myself absent from the Council), he told me, and with some concern, that nothing was yet being formulated, and that he was having no success in his efforts to expedite the affair. I thought it better, therefore, to be silent for a time than to write at once what I knew would be annoying to you, and this in the expectation of afterwards being able to write, with full satisfaction, what *I* wanted to write and *you* so much desired. Today, as I hope, I have brought things to a conclusion; for after I had in the Council once or twice reminded the President[4] of your business, he reported it immediately, and with such effect that tomorrow is appointed for

were most gladly granted by the Parliament of the Commonwealth of England. In whose name these are commanded to be signed.
      'Henry Scobel, Clerk of the Parliament.'—Columbia *Milton*, Vol. XIII, pp.115–117.
2 From Scotland Yard to a house 'in Petty France in Westminster, next door to the Lord Scudamore's and opening into St. James' Park.' Edward Phillips.—Darbishire, *Early Lives*, p.71.
3 Gualter Frost, the elder, General Secretary to the Council of State, and hence Milton's near colleague and superior.
4 Whitlocke, who was appointed President of the Council for the coming month on December 29, 1651. He was succeeded by Sir Arthur Haselrig, January 28, 1651/2.—The Council Order Books, in Masson, *Life*, Vol. IV, pp.421, 423.

the consideration of an answer to be given to you as speedily as possible. And that consideration I venture to say will be very brief, unless you insist upon defining that word *brief* too precisely, as if in
arithmetic. I thought that if I were the first, as was my purpose, to
give you this information, you would be greatly pleased, and it
would also be a sign of my regard for you. Most zealous for your
affairs and honour,

John Milton.

Petty France, Westminster: January 2, 1651/2.

138. Milton to Mylius. 1651/2.

From the Latin.

Most noble sir, this safeguard, suitably phrased to the best of my
ability (for I used for the most part your own words), I send you to
be read over. Some points I found it necessary to insert, others I
abbreviated; I hardly think the Council wishes it to be more detailed; more succinct I could not make it, since in all things I wish
it to be satisfactory to you. I send you the identical copy which I am
to show this evening at the meeting of the Council; so unless it be
sent back to me by the second hour this afternoon, I fear I may not
carry the matter through today. Most zealous for your fame,

John Milton.

January 8, 1651/2.

139. From Milton to Mylius. 1651/2.

From the Latin.

Most noble sir, yesterday I attended the meeting of the Council
according to my wont, with your documents; and when finding opportunity I explained the matter to the President,[5] he at once laid
before the Council the reading of them in both languages; and nothing seemed likely to be denied, provided care be taken to guard the

5 Whitlocke.

interests of our friends the people of Bremen, against whom some, I know not why, seem to suspect my Lord Count of plotting.

140. Milton to Mylius. 1651/2.

From the Latin.

Most noble sir, what I promised you yesterday, I fulfilled punctiliously; I spoke about your business with the individuals to whom I knew it had been referred. Most of them seemed to me not to have given it sufficient attention, rather than to have been unwilling to grant you what you ask, for they also thought that they had granted you in that document just what you wished. But I was not able to secure another discussion of the subject yesterday in the Council, nor do I feel sure on what day I shall achieve this. Thus it remains for you not to neglect your own interests, but to write to the Council about that postponement; for I have omitted naught which in me lies. Most zealous for your honour and plans,

John Milton.

February 10, 1651/2.

141. Milton to Mylius. 1651/2.

From the Latin.

Yesterday, my most respected Hermann, after you left, there came to me an order of the Council, by which I was commanded to compare the Latin copy with the English and take care that they agree with each other; then to send both to Mr. Whitlocke and Neville to be read. I both did this and at the same time wrote fully to Mr. Whitlocke about what you wished to be inserted, namely that provision be made for the successors and descendants of the Lord Count, in the very formula which you yourself suggested: I added besides the reasons you advanced why, if this were not done, nothing would seem to have been accomplished. What afterwards happened in the Council, I do not positively know, for I was not present, being kept away by yesterday's rain. If you send some of your people to the secretaries of the Council, or better to Mr. Frost, I believe you will hear from them, or in any case you shall learn in the evening from me. Your most devoted,

John Milton.

February 13, 1651/2.

142. From the English Correspondence, Milton to Whitlocke. 1651/2.

My Lord,

By an order of the Council, which I received this morning, I am appointed to look over the Latin copy of the safeguard granted to the Count of Oldenburgh, and to bring it to Your Lordship and Mr. Neville to be perused. The agent himself was with me this morning and desired earnestly to see the copy, which because it was a thing granted to him by the Council at his request, I thought it could be no trespass to let him see, and it pleased him well enough when he had read it; only he desired that where the two marks be on the margent of the English copy this clause might be inserted, 'Together with his successors either in fee or his own proper right, provided they act or design nothing against the Commonwealth of England': and he alleges this reason, because his Lord is very old, and desires as well to provide for his posterity as for himself, and if he should chance to die ere the agent should return home or soon after, that then all his pains here and time spent, would prove to no purpose. If for this reason, which seems but just, this clause concerning his successors may be inserted, I believe it will content him, else not. Which I thought with the soonest to communicate to Your Lordship, with the papers themselves, and the Latin made agreeable to the English, with the addition of some few words in the beginning, and in another place toward the end which I believe were left out by chance in the English, and so take leave.

Your Lordship's faithful servant,

John Milton.

February 12, 1651/2.

143. Milton to Mylius. 1651/2.

From the Latin.

Most noble sir, it is now three days since I sent those documents you wish to see to the secretaries of the Council to be copied; the diploma which I sent to Mr. Whitlocke to be read for the last time in Parliament, I have not seen since then. Mr. Frost told me that everything was granted in it according to your desire. There remains nothing, so far as I know, but for the documents to be sent by the Secretary of the Council to the Clerk of the Parliament to be signed; if this be not yet done, I will on Monday, when I go to the Council, see that it be done as soon as may be, when I have once made sure that the clause which you wished to be put in has been inserted. Heartily zealous for you,

John Milton.

February 21, 1651/2.

144. From the English Correspondence, Milton to Bradshaw. 1652/3.

My Lord,

But that it would be an interruption to the public, wherein your studies are perpetually employed, I should now and then venture to supply this my enforced absence with a line or two, though it were my only business, and that would be no slight one, to make my due acknowledgements of your many favours; which I both do at this time and ever shall; and have this farther which I thought my part to let you know of, that there will be with you tomorrow upon some occasion of business a gentleman whose name is Mr. Marvile,[6] a man whom both by report, and the converse I have had with him, of singular desert for the state to make use of; who also offers himself, if there be any employment for him. His father was the minister of Hull, and he hath spent four years abroad in Holland, France, Italy, and Spain, to very good purpose, as I be-

6 Andrew Marvell.

lieve, and the gaining of those four languages; besides he is a scholar and well read in the Latin and Greek authors, and no doubt of an approved conversation; for he comes now lately out of the house of the Lord Fairfax who was General, where he was entrusted to give some instructions in the languages to the Lady his daughter. If upon the death of Mr. Wakerley[7] the Council shall think that I shall need any assistant in the performance of my place (though for my part I find no encumbrance of that which belongs to me, except it be in point of attendance at conferences with ambassadors, which I must confess in my condition I am not fit for), it would be hard for them to find a man so fit every way for that purpose as this gentleman, one who I believe in a short time would be able to do them as good service as Mr. Ascan.[8] This my Lord I write sincerely without any other end than to perform my duty to the public in helping them to an able servant, laying aside those jealousies and that emulation which mine own condition might suggest to me by bringing in such a coadjutor; and remain,

My Lord, your most obliged and faithful servant,

John Milton.

February 21, 1652/3.
For the Honourable the Lord Bradshaw.

145. From Familiar Letter 19, to Richard Jones. 1656.

From the Latin.
  Richard Jones, who later became third Viscount and first Earl of Ranelagh, was one of Milton's pupils, sent by his mother, Lady Ranelagh, who was also influential in sending to Milton her nephew, the Earl of Barrimore.[9]

7 George Weckherlin, Milton's assistant in the Secretaryship, March 11, 1652 until the end of November. Thurlow was given an additional salary, December 1, 1652, for taking over Weckherlin's work. Marvell became Milton's assistant by appointment of Cromwell, but not until 1657.
8 Perhaps Anthony Ascham, the English Resident in Madrid, who had been assassinated May 27, 1650. Milton's amanuensis on this occasion was not skilful.
9 Masson, *Life*, Vol. III, pp.658–660.

Preparing again and again to reply to your last letter, I was first prevented, as you know, by some sudden pieces of business, of such a kind as are apt to be mine;[10] then I heard you were off on an excursion to some places in your neighbourhood; and now your most excellent mother, on her way to Ireland—whose departure ought to be a matter of no ordinary regret to both of us (for to me also she has stood in the place of all kith and kin)—carries you this letter herself. That you feel assured of my affection for you, right and well; and I would have you feel daily more and more assured of it, the more of good disposition and of good use of your advantages you give me to see in you. . . .

Victories of princes, which you extol with praises, and matters of that sort in which force is of most avail, I would not have you admire too much, now that you are listening to philosophers. For what should be the great wonder if in the native land of *wethers* there are born strong horns, able to *ram* down most powerfully cities and towns? Learn you, already from your early age, to weigh and discern great characters not by force and animal strength, but by justice and temperance. Farewell; and please to give best salutations in my name to the highly accomplished Henry Oldenburg, your chamber-fellow.

Westminster: September 21, 1656.

146. Familiar Letter 27, to Peter Heimbach. 1657.

From the Latin.

    Masson surmises from a letter of 1656 (extract 36) that Heimbach perhaps served Milton as amanuensis during a visit to London.[11] The present letter he discusses as a courteous discouragement of further requests from Heimbach and for the light it throws upon Milton's relationship to the Council.[12] Milton writes Heim-

10 It is for this sentence, Milton's only comment of the kind upon his duties as secretary, that this extract is placed in this section rather than among Milton's comments upon his friendships.
11 *Life*, Vol. V, pp.279–280.
12 Ibid., Vol. V, pp.380–382.

bach again in 1666 (extract 157), neither here nor then so cordially as in the first letter, in 1656.

I have received your letter dated the Hague, December 18, which, as I see it concerns your interests, I have thought I ought to answer on the very day it has reached me. After thanking me for I know not what favours of mine—which, as one who desires everything good for you, I would were really of any consideration at all—you ask me to recommend you, through Lord Lawrence,[13] to our minister appointed for Holland. I really regret that this is not in my power, both because of my very few intimacies with the men of influence, almost shut up at home as I am, and as I prefer to be, and also because I believe the gentleman is now embarking and on his way, and has with him in his company the person he wishes to be his secretary—the very office about him you seek. But the post is this instant going. Farewell.

Westminster: December 18, 1657.

Milton's activities as Latin secretary are also mentioned in extracts 2, 46, and 95.

13 Henry Lawrence, President of the Council during the first protectorate and a member of Oliver's privy council during the second. It was to his elder son, Milton's pupil, that Milton's sonnet XVII (extract 32) was addressed. The minister referred to is George Downing.

XII. MISCELLANEOUS

But fie my wandring Muse how thou dost stray!

147. Elegy I, to Charles Diodati. 1626.

From the Latin.

AT last, dear friend, your letter has come to my hand, and its sheets, serving as messenger, have brought your voice to my ears, aye, brought it from afar, from the western bank of the Dee, by Chester, where the Dee with down-darting waters makes for the Vergivian [Irish] main. Much, believe me, much does it pleasure me that lands remote have nurtured a heart so full of love for me, a soul so loyal, and that a quarter of the world far off owes me a charming comrade, a quarter far off, yes, but minded at command to deliver him soon to me.

I am detained in the city that the Thames laves with its refluent waters; possessed am I, though not against my will, by the charming city of my birth. Not now am I concerned to revisit the reedy Cam, nor am I harrowed now by love of my Lares there, this long time denied me. I find no pleasure in fields that are naked and that refuse soft shade; how ill-adapted is such a place to the worshippers of Phœbus! I am not minded to bear unceasingly the threats of an unbending teacher and all the other trials that are not to be met by a nature such as mine. If it be exile for a man to visit his home, his father's house, and free of all anxieties to pursue the delights of leisure, then I refuse not the name of exile, nor, if you will, the *lot* of exile; nay, right merrily I enjoy the terms imposed by 'exile.'[1] Would to heaven the bard had ne'er borne heavier lot, that famous

---

[1] This is the only reference in Milton's writings to his rustication from Cambridge. What other information we have about it comes from Aubrey, who claims as his authority, Milton's brother, Christopher Milton: 'And was a very hard student in the university, and performed all his exercises there with very good applause. His first tutor there was Mr. Chappell, from whom

bard who was exile in Tomis' borders: he had not then yielded
aught to Ionia's son, Homer's self, and you, Maro, had been out-
done, and the first meed of praise would not now be yours! [I enjoy
my 'exile'], for I am privileged now to give, here, hours free of all
else to the calm Muses, and my books—my true life—sweep me off
with them, mastering me utterly. Presently, when I am weary
grown, the splendour of the rounded theatre welcomes me, and
summons me to sound its plaudits, whether I am listening to some
canny ancient, or to a spendthrift heir, or a suitor is on the boards,
or a soldier with his casque now laid aside, or if some lawyer, grown
rich through a suit ten years prolonged, thunders out in an uncouth
court outlandish words, or if some roguish slave comes to the aid of
a love-struck son, and at every turn tricks the nose of the lad's unbending father. Oft-times there a maiden, marvelling at new fires,
knows not what love is, yet while she knows not, loves. Mayhap
Tragedy, distraught, shakes her blood-dyed staff, her locks the
while flung loose, her eyes rolling wildly. It pains me, and yet I
look, and find pleasure in looking though it pains me. Sometimes
there is a sweet bitterness in the tears I shed if some hapless lad
leaves joys untasted and falls in death, fit subject thus for tears,
through the rending of his love, or if some merciless avenger of
crime, issuing from the darkness, traverses again the Styx, and with
his funeral brand affrights conscience-stricken souls, or if sorrow
o'erwhelms the house of Pelops or the lordly house of Ilium, or if
Creon's court makes atonement for incestuous forebears.

Yet I hide not always 'neath a roof or within the city, nor do the
hours of spring slip by void of all profit for me. A grove too claims
me, a grove thick grown with elms, near the city, and the glorious
shade of some spot not remote from the town. There o'er and o'er
one may see troops of maidens pass, stars, these, that breathe forth
alluring fires. Ah, how oft have I gazed spellbound on some marvellous form, form fit to have power to renew the ravages of age, even

receiving some unkindness (whipt him), he was afterwards (though it
seemed against the rules of the college) transferred to the tuition of one
Mr. Tovell, who died parson of Lutterworth.'—Darbishire, *Early Lives*,
p.10.

in Jupiter's self! [2] Ah, how oft have I seen eyes that outdid jewels and the fires that either pole keeps in revolution, and necks that surpassed [in whiteness] the [ivory] arms of Pelops, twice alive, and that streaming Way which is steeped in nectar undilute! How oft have I seen peerless beauty of brow, and dancing tresses, the golden nets that Cupid, prince of tricksters, spreads, and seductive cheeks —matched with such cheeks the hyacinth's crimson beauty, even the blushing hues of your own flower, Adonis, seem dull and tarnished. Yield, ye heroic maidens, once lauded so oft, yield, too, every maid that e'er enthralled wide-wandering Jove! Yield, ye maids of Achæmenia, maids with foreheads turret-crowned! Yield, all ye maids that dwell in Susa, and in Memnon's Nineveh! Yield ye, too, nymphs of Greece, lower your *fasces*; yield ye, maids of Ilium, and daughters of Romulus! Let not now the Tarpeian Muse boast of Pompey's Columns, or of the theatres crowded with Ausonian stoles! 'Tis to the maids of Britain that first glory [in beauty] is due! Count it enough, women of other lands, that you can follow them [in beauty]. You, London, city reared by Dardan settlers, made conspicuous far and wide by your towered head, blessed, all too blessed, you enclose within your walls whatever beauty the pendent earth possesses. The stars that flash for you in the unclouded skies—the host that serves Endymion's goddess—number not so many as the maids who, resplendent with beauty of person and with gold, flash radiant on all eyes throughout your streets. Men believe the tale that Venus, giver of life, made her way to this city, riding in a car drawn by twin doves, guarded by her quiver-bearing warriors, because she was minded to set below this city Cnidus, and the vales bedewed by Simoïs' stream, Paphos, too, and Cyprus, land of roses.

Yet while the indulgent kindness of the blind lad permits, I am making ready to leave with all suddenness these walls, and employing the aid of *moly*, plant divine, to evade in a place far distant the ill-famed halls of deceptive Circe. [3] I am resolved, also, to make my

2 Cf. Elegy VII (extract 6).
3 Cf. *Comus*, ll.618-647. 'The shepherd lad' to whom the Attendant Spirit

way back to the reedy marshes of the Cam and again to face the uproar of the noisy School.

Meanwhile, take this gift, humble, yes, but sent by a loyal friend,
a word or two forced into elegiac measures.

148. From the Third Prolusion. 1627 or 1628?

From the Latin.

> Less personal, perhaps, than most of the utterances of Milton
> collected in this volume, this is nevertheless an extremely impor-
> tant evidence of Milton's discontent at Cambridge, for it was the
> scholastic education that he found there.[4]

I was seeking lately with all my might, fellow collegians, very anx-
iously, how I might entertain you, my auditors, with the best possible exhibition of language, when suddenly there came into my mind
an expression which Marcus Tullius, from whom by a fortunate
omen my oration begins, frequently set down in his books; namely,
that the function of the speaker has been established and determined as follows: that he instruct, please, and finally persuade. Accordingly, with that in view, I proposed to myself the task of departing as little as possible from this threefold requirement of the
orator. But since to teach you, men accomplished in every way, is
not what I should undertake, nor is it what you would endure, I may
be permitted at least (what is nearest to it) to suggest something perchance not altogether foreign to the occasion. Meanwhile, to please,
which I really fear very much is my weak point, will be nevertheless
the height of my desire, which, if I shall attain it, certainly will be

is indebted for the herb hæmony in *Comus* has been identified by some as
Diodati and the passage thus interpreted becomes a tribute to Diodati's
botanical knowledge as well as a record of the friendship. Professor Hanford suggests, however, that—here and in *Comus*—the 'virtuous plant'
represents 'the sure guidance of Christian ethics,' to which Milton has
'hitherto owed his safety amid the strongly felt allurements of the senses'
(*Youth of Milton*, p.113). Since it was by means of moly that Ulysses is
made immune to the charms of Circe in the tenth book of the *Odyssey*, this
is the more tempting interpretation; and the identification of Diodati in the
Comus passage becomes very doubtful if the herb there, 'more medicinal'
than moly, also stands for 'the sure guidance of Christian ethics.'

4 See Tillyard, *Correspondence and Academic Exercises*, pp.xxii–xxiv.

equal to persuasion. I will indeed persuade you fully at this time to my opinion, if I shall be able to induce you, my listeners, to open with sparer hand those huge and almost monstrous tomes of the, as they say, subtle doctors, and to indulge a little more mildly in the warty controversies of the sophists. But although it is well known to everybody how that which I advocate is just and honoured, I will show briefly during my little half hour that, by those studies mentioned, the mind is neither delighted nor instructed, nor indeed is any common good promoted.

And certainly at the beginning I challenge you, collegians, if by any means it can be done in accordance with my conception of your ability: what pleasure, I ask, can there be in these joyous wranglings of crabbed old men, which, born if not in the cave of Trophonius, then certainly in the cells of monks, are betrayed by their odour and exhale the savage sternness of their authors and exhibit the frowns of the fathers; and which, prolix beyond measure, in the midst of extreme brevity awaken disgust and loathing? Moreover, if ever more verbose authors are read, then indeed they breed in the readers an aversion almost natural and whatever is beyond of inborn hatred. Frequently, my hearers, when by chance at different times the necessity of investigating a little while these quibbles was forced upon me, after the keenness of my eyes and mind had been dulled by long reading—frequently, I say, I halted to catch my breath, and repeatedly measuring the weight with my mind's eye, I have sought a wretched relief from my disgust. But when I always saw more in sight than I had finished in my reading, often indeed I preferred, instead of these crammed-in fooleries, to clean out the Augean stables; and I declared Hercules a happy man, to whom the good-natured Juno had never set an exhausting hardship of this kind.

Nor does a more flowery style uplift from the earth or elevate this nerveless, languid, creeping stuff; but a diction dry and juiceless accompanies in such very close fashion the insignificance of the material that I could certainly believe without difficulty it had been written under gloomy Saturn, unless the harmless simplicity of that age was quite ignorant of those delusions and trifling inconsistencies with which these books everywhere abound. Believe me, most illustrious young men, sometimes while I survey unwillingly these empty little questions, I seem to myself to be undertaking a journey through rugged deserts and uneven roads and through vast solitudes and precipitous passes of mountains, because it is not likely that the charming and elegant Muses preside over these shrivelled and obscure subjects or that the silly followers of these lay claim to their patronage. On the contrary, I think there never was a place for them on Parnassus, except perhaps some neglected corner at the bottom of the hill, dismal, rough and wild with brambles and thorns, covered over with thistles and dense nettles, far distant from the chorus and assembly of the goddesses—a place which neither yields laurels nor produces flowers, where in short the sound of Phœbus' lyre shall never reach.

149. From Familiar Letter 8, to Benedetto Bonmattei. 1638.

From the Latin.

Bonmattei is one of the unforgettable friends mentioned in the *Second Defence*. The omitted beginning of this letter is an abstract discussion in praise of grammarians. Milton is writing Bonmattei of that scholar's projected *Della Lingua Toscana*, published in 1643.

I will now speak of foreigners. For obliging them, if that is at your heart, most certainly at present an ample opportunity is offered, since what one is there among them that, happening to be more blooming than the rest in genius or in pleasing and elegant manners, and so counting the Tuscan tongue among his chief delights, does not also consider that it ought to have a place for him in the solid part of his literature, especially if he has imbibed Greek and Latin either not at all or but in slight tincture? I, certainly, who have not wet merely the tips of my lips with both those tongues, but have, as much as any, to the full allowance of my years drained their deeper draughts, can yet sometimes willingly and eagerly go for a feast to that Dante of yours, and to Petrarch, and a good few more; nor has Attic Athens herself, with her pellucid Ilissus, nor that old Rome with her bank of the Tiber, been able so to hold me but that I love often to visit your Arno and these hills of Fæsule. See now, I entreat, whether it has not been with enough of providential cause that I have been given to you for these few days, as your latest guest from the ocean, who am so great a lover of your nation that, as I think, there is no other more so. Wherefore you may, with more reason, remember what I am wont so earnestly to request of you— to wit, that to your work already begun, and in greater part finished, you would, to the utmost extent that the case will permit, add yet in behalf of us foreigners some little appendix concerning the right pronunciation of the language. For with other authorities in your tongue hitherto, the intention seems to have been to satisfy only their own countrymen, without care for us. Although, in my opinion, they would have consulted both their own fame and the glory of the Italian tongue much more certainly had they so delivered their precepts as if it concerned all mankind to acquire the knowledge of that language, yet, in so far as has depended on them, you might seem, you Italians, to regard nothing beyond the bounds of the Alps. This praise, therefore, untasted by anyone before, will be wholly your own, and keeps itself till now untouched and entire for you; nor less another which I will venture to mention. Would you consider it too much trouble if you were to give information separately on such points as these: who, in such a crowd of writers, can justly claim for himself the second place, next after the universally celebrated authors of the Florentine tongue; who is illustrious in tragedy; who happy and sprightly in comedy; who smart or weighty in epistles or dialogues; who noble in history? By this means the choice of the best in each kind would not be difficult for the willing student, while, whenever it might please him to range more widely, he would have ground on which to step intrepidly. In this matter you will have, among the ancients, Cicero and Fabius for examples; but whether any of your own men I know not. Though I believe I have already (unless my memory deceive me) made these demands of you every time we have fallen on the matter in talk—such is your politeness and kindly disposition—, I am unwilling to regard that as any reason for not entreating the same in set phrase, so to speak, and in an express manner. For while your own worth and candour would assign the lowest value and the lowest estimation to your own labours, my wish is that both their inherent dignity and my individual respect should set the just and exact value upon them; and certainly it is but fair everywhere that the more easily one admits a request the less defect should there be of due honour to his compliance. For the rest, should you perchance wonder why on such a subject I use the Latin tongue rather than yours, please to understand that it is precisely because I wish to have this Italian tongue of yours cleared up for me in precepts by yourself that I employ Latin openly in my confession of poverty and want of skill. By this very method I have hoped to prevail more with you, not without a belief at the same time that by the very act of bringing with me that hoary and venerable mother from Latium as my helper in her daughter's cause, I should make sure that you would deny nothing to her venerable authority, her majesty august through so many ages. Farewell.

Florence: September 10, 1638.

150. From *An Apology for Smectymnuus*. 1642.

> Another expression of disdain for argument from mere authority or from the authority of the councils parallel to that in the *Reason of Church Government* (extract 1), where Milton's opponents are described as 'men whose learning and belief lies in marginal stuffings, who when they have like good sumpters laid ye down their horseloads of citations and fathers at your door . . ., ye may take off their packsaddles, their day's work is done. . . .'

And here first it pleases him much that he hath descried me, as he conceives, to be unread in the councils. Concerning which matter it will not be unnecessary to shape this answer: that some years I had spent in the stories of those Greek and Roman exploits, wherein I found many things both nobly done and worthily spoken, when coming in the method of time to that age wherein the church had obtained a Christian emperor, I so prepared myself as being now to read examples of wisdom and goodness among those who were fore-most in the church, not elsewhere to be paralleled. But to the amazement of what I expected, readers, I found it all quite con-trary; excepting in some very few, nothing but ambition, corrup-tion, contention, combustion: insomuch that I could not but love the historian Socrates, who in the proem to his fifth book professes he was fain to intermix affairs of state, for that it would be else an extreme annoyance to hear in a continued discourse the endless brabbles and counterplottings of the bishops. Finding therefore the most of their actions in single to be weak and yet turbulent, full of strife and yet flat of spirit, and the sum of their best councils there collected to be most commonly in questions either trivial and vain, or else of short and easy decision without that great bustle which they made, I concluded that if their single ambition and ignorance was such, then certainly united in a council it would be much more; and if the compendious recital of what they there did was so tedi-ous and unprofitable, then surely to sit out the whole extent of their tattle in a dozen volumes would be a loss of time irrecoverable. Be-sides that which I had read of Saint Martin, who for his last sixteen years could never be persuaded to be at any council of the bishops. And Gregory Nazianzen betook him to the same resolution, affirm-ing to Procopius, that of any council or meeting of bishops he never saw good end, nor any remedy thereby of evil in the church, but rather an increase. 'For,' saith he, 'their contentions and desire of lording no tongue is able to express.' I have not therefore I confess read more of the councils save here and there; I should be sorry to have been such a prodigal of my time: but that which is better, I can assure this confuter: I have read into them all. And if I want any-thing yet, I shall reply something toward that which in the defence of Muræna was answered by Cicero to Sulpitius the lawyer. If ye provoke me (for at no hand else will I undertake such a frivolous la-bour) I will in three months be an expert councilist. For be not de-ceived, readers, by men that would overawe your ears with big names and huge tomes that contradict and repeal one another, be-cause they can cram a margent with citations. Do but winnow their chaff from their wheat, ye shall see their great heap shrink and wax thin past belief.

151. From *An Apology for Smectymnuus*. 1642.

For this good hap I had from a careful education to be inured and seasoned betimes with the best and elegantest authors of the learned tongues, and thereto brought an ear that could measure a just cadence and scan without articulating, rather nice and humorous in what was tolerable, than patient to read every drawling versifier.

152. From *An Apology for Smectymnuus*. 1642.

For me, readers, although I cannot say that I am utterly untrained in those rules which best rhetoricians have given, or unacquainted with those examples which the prime authors of eloquence have written in any learned tongue, yet true eloquence I find to be none but the serious and hearty love of truth: and that whose mind soever is fully possessed with a fervent desire to know good things, and with the dearest charity to infuse the knowledge of them into others, when such a man would speak, his words (by what I can express) like so many nimble and airy servitors trip about him at command, and in well-ordered files, as he would wish, fall aptly into their own places.

153. Familiar Letter 12, to Leonard Philaras.[5] 1652.

From the Latin.

    Milton here refuses a request from Philaras for the assistance of his pen in the freeing of the Greeks from Turkish rule on the basis of his confidence that only those people are slaves who deserve to be. Cf. the *Second Defence* (extract 124): 'These men were never let loose by a contempt or violation of the laws to an unreigned licence; they were inflamed by no delusive vision of virtue and of glory or by any foolish emulation of the ancients for the empty name of liberty; they were taught the straight and only way to true liberty, by innocence of life and sanctity of manners. . . .'

5 Mr. Tillyard analyses this letter as an example of Milton's quite remarkable urbanity, of his skill as a letter writer: *Correspondence and Academic Exercises*, pp.xi–xii.

Your good will towards me, most honoured Leonard Philaras, as well as your high opinion of our *Defence for the English People*, I learned from your letters, written partly on that subject, to Mr. Augier,[6] a man illustrious among us for his remarkable fidelity in diplomatic business for this republic: after which I received, through the same, your kind greeting, with your portrait and the accompanying eulogium, certainly most worthy of your virtues— and then, finally, a most polite letter from yourself. Be assured that I, who am not in the habit of despising the genius of the Germans or even of the Danes or Swedes, cannot but value very much such an opinion of me from *you*, a native of Attic Athens, who have besides, after happily finishing a course of literary studies among the Italians, reached such ample honours by great handling of affairs. For, as the great Alexander himself, when carrying on war in the remotest parts of the earth, declared that he had undergone such great labours for the sake of the good opinion of the Athenians, why should not I congratulate myself and think myself honoured to the highest in having received praises from one in whom singly at this day the arts of the old Athenians and all their celebrated excellencies appear after so long an interval to revive and rebloom? Remembering how many men of supreme eloquence were produced by that city, I have pleasure in confessing that whatever literary advance I have made I owe chiefly to steady intimacy with their writings from my youth upwards. But were there in me by direct gift from them, or a kind of transfusion, such a power of pleading that I could rouse our armies and fleets for the deliverance of Greece, the land of eloquence, from her Ottoman oppressor—to which mighty act you seem almost to implore our aid—truly there is nothing which it would be more or sooner in my desire to do. For what did even the bravest men of old, or the most eloquent, consider more glorious or more worthy of them than, whether by pleading or by bravely acting, to make the Greeks free and self-governing? There is, however, something else besides to be tried, and in my judgement far the

6 René Augier, at one time Resident Agent in Paris for the English parliament.

most important: namely that someone should, if possible, arouse and rekindle in the minds of the Greeks by the relation of that old story the old Greek valour itself, the old industry, the old patience of labour. Could someone do *that*—and from no one more than yourself ought we to expect it, looking to the strength of your feeling for your native land and the combination of the same with the highest prudence, skill in military affairs, and a powerful passion for the recovery of the ancient political liberty—then, I am confident, neither would the Greeks be wanting to themselves, nor any other nation wanting to the Greeks. Farewell.

London: June, 1652.

154. Familiar Letter 17, to Ezekiel Spanheim. 1654/5.

From the Latin.
 Spanheim, a Geneva enemy of Alexander More, has apparently sent Milton information about More.

I know not by what accident it has happened that your letter has reached me little less than three months after date. There is clearly extreme need of a speedier conveyance of mine to you; for, though from day to day I was resolving to write it, I now perceive that hindered by some constant occupations I have put it off nearly another three months. I would not have you understand from this my tardiness in replying that my grateful sense of your kindness to me has cooled, but rather that the remembrance has sunk deeper from my longer and more frequent daily thinking of my duty to you in return. Late performance of duty has at least this excuse for itself, that there is a clearer confession of obligation to do a thing when it is done so long after than if it had been done immediately.

You are not wrong, in the first place, in the opinion of me expressed in the beginning of your letter—to wit, that I am not likely to be surprised at being addressed by a foreigner; nor could you, indeed, have a more correct impression of me than precisely by thinking that I regard no good man in the character of a foreigner or a stranger. That you are such I am readily persuaded by your being the son of a most learned and most saintly father,[7] also by your being well esteemed by good men, and also finally by the fact that you hate the bad. With which kind of cattle as I too happen to have a warfare, Calandrini [8] has but acted with his usual courtesy, and in accordance with my own sentiment, in signifying to you that it would be very gratifying to me if you lent me your help against a common adversary. This you have most obligingly done in this very letter, part of which, with the author's name not mentioned, I have not hesitated, trusting in your regard for me, to insert by way of evidence in my forthcoming *Defensio*.[9] This book, as soon as it is published, I will direct to be sent to you if there is anyone to whose care I may rightly entrust it. Any letters you may intend for me, meanwhile, you will not, I think, be unsafe if you send under cover to Turretin of Geneva, now staying in London, whose brother in Geneva you know, through whom as this of mine will reach you most conveniently, so will yours reach me. For the rest I would assure you that you have won a high place in my esteem, and that I particularly wish to be loved by you yet more.

Westminster: March 24, 1654/5.

155. Familiar Letter 21, to Emeric Bigot. 1656/7.

From the Latin.

Except that it is apparent that Bigot had called on Milton during a visit to England, I know nothing of their relationship. Bigot was a French scholar, at this time about thirty years old.

That on your coming into England I had the honour of being thought by you more worth visiting and saluting than others was truly and naturally gratifying to me; and that now you renew your salutation by letter, even at such an interval, is somewhat more gratifying still. For in the first instance you might have come to me perhaps on the inducement of other people's opinion; but you could hardly return to me by letter save at the prompting of your own

7 Spanheim's father had been Professor of Theology at Geneva. Both Spanheims were enemies of Alexander More.

8 An Italian merchant in Geneva.

9 The *Defence of Himself*.

judgement, or, at least, good will. On this surely I have ground to congratulate myself. For many have made a figure by their published writings whose living voice and daily conversation have presented next to nothing that was not low and common: if, then, I can attain the distinction of seeming myself equal in mind and manners to any writings of mine that have been tolerably to the purpose, there will be the double effect that I shall so have added weight personally to my writings, and shall receive back by way of reflection from them credit, how small soever it may be, yet greater in proportion. For, in that case, whatever is right and laudable in them, that same I shall seem not more to have derived from authors of high excellence than to have fetched forth pure and sincere from the inmost feelings of my own mind and soul. I am glad, therefore, to know that you are assured of my tranquillity of spirit in this great affliction of loss of sight, and also of the pleasure I have in being civil and attentive in the reception of visitors from abroad. Why, in truth, should I not bear gently the deprivation of sight, when I may hope that it is not so much lost as revoked and retracted inwards,[10] for the sharpening rather than the blunting of my mental edge? Whence it is that I neither think of books with anger, nor quite intermit the study of them, grievously though they have mulcted me —were it only that I am instructed against such moroseness by the example of King Telephus of the Mysians, who refused not to be cured in the end by the weapon that had wounded him. As to that book you possess, *On the Manner of Holding Parliaments*, I have caused the marked passages of it to be either amended, or, if they were doubtful, confirmed, by reference to the manuscript in the possession of the illustrious Lord Bradshaw, and also to the Cotton MS., as you will see from your little paper returned herewith. In compliance with your desire to know whether also the autograph of

---

10 Mr. Tillyard (*Correspondence and Academic Exercises*, p.131) points out the parallel between this sentence and *Paradise Lost*, Book III, ll.51–53 (extract 47):

> So much the rather thou celestial Light
> Shine inward, and the mind through all her powers
> Irradiate; there plant eyes.

this book is extant in the Tower of London, I sent one to inquire
of the herald who has the custody of the deeds, and with whom I am
on familiar terms. His answer is that no copy of that book is extant
among those records. For the help you offer me in return in procuring literary material I am very much obliged. I want, of the Byzan-
tine historians, *Theophanis Chronographia* (folio: Greek and Latin),
Constantini Manassis Breviarium Historicum, with *Codini Excerpta
de Antiquitatibus Constantinopolitanis* (folio: Greek and Latin),
Anastasii Bibliothecarii Historia et Vitæ Romanorum Pontificum
(folio); to which be so good as to add, from the same press, *Michael
Glycas*, and *Joannes Cinnamus*, the continuator of Anna Comnena,
if they are now out. I do not ask you to get them as cheap as you can,
both because there is no need to put a very frugal man like yourself
in mind of that, and because they tell me the price of these books is
fixed and known to all. Mr. Stoupe[11] has undertaken the charge of
the money for you in cash, and also to see about the most convenient mode of carriage. That you may have all you wish, and all you
aspire after, is my sincere desire. Farewell.

Westminster: March 24, 1656.

156. Familiar Letter 24, to Henry Oldenburg. 1657.

From the Latin.

I am glad you have arrived safe at Saumur, the goal of your travel,
as I believe. You are not mistaken in thinking the news would be
very agreeable to me in particular, who both love you for your own
merit, and know the cause of your undertaking the journey to be so
honourable and praiseworthy.

As to the news you have heard, that so infamous a priest has been
called to instruct so illustrious a church,[12] I had rather anyone else
had heard it in Charon's boat than you in that of Charenton; for it is

---

11 A 'travelling agent' employed by Cromwell and Thurlow.—Masson, *Life*,
   Vol. V, pp.287–289.
12 Alexander More has been called to serve as minister to the Protestant
   church at Charenton, near Paris—'the main Protestant church of Paris
   itself and the most flourishing representative of French Protestantism
   generally.'—Masson, *Life*, Vol. V, p.368.

mightily to be feared that whoever thinks to get to heaven under the auspices of so foul a guide will be a whole world awry in his calculations. Woe to that church (only God avert the omen!) where such ministers please, mainly by tickling the ears—ministers whom the church if she would truly be called reformed would more fitly cast out than desire to bring in.

In not having given copies of my writings to anyone that does not ask for them, you have done well and discreetly, not in my opinion alone, but also in that of Horace:

> Err not by zeal for us, nor on our books
> Draw hatred by too vehement care.

A learned man, a friend of mine, spent last summer at Saumur. He wrote to me that the book was in demand in those parts; I sent only one copy; he wrote back that some of the learned to whom he had lent it had been pleased with it hugely. Had I not thought I should be doing a thing agreeable to them, I should have spared you trouble and myself expense. But,

> If chance my load of paper galls your back,
> Off with it now, rather than in the end
> Dash down the panniers cursing.

To our Lawrence,[13] as you bade me, I have given greetings in your name. For the rest, there is nothing I should wish you to do or care for more than see that yourself and your pupil[14] get on in good health and that you return to us as soon as possible with all your wishes fulfilled.

Westminster: August 1, 1657.

157. Familiar Letter 31, to Peter Heimbach.[15] 1666.

From the Latin.

> This is the only extant letter written after the Restoration. Milton's disillusionment is complete.[16]

13 Milton's pupil, Edward Lawrence, to whom Sonnet XX (extract 32) is addressed.
14 Richard Jones, 'Young Ranelagh.'
15 See headnote, extract 146.
16 See Tillyard, *Correspondence and Academic Exercises*, p.xv, for comment

Small wonder if, in the midst of so many deaths of my countrymen, in a year of such heavy pestilence, you believed, as you write you did, on the faith of some special rumour, that I also had been cut off. Such a rumour among your people is not displeasing if it was the occasion of making known the fact that they were anxious for my safety, for then I can regard it as a sign of their good will to me. But, by the blessing of God, who had provided for my safety in a country retreat,[17] I am still both alive and well, nor useless yet, I hope, for any duty that remains to be performed by me in this life.—That after so long an interval I should have come into your mind is very agreeable; although, from your exuberant expression of the matter, you seem to afford some ground for suspecting that you have rather forgotten me, professing as you do such an admiration of the marriage-union in me of so many different virtues. Truly, I should dread a too numerous progeny from so many forms of the marriage-union as you enumerate, were it not an established truth that virtues are nourished most and flourish most in straitened and hard circumstances; albeit I may say that one of the virtues on your list has not very handsomely requited to me the hospitable reception she had. For what you call 'policy,' but I would rather have you call 'loyalty to one's country'—this particular lass, after inveigling me with her fair name, has almost expatriated me, so to speak. The chorus of the rest, however, makes a very fine harmony. One's country is wherever it is well with one.—And now I will conclude, after first begging you, if you find anything incorrectly written or without punctuation here, to impute that to the boy who has taken it down from my dictation, and who is utterly ignorant of Latin, so that I was forced, while dictating, not without misery, to spell out the letters of the words one by one. Meanwhile I am glad that the merits of one whom I knew as a young man of excellent hope have raised him to so honourable a place in his prince's favour; and I desire and hope all prosperity for you otherwise. Farewell!

London: August 15, 1666.

on this letter as 'in the mood of *Paradise Regained*,' Milton's patriotism being for the time completely extinguished.   17 Chalfont St. Giles.

APPENDIX A

The following are references to the Columbia MILTON for all extracts

EXTRACT	REFERENCE	EXTRACT	REFERENCE
1.	III, pt. I, pp.231–242.	29.	XVIII, p.270.
2.	VIII, pp.111–139.	30.	XVIII, p.271.
3.	I, pt. I, p.283.	31.	XII, pp.59–61.
4.	VIII, pp.59–63.	32.	I, pt. I, p.67.
5.	IX, pp.123–125.	33.	I, pt. I, pp.67–68.
6.	I, pt. I, pp.215–223.	34.	XVIII, p.270.
7.	I, pt. I, p.223.	35.	XII, pp.77–79.
8.	I, pt. I, p.47.	36.	XII, pp.83–85.
9.	I, pt. I, p.49.	37.	XVIII, p.270.
10.	I, pt. I, p.51.	38.	XII, pp.225–227.
11.	I, pt. I, p.53.	39.	XII, pp.241–243.
12.	I, pt. I, p.55.	40.	XVIII, p.271.
13.	I, pt. I, p.57.	41.	III, pt. I, pp.295–307.
14.	I, pt. I, p.59.	42.	III, pt. I, pp.342–343.
15.	XII, pp.5–7.	43.	IX, pp.161–187.
16.	I, pt. I, pp.187–189.	44.	I, pt. I, pp.66–67.
17.	XII, pp.119–123.	45.	XII, pp.65–71.
18.	XII, pp.205–217.	46.	VIII, pp.63–77.
19.	XII, pp.9–13.	47.	II, pt. I, pp.77–79.
20.	XII, pp.13–15.	48.	I, pt. I, p.68.
21.	I, pt. I, p.207.	49.	I, pt. I, pp.68–69.
22.	XII, pp.15–17.	50.	XII, p.247; I, pt. I,
23.	XII, pp.19–23.		pp.19–21.
24.	I, pt. I, pp.283–285.	51.	I, pt. I, pp. 213–215.
25.	I, pt. I, p.287.	52.	XII, pp.247–251.
26.	XII, pp.39–45.	53.	XII, pp.320–322.
27.	I, pt. I, pp. 295–301.	54.	XII, pp.322–325.
28.	XII, pp.45–53.	55.	I, pt. I, pp.269–279.

EXTRACT	REFERENCE	EXTRACT	REFERENCE
56.	I, pt. I, pp.76–83.	90.	V, pp.291–294.
57.	XII, pp.23–29.	91.	VII, pp.3–13.
58.	I, pt. I, pp.289–295.	92.	IX, pp.3–9.
59.	I, pt. I, pp.307–315.	93.	IX, pp.11–15.
60.	III, pt. I, p.148.	94.	IX, pp.85–89.
61.	I, pt. I, pp.60–61.	95.	VI, pp.1–3.
62.	I, pt. I, p.25.	96.	VI, pp.43–45.
63.	I, pt. I, p.155.	97.	VI, pp.46–48.
64.	I, pt. I, pp.317–325.	98.	VI, p.101.
65.	XII, pp.63–65.	99.	VI, p.106.
66.	II, pt. I, pp.8–9.	100.	VI, pp.111–112.
67.	II, pt. I, p.6	101.	VI, p.151.
68.	I, pt.2,pp.331–333.	102.	XIV, pp.3–15.
69.	I, pt. I, pp.195–197.	103.	III, pt. I, p.10.
70.	III, pt. I, p.183.	104.	III, pt. I, pp.105–108.
71.	III, pt. 2, pp.493–494.	105.	III, pt. I, pp.281–289.
72.	IV, pp.11–15.	106.	IV, pp.60–61.
73.	IV, pp.16–17.	107.	IV, pp.63–69.
74.	II, pt. I, pp.211–213.	108.	IV, p.230.
75.	II, pt. 2, pp.260–262.	109.	IV, p.235.
76.	II, pt. 2, p.405.	110.	IV, p.238.
77.	III, pt. 2, p.369.	111.	IV, p.267.
78.	III, pt. 2, pp.371–372.	112.	IV, pp.271–273.
79.	III, pt. 2, pp.377–379.	113.	V, pp.86–87.
80.	III, pt. 2, p.384.	114.	V, p.121.
81.	IV, pp.275–277.	115.	IX, pp.99–101.
82.	IV, pp.19–20.	116.	IX, pp.107–113.
83.	IV, p.293.	117.	IX, pp.129–133.
84.	IV, pp.329–331.	118.	VI, pp.40–41.
85.	XVIII, p.269.	119.	VI, p.165.
86.	XVIII, p.269.	120.	VII, pp.555–559.
87.	V, pp.4–5.	121.	I, pt. I, p.62.
88.	V, pp.63–65.	122.	I, pt. I, pp.62–63.
89.	V, p.276.	123.	VII, p.551.

EXTRACT	REFERENCE	EXTRACT	REFERENCE
124.	VIII, pp.3–23.	141.	XII, p.375.
125.	VIII, pp.83–87.	142.	XII, pp.326–327.
126.	VIII, pp.99–109.	143.	XII, p.377.
127.	VIII, pp.187–193.	144.	XII, pp.329–330.
128.	VIII, pp.201–203.	145.	XII, pp.79–83.
129.	VIII, p.253.	146.	XII, pp.103–105.
130.	XII, pp.71–73.	147.	I, pt. I, pp.169–175.
131.	IX, pp.221–227.	148.	XII, pp.159–163.
132.	XII, p.105.	149.	XII, pp.35–39.
133.	XII, p.109.	150.	III, pt. I, pp.357–358.
134.	VI, pp.148–149.	151.	III, pt. I, p.328.
135.	XVIII, p.366.	152.	III, pt. I, p.362.
136.	XII, pp.349–351.	153.	XII, pp.55–59.
137.	XII, pp.353–355.	154.	XII, pp.75–77.
138.	XII, p.361.	155.	XII, pp.85–89.
139.	XII, pp.363–365.	156.	XII, pp.97–99.
140.	XII, pp.369–371.	157.	XII, pp.113–115.

APPENDIX B

Reference to the works most frequently consulted in the Introduction and notes is made in the following short forms:

Darbishire, Helen, *The Early Lives of Milton*. London, 1932   Darbishire, *Early Lives.*

Hanford, James Holly, *A Milton Handbook*, Revised Edition. New York, 1933   Hanford, *Handbook.*

Hanford, James Holly, 'The Youth of Milton,' in *Studies in Shakespeare, Milton, and Donne*. New York, 1925   Hanford, *Youth of Milton.*

Liljegren, S.B., *Studies in Milton*. Lund, 1918   Liljegren, *Studies in Milton.*

MacKellar, Walter, *The Latin Poems of John Milton*. New Haven, 1930   MacKellar, *Latin Poems.*

Masson, David, *The Life of John Milton*. London, 1859–1894. 7 vols. Second edition of Volume I, 1881   Masson, *Life.*

Masson, David, *The Poetical Works of John Milton*. London, 1874. 3 vols.   Masson, *Works.*

Patterson, Frank A., and others, *The Works of John Milton*. New York, 1931–1938. 18 vols.   Columbia *Milton.*

Smart, John S., *The Sonnets of Milton.*
Glasgow, 1921   Smart, *Sonnets.*

Tillyard, E.M.W., *Milton.*
London, 1934   Tillyard, *Milton.*

Tillyard, Phyllis B. and E.M.W.,
Milton: Private Correspondence and
Academic Exercises. Cambridge, 1932   Tillyard, *Correspondence*
                                 and Academic Exercises.

INDEX

Throughout the Index Milton's name has been omitted from entries.
Headnotes are referred to by 'h.,' footnotes by 'n.'

281